POST-SOVIET POLICY PERSPECTIVES

POST-SOVIET POLICY PERSPECTIVES

EDITED BY
ALEXEI D. VOSKRESSENSKI

NOVA SCIENCE PUBLISHERS, INC.
COMMACK, NEW YORK

Assistant Vice President/Art Director: Maria Ester Hawrys
Graphics: Frank Grucci
Editorial Production: Susan Boriotti
Office Manager: Annette Hellinger
Acquisitions Editor: Tatiana Shohov
Book Production: Ladmila Kwartirof, Christine Mathosian,
Joanne Metal and Tammy Sauter
Circulation: Iyatunde Abdullah, Cathy DeGregory and
Annette Hellinger

Library of Congress Cataloging–in–Publication Data
available upon request

ISBN 1-56072-495-1

6080 Jericho Turnpike, Suite 207
Commack, New York 11725
Tele. 516-499-3103 Fax 516-499-3146
E-Mail: Novascience@earthlink.net

Printed in the United States of America

CONTENTS

Chapter 10 Nato Enlargement: A Critical View from Belarus **185**
Denis Krivosheev

PREFACE

The research for this project was supported in part by the International Science (Soros) Foundation and The Victoria University of Manchester (UK). This support enabled relatively young researchers (Mr. Denis Krivosheev, Belarus) together with more established researchers (Victor Stepanenko, Institute of Sociology, National Academy of Science, Ukraine and Irina A. Denisova, Central Institute of Economics and Mathematics, Russian Academy of Science) to voice their views on different problems confronting what is sometimes called "The Post-Soviet World." This entity is struggling with the aftermath of the Cold War trying to find out what is post-Communist/post-Soviet identity. These questions are dealt with by Victor Stepanenko. The evolving civil society in these countries shows the way to a more humane and rational world. General problems relating to economic-security nexus in East-Central Europe are analyzed in the next paper by Denis Krivosheev, and more specific questions of monetary policy transmission in Russia in the paper by Irina A. Denisova. Two security questions are analyzed: NATO enlargement and a more broad question of the 'security indivisibility' thesis which is questioned by Denis Krivosheev in view of a new strategic context in Europe. The book is fleshed out by important views and analyses provided by K. Roberts et al., as well as by S.D. Goldman et al., and A.F. Woolf.

The editorial work was enabled in part by the combination of different research grants and intellectual support provided by such organizations as International Science Foundation, Netherlands Institute for Advanced Study in the Humanities and Social Sciences (Royal Netherlands Academy of Arts and Sciences), Carnegie Endowment for International Peace (Washington and Moscow Centers), Council on Regional Studies of Princeton University, Centre of Post-Soviet Studies of the University of Reading (UK), the Institute of Far Eastern Studies (Russian Academy of Sciences, Moscow) and Moscow School of Social and Economic Studies. The editor is grateful to Professors Sherman Garnett and Gilbert Rozman for intellectual stimulation.

The statements and views expressed herein are those of the authors and not of the above mentioned organizations or the states from where the authors are from.

Alexei D. Voskressenski
Manchester-Moscow, July 1997

CHAPTER 1

POST-COMMUNIST IDENTITY IN A POSTMODERN PERSPECTIVE: CONCEPTUALIZING POST-SOVIET EXPERIENCE

VICTOR P. STEPANENKO
Kyiv, Ukraine - Manchester, UK

The fundamental transformation currently taking place in the political and socio-economic systems, culture, psychological attitudes and way of life, in central and eastern Europe provides an unique opportunity to re-examine some traditional theoretical questions. This becomes especially evident in the case of the newly created independent states in the territory of the former Soviet Union. Almost all of these states face the problem of seeking their own identity (cultural, ethnic, political). Almost all of them have officially declared their political transformation to democracy and market economy. The process of 'rediscovering the past', of 'restoring the historical memory of the people' and the 'historical truth' is supplemented by the creation of new traditions and attempts to transfer the 'Western experience' (associated with the tradition of liberal capitalism) onto native soil.

In fact, the social construction of new cultural, ethnic and political identities is taking place. This process is primarily associated with the political transition towards a democratic order and a new civic culture. However, while the process of democratic transformation of eastern European countries, and particularly post-Soviet countries, has still many specific traits it reveals some common characteristics in the post-communist experience. Basing on the example of a post-communist transformation in Ukraine, I would like to show these common characteristics which might be combined in the concept of 'post-communist identity'.

Post-communist identity is a valuable theoretical construct which implies both the meaning of the process's genealogy and its self-reflexivity. There are two theoretical premises which might be helpful in the subsequent analysis:

1. It is impossible to understand anything in the contemporary post-Soviet situation without referring to its origin. From this angle the post-Soviet cases (Ukrainian, Russian, Belorussian, and so forth) might be considered as a particular examples of the recent transformation of the former Soviet identity. The current new ethnic

and cultural identities are only in the course of (self-) construction and they are still submerged in the post-communist sociocultural context.

2. This understanding inevitably implies the problem of self-reflexivity or an ideal observer which is possible only with a certain historical distance from and non-involvement in the cultural situation. The challenge is to represent social change as an intelligible object for consciousness, which itself is constantly changing. Hence, post-communism is the theoretical conditions and actual practice of the altered states of mind and identities of both the researcher and the society. This is the project of becoming rather than being.

THE NATURE OF POST-COMMUNIST TRANSFORMATION: SOCIOCULTURAL ASPECT

Indeed, a post-communist experience is an uncomfortable but, at the same time, for many analysts an attractive theme for conceptualization . The very fact of the plurality of theoretical models, aimed to theorise this grandiose sociocultural and political shift proves the complex nature of the phenomenon (See, for example: Schoplin, 1993; Whitefield ed., 1993; Bryant and Mokrzycki eds., 1994; Polokhalo ed., 1995). However, questions relating to the reasons for and the nature of post-communist transformations in the countries of central and Eastern Europe are still open. In this respect the most intriguing historical turning point, which has to be mentioned is the initiation of the so called *perestroika* started in the former Soviet Union at the middle of 1980s and which triggered the processes of democratic changes in eastern Europe. Leaving apart the meanings of perestroika which oscillate between deliberate revolution and a forced attempts of liberalise the system, I would stress that the process was initiated from above and aimed, in fact, to adjust a political order to the new emerging sociocultural situation. This situation was a result of an actual profound structural shift in values and cultural orientations, attitudes, way of life, psychology and patterns of behaviour of being still formally the Soviet people. (The reasons, motivations and driving forces behind this shift is a problem for special analysis). But my principal point is that political arrangements (and political will) were, to some extent, the consequences rather than reasons of the gradual silent revolution in the minds of the people which, however, was reinforced and legitimized by political arguments and decision-makings.

Hence, my approach involves an understanding of the post-communist experience as not only political but above all as a sociocultural transformation. The principal questions here are: What is the nature and meaning of this transformation? Could it be understood and theorised in terms and concepts of classic theoretical discourse, above all in the framework of the traditional/modern model? And, if not, how is it possible to conceptualize the contextual model which is supposed to be commensurable within a new cultural globalization and theoretical convention?

In attempting to conceptualize communism and communist identity in terms of classic discourse on tradition and modernity, Gellner's perspective can serve as a point of departure. Gellner (1988, p.127) distinguishes pre-industrial and industrial societies and assumes a different role and meaning of culture within these societies. According to him, the signs of the industrial culture are the following: the division of labour, occupational mobility, the importance of education as a preconditions of economic and political citizenship, the pervasive influence of the mass media (Ibid., p.128). The late communist situation closely approximated to these characteristics, which I would prefer to locate in the typology of modern society and modernity. At the same time, this situation, particularly in the Soviet case, can be characterized, also, as a culture with significant remnants of the traditional order'. The ideological doxa which determined all spheres of life, played formally a similar role as a tradition and a mythology in a traditional, pre-modern society. This doxa was also supposed to provide the set of classifications and identifications in a communist society. The cliché of Soviet man constituted the most general ideal type of social, political and cultural identity. As Vladimir Iadov (1994: p.36-37) puts it, bluntly: In its classic phase of totalitarianism, Soviet society resembled a traditional society in its principal quality: individual had none of the attributes of a subject. Hence, in his interpretation the breakdown of established social identification resembles in its mechanism processes, which were analogous to the cultural historical transition from a stagnant, traditional society to a modern - that is, dynamic- society (ibid.: p.38).

This theoretical scheme, however, exaggerates pre-industrial, traditionalist side of communism by opposition to its entirely modern nature. (The specificity of a communist modernization is another question). The very attempt at the uniform incorporation of the differences within the project of *Sovietness* was a characteristic historical way of modernising traditional identities, above all ethnic ones. While, in a paradoxical way some post-communist oversimplifications are affected partly by the same type of logic (and implicitly, identity) which presumably should be overcome by them. This logic, which is in essence the logic of modernity and continuity, operates mostly with rational constructs and ideal typologies. In the case of communist modernization the ideal typology (in particular Soviet man) was both a product of the political imposition of total abstractions upon social reality and justification of that practice. Theoretical generalizations correspond perfectly to the politics of totalities and macro-entities. Stressing the anti-backward, in fact, modern nature of Soviet identity, Tamara Drabadze (1987: p.158) notes: Officially, there is supposed to be equality between sexes and harmony between generations throughout the Soviet Union. There must be love between all the ethnic and regional groups within the country, the mutual respect between the city and village. Furthermore, there should be definite indications of a convergence of thought and customs by all Soviet people, characterized by secularization, even though it is conceded that the different nationalities have for along time had particular ways which are national in form although socialist in content (Stalin's formula). All evidence to the contrary is officially considered to be a sign of backwardness while evidence supporting the fulfilment of these directives is applauded as progressive. So, there are two positions (both plausible) which stress, the traditional character of Soviet socio-culture, on the one hand, and its modernity, on the other.

It seems, however, that the Soviet experience, a strange mixture of traditional and modern (or even pre-modern) orders, cannot be fitted properly into the classic scheme of social typology, based on the dichotomy traditional/modern. The concept of Soviet modernization is an attempt at re-evaluating this scheme. The arguments which developed within the framework of this concept stressed the specificity of the Soviet case and, therefore, the particular nature of the modernization in the Soviet and, more broadly, communist conditions. If technical development or industrialization alone were taken as the decisive criteria of modernisation then the former Soviet Union could be considered as a fairly successful case of rapid industrialization on the basis of a socialist economy. But recent attempts at a market-oriented modernization of the former Soviet industry in Ukraine (which had inherited a disproportionate number of Soviet era 'industrial dinosaurs[1]) failed. Instead, the 'party of power', representing mainly the former Soviet *nomenclature* in Ukraine, 'has achieved something that many might have thought impossible: to invent an economic system that is more inefficient than the former economy of the old Soviet Union' (Unruly Child, 1994: p.4).

'Modernization' (and rationalization) are not only concepts of technical and economic development but rather notions of sociocultural dimension associated with Weber's understanding of the phenomena. Giddens (1991: p.15) proceeds in the same direction insofar as he defines modernity as 'roughly equivalent to the industrialized world, so long as it be recognized that industrialism is not its only institutional dimension'. However, the Soviet modernization (or the Soviet modernity) in comparison with its Western historical counterpart was conducted in different sociocultural circumstances and effected, above all, by severe political and ideological state control. The consequences were a hyper-centralization of power and a politics of homogenization of life in the former Soviet Union. Apparently, this was one of the main reasons for further stagnation and degradation of economics and policy in the former Soviet Union. According to George Schopflin (1993: p.5) 'backwardness' is also a common characteristic of Soviet influence in eastern Europe. (However, his distinction between the countries of eastern Europe and the countries of the former Soviet Union is noteworthy - Ibid.). Schopflin points out further: 'This backwardness manifested itself notably in the significantly different relationship between state and society to what had evolved in Western Europe, in attitudes towards modernity and the definition of modernity, as well as the demands that modernization makes on any society' (Ibid.) The concept of the Soviet backwardness within the discourse of modernization restores in an indirect way the traditional/modern dichotomy which is substituted by the opposition undeveloped/developed societies.

However, it has become clear that the conceptualization of the modernity project in its communist modification inevitably implies the re-examination of theoretical notions of traditional (pre-modern) and modern (allegedly, non-traditional) and, more broadly, the very logic of this conceptualization. This logic involves a shift from radical to coexistence type of theorizing (Heelas, 1996: p.3). So far the communist project and identity was neither traditionalist, nor modern in Western meanings of the term. *Sovietness* had its own

1 According to 'The Economist' survey Ukraine produced in 1989 34% of the Union's steel, 46% of its iron ore, 36%of its televisions and 53% of its sugar (Unruly Child,,1994: p.3)

particular meaning and implied its own contextuality in every concrete case of sociocultural and political translation of the traditional national contents into a socialist modern form. Moreover, if one takes as a basic assumption the idea that a tradition is a historical, sociocultural phenomenon, created as a result of economic, political, cultural and psychological interaction between people and their social and discursive practices, the *Soviet* and *communist* have themselves acquired a meaning of tradition under which at least three generations of people have grown up. In the Ukrainian case the suture identity of *Soviet Ukrainian* or *Ukrainian Soviet* might be proper expressions of this social hybridization.

The social change, termed conventionally post-communist transformation reinforced the sociocultural complexity of new identities and aggravated the problem of their conceptualization. The attempt to explain post-communist changes by analogy with the historical process arising out of industrial societies and the development of capitalism in the nineteenth century proved inadequate. Bryant and Mokrzycki (1994), comparing the theoretical analysis of the great transformation given by Carl Polanyi with the new great transformation, came to the conclusion that there were substantial historical and cultural differences between the two processes. Their arguments are centred on three main distinctions. Firstly, the social change which in western Europe took nearly a century is occurring within the active life of one generation in the eastern-European case. Secondly, democratic reforms and establishment of liberal states in the West were preceded by economic transformation of the societies. Instead, in the post-classic case, political transformation, excluding perhaps Hungary, took place before the onset of economic transformation. And, finally, the cultural legacy of the pre-capitalist West has diverged greatly from the historical and cultural legacies of real socialism in Eastern Europe. (Bryant, Mokrzycki, 1994: p.5-6). Indeed, the concept of post-communism cannot be fitted into a simple two-way choice between socialism and capitalism, between traditional and modern. In addition the conceptualization of this change cannot be adjusted to fit a simple analogous scheme.

POST-COMMUNISM IN THE CONTEXT OF POST-MODERNITY

Post-communism is relative to and could be understood only in the context of a global cultural shift. A new global emerging cultural order is termed in various theoretical constructions as a post-industrial society, late, high or reflexive modernity or, in the most common way post-modernity. Despite the vast range of definitions and their entirely conventional character, post-modern theories are common in their understanding of contemporaneity as a qualitatively new stage in social and cultural development which puts in doubt the existence of a progressive and linear logic in modern historical development. In this respect a post-communist experience is both a mutation and a catalyst of global change. Moreover, the very notion of post-communism is the creation of the post-modern logic of conceptualization, in which the *post-* is a manifestation of ambivalence, betweenness and of the partial character of truth and culture (Clifford, 1986;

Bhabha, 1996: p.54). As post-modernity reveals the incompleteness of the modernity project and its own open nature, a post-communist experience is taking place within in-between stage, the stage of luminality, where neither the old nor the new rules apply (Bauman, 1994: p.16). Despite the controversy within post-modern discourse, which itself, sometimes, pretends to be a new fixed theoretical construct, I will attempt to conceptualize further some post-communist phenomena in terms of post-modernity.

In fact, post-communist and post-modern experiences are entirely at one in their articulation of two particular meanings. In the course of theoretical conceptualization as in reality these meanings constantly intersect and overlap. These are individualization or subjectivization of social life and practice, on the one hand, and reflexivity of social and individual Self, on the other.

Individualization in both cases means the disintegration of previously existing social forms (either traditional or modern) or, as Beck and Beck-Gernsheim (1996: p.24) put it, the increasing fragility of such categories as class and social status, gender roles, family, neighbourhood, etc. and the collapse of state-sanctioned normal biographies, frames of reference, role models. A post-modern individualization also coincides with globalizing influences. In Giddens version, this combination of two extremes makes possible a situation in which humankind in some respect becomes a we, facing problems and opportunities where there are no others (Giddens: 1991: p.27). However, the most distinctive characteristic of the post-modern individualization by comparison with a simple (Lash, 1994: p.113) or traditional modernization is its reflexive character. Summarising the arguments for the distinctive and particular character of present-day modernization, Scott Lash notes: ...If simple modernization means subjugation, then reflexive modernization involves the empowerment of subjects. If simple modernization gives us Foucaults scenario of atomization, normalization and individuation, then the reflexive counterpart opens up a genuine individualization, opens up positive possibilities of autonomous subjectivity in regard to our natural, social and psychic environments (Ibid.).

This comparison between simple (allegedly bad) and reflexive (implicitly good) modernizations is valuable for my further consideration. It reveals a juxtaposition of a new reflexive logic which suffers as result of its global nature from a certain rigidity and the neglect of the cultural context. I will show this on the example of post-Soviet transformation. But here I will continue with the analysis of reflexivity in a post-modern and, then, in a post-communist contexts.

Reflexivity and self-reflexivity are the most popular terms in a post-modern discourse. Despite a broad variety of interpretations of the notion, different theoretical approaches converge in a recognition that reflexivity is entirely about global re-evaluation, re-theorization, re-vision, re-thinking and re-conceptualization of the nature of modernity, knowledge and the self in conditions of social change at the turn of twenty-first century. According to this approach, the self, like the broader institutional contexts in which it exists, has to be reflexively made (Giddens, 1991: p.3). The self constitutes the centre of this reflexive imperative as both its subject and object. As Giddens (1991: p. 33) further elaborates: the altered self has to be explored and constructed as part of reflexive process of connecting personal and social change. There are two main orientations of this reflexive process. First one is an outwards reflection of the self on social arrangements, constraints and social structure, or, in more general terms, on self's social conditions of existence. Scott Lash terms this structural reflexivity (1991: p.115). The second orientation is associated with inwards reflection (or self-reflexivity) in which the self (a subject or agency) reflects on itself (Ibid.).

In fact, the self-reflexive practices are close to what Hegel called self-consciousness (*Selbstbewusstsein*) - the reflection of the subject on the subject itself. But in a post-modern (or late modern) paradigm the notion of self-reflexivity acquired its distinctive meaning which implied a global search for self-identity - the process which involves both a person and a society. This movement for self-identity becomes reflexively organized endeavour (Giddens, 1991: p.5). Meanwhile the very concept of identity has changed in post-modern conditions. According to Bauman (1996: p.18), if the *modern* problem of identity was how to construct an identity and keep it solid and stable, the *post-modern* problem of identity is primarily how to avoid fixation and keep the options open. Post-modern discourse on self-reflexity and self-identity centres around the possibility to choose, create (or rather re-create), recycle, continuously revise and even invent or imagine identities in the context of multiple choice. Self-reflexivity and self-identity become self-narrative of his or her biography which can be re-written, re-told or re-interpreted in terms of text or story. The normal biography becomes the reflexive biography (Giddens), the elective biography, the do-it-yourself biography (Beck). In post-modern approach this shift is justified by the ever-increasing power and role of social actor, agency and human subjectivity, that is with a help of the same arguments which construct the theory of post-modern individualization.

However, there are two principal deficiencies in this approach to the interpretation of the post-modern self and identity. Firstly, a neglect of the role of tradition in a post-modern society. As Heelas (1996: p.216) fairly notes theorization of detraditionalization must interplay with theorization of tradition-maintenance, construction and re-construction. The core of contra-Giddens arguments is the co-existence and mutual implication of tradition, order and control with reflexivity, disorder, flux and uncertainty of postmodernity (Adam, 1996: p.135). The co-existence thesis is especially relevant in the consideration of identity formation (both in the self and collective appearances). This is the process (and practice) which can never start suddenly; it always builds upon a pre-existing set of symbolic materials transmitted from the past. In a sense, a tradition is indeed contextual, as Giddens (1994: p.79), nevertheless, acknowledges.

Hence, a neglect of the traditional side of identity formation overlaps with another shortcoming in post-traditional discourse, namely its disregard of context (political, cultural, historical) in the search for identity. A neglect of social context leads to an over-simplification and over-generalization of theoretical schemes purporting to be universal for humankind. As a result, all particularities, differences and nuances of specific cases are dissolved in an abstract theoretical formalism. The statement 'the self is not a passive entity, determined by external influences; in forging their self-identities, *no matter how local their specific contexts of action* (*italics* is mine-V.S.), individuals contribute to and directly promote social influences that are global in their consequences and implications'

(Giddens, 1991: p.2) is correct in general, but demands its own justification in every concrete case. The thesis that post-modern processes not only permit, but demand, an active contribution by individuals who must be able to plan for the long term and adapt to change, must organize and improvise, set goals, recognize obstacles, accept defeats and attempt new starts, who need initiative, tenacity, flexibility and tolerance of frustration (Beck and Beck-Gernsheim, 1996: p.27) might be seen as a just good intention only unless it specifies its correspondence to a concrete case.

POST-SOVIET EXPERIENCE: GIVING A SUBSTANCE TO A POST-MODERN CONCEPTUALIZATION

Post-communist experience, in particular in its Soviet variation is a great challenge for a post-modern conceptualization insofar as it is not only a part of post-modernity, but a part with its own meaning and contextuality. The problem is not to adjust post-modern theoretical constructs to post-communist reality, but rather to represent this reality in the notions of post-modernity. Post-communism is not a marginal or side effect of the post-modern dominant trend, but its substantial and representative appearance which was often neglected or served only as an illustration for global conceptualizations. Moreover, some post-modern concepts, such as the end of history, individualization, detraditionalization, search for identity, (self-) reflexivity, disembedding, separation of time and space, risk society, survival, victimization and others acquire their justification and even plausibility mostly in the wake of the post-communist experience. I will attempt here to concretise some post-modern concepts, in particular with regard to (self-)identity and (self-) reflexivity in their post-communist variations and to show similarities and differences between the ideal (implicitly, Western) model of post-modernity and its post-Soviet counterpart.

The structural post-communist transformation, as I have argued above, began much earlier than its official proclamation by the politics of perestroika in the mid-1980s. It seems that the deconstruction of the communist ideal is connected with the first attempts at liberalization of the communist order in the post-Stalinist era. The short period at the beginning of the 1960s which later was symbolically termed the thaw (*ottepel*), was associated with controversial political efforts by the communist authority to attach a human dimension to communist doctrine and to create the image of socialism with a human face. In spite of the contradictions and inconsistencies of these attempts, manifested by the first sharp criticism of Stalinism as a political doctrine and practice, they had a great impact on the former Soviet society and on the new generation of intellectuals who called themselves somewhat proudly the children of the thaw. In fact, de-Stalinization of the 1960s brought about mass first historical experience of mass re-thinking and de-construction of communist principles and formed the new generation of people whose allegedly clear communist identities and loyalties were fractured and spoiled somewhat by the seeds of doubt and the ability to criticize and reflect.

The doctrine of new thinking associated with the perestroika found, to some extent, its own justification in this historical and psychological turn, though its consequences were postponed to the next generation. As, was officially acknowledged, new thinking- this Soviet version of reflexive modernization- had arisen alongside ever-increasing mass social criticism and self-reflexivity. These processes were officially characterised in the following way: The people representing the working class, the peasantry, the intelligentsia, the party apparatus, in the centre and in the province, gradually began to reflect seriously on what was going on in the country; an understanding of the impossibility to live in such a way was growing. There were increased misgivings and indignation over neglecting great values, which were born in the socialist revolution of 1917' (Gorbachev, 1988: p.19). The premises of new thinking includes a recognition of universal human values in their paradoxical combination with traditional communist class priorities; an acknowledgement of the principles of pluralism, mainly in the cultural sphere; and official claim to adhere to the ideas of democracy and civil society, though on the basis of the communist interpretation.

However, in spite of its inconsistencies and contradictory character new thinking was a first official prototype of post-communist (and in this context post-modern) conceptualization restricted, at the same time, by the general framework of communist doxa and rhetoric. The result of that synthesis appeared in the ambiguous, ambivalent and multi-dimensional nature of the concepts and declarations of the new thinking exemplified by the slogans *more socialism, more democracy*, *renovation of values, acceleration, glastnost* and others. These ambivalent concepts constituted an ever broadening field for reinterpretation. Polyvariety, multi-meaning and controversy of many official statements created a new cultural situation, in which these statements could not be transformed into clear directives and direct prescriptions, in the traditional way. As a result, the breakdown of the systems logic began. A deep crisis in the traditional communist schemes of conceptualization and normalization and their inability to adapt to the new, emerging circumstances was an acknowledgement of the open, uncertain nature of the transformation and its consequences. When faced with the crucial question: what are we striving for in perestroika, what are its objectives? Initiators of the process responded: It is hard to respond to that question in a detailed, pedantic way. It is not in our tradition (?-V.S.) to deal with prophecy and try to identify beforehand all the architectural elements of that social building which we shall erect in the process of perestroika (Gorbachev, 1988: p. 31). This is indeed a remarkable revelation which touched upon the transformation of one of the main characteristics of the communist mind and identity, namely its teleological and logocentric nature.

Perestroika revealed the deep crisis of ideological representations of the self and social realities which were based on the social totemism of words and on political myth-making. In the late communist conditions the post-modern phenomenon termed by Lyotard as the collapse of grand narratives or, using Bourdieus metaphor, the breakdown of the Oracle effect appeared in the most persuasive way. Official inefficiency in the creation of new narratives or in the restoration of traditional ones, the decline in former rhetoric and representative practices to seek to explain *what is happening?* and *who we now are?*, led to characterizing the social situation in terms of ontological chaos and social schizophrenia

(Golovakha and Panina, 1994: p.3). The experience of the biggest world catastrophe at the Chernobyl nuclear power in Ukraine in 1986 contributed to the feelings of mass victimization and formed a perspective of the uncertain future on the fragile planet in a post-modern age. This again revealed the hypocrisy and cynicism of the allegedly new system of communist democracy that had tried to cover-up the actual scale and danger of the catastrophe.

If Chernobyl became the symbol of the risk society and of the fragility of human life two crucial historical events of 1991 had acquired the symbolic meaning of deconstruction in post-communist and post-modern history. These were the destruction of the Berlin Wall and the collapse of the Soviet Union as a political and state unity. The first meant not only an abolition of a last political frontier (the so called iron curtain), separating the European East from the West, but, above all, the realization of the globality and openness to the world involving a mass experience in a discovery of Otherness (political, cultural, ethic, ideological, economical) on both sides of the Walls. The collapse of the USSR which had become the historical fact after Ukraine's vote for its own independence at the end of 1991 brought a political end to the last world empire and the end of history characterized by active and open military confrontation. And above all it was accompanied by a dramatic mass experience of transformation in the most basic meanings of identity, including that of social being, time and space.

The foundations of traditional meanings, identity references and social coherence, such as socialism and socialist state, socialist camp, fraternal multinational family of the people and others were shattered. The value system of the Soviet man which included an unqualified acceptance and demonstration of state-approved beliefs, judgements and evaluations; a ritualized demonstration of common popular enthusiasm; a set of symbols acknowledging individual success by the state and other bureaucratic structures; and, finally, the ideology condemning enemies of the people and dissidents (Levada, 1993) was crushed. Instead, new social meanings and knowledge which can be considered as forming axiomatic and referenial constructs have not yet been created. The ontological chaos and existential vacuum of post-communist society appeared vividly in the problematic character of meanings referring to collective and group identities. The analysts of post-Soviet society consider this to be an indication of profound change in mass conscience and in the values of the people. This change is characterised in terms of particularization, fragmentation, privatization, individualization, capitalization of mass conscience - the process which is related to the post-modern characteristic of individualization. However, the post-communist and, in particular, post-Soviet practice of individualization was opposed in larger measure by the strengthening of abstract systems of state and governmental bureaucracy. Along with a development of self-reflexivity at individual level the processes of ever-increasing institutional reflexivity had begun. Giddens defines this phenomenon as the regularised use of knowledge about circumstances of social life as a constitutive element in its organization and transformation (1991: p.20). Inasmuch as the processes of social transformation were submitted to and governed predominantly by the new state's infrastructures the practice of post-communist institutional reflexivity involved the creation of new subjections and fabrication of social thought and meanings.

The new collective social actors, above all, newly created nation-states, monopolize the production of new identities and attempt to invest them with new meanings to fill the ideological and cultural vacuum in society. In this context Iadov argues that post-Soviet countries are experiencing the genesis of a new social subjectivity. However, he continues, since a civil society has not yet been formed, and the mechanism defending the rights of diverse groups of population has been exclusively the prerogative of bureaucratic structures, any truly common interest is perceived today with extreme suspicion, as one more version of intrigue by the plutocracy or by another group pursuing its own self-interested objectives. (Iadov, 1994: p. 37). Politics of identity and its representation has become one of the main practical and theoretical domains of institutional reflexivity in post-communist conditions.

CONCEPTUALIZING THE PATTERNS OF POST-COMMUNIST IDENTITY AND REFLEXIVITY

The overlapping of individual and institutional reflexivity in regard to the practice of social transformation can be found in the various models of post-communist theoretical conceptualizations. One of them, the so-called psychiatric discourse constituted an attempt to synthesise micro- and macro- approaches, individual and institutional dimensions of social changes. Psychiatric discourse has been originally developed in the course of new thinking and was based on the recognition of the complex and profound nature of post-communist transformation as, above all, the problem of a human factor, a change of consciousness and breaking of mental structures both on individual and social levels. One of the prophets of the new thinking proclaimed: the greatest difficulty on the path of social re-building lies in our thinking, which was formed in former times (Gorbachev, 1988: p.62). The theme of social-psychiatric treatment, which are clearly represented in official rhetoric, gained popularity in the post-communist mass media, culture and in every-day communicative practice. The refrain of the popular song of the perestroika time: *...mother, we all are seriously ill...* became leitmotiv of the mass psychiatric movement and numerous attempts of social diagnostics of post-communist changes. The very term diagnosis replaces in this context the term theorization. Golovakha and Panina (1994: p.7) describe the mass psychiatric shift of post-perestroika time in the following way: To declare that the country went mad, that the people got crazy and all things that are going on is close to delirium became the good style in numerous public statements of quite respectable representatives of political and spiritual elite. Indeed, the outbreak of active interest in the issues of collective and individual psyche and identity in periods of historical changes and revolutions is an interesting phenomena.

I do not attempt here to provide a full explanation of the nature of post-communist psychiatric shift based partly on real psychological tensions of consciousness in the adaptation to social changes that have been concentrated within an extremely short period of time. I will focus rather upon the intersection of individual and institutional reflexivity, which is represented by theoretical discourse. There is no watershed between them. The so called theoretical consciousness is always immersed in the context of day-to-day routine practice and the common sense reflexivity of individuals. The post-communist psychiatric movement, even in its most theoretical and sophisticated forms, was based on the intention to legitimise an oppressed common sense in contrast to ideological and political speculations. The notion common sense itself, which is literally translated in Russian and Ukrainian as the *healthy sense* stresses the hypothetical and desirable order of social normality in contrast to the former, alleged social clinic which must be overcome with the help of psychiatric arguments. The task of shattering, deconstructing, eliminating and reducing dogmatic schemes imposed on the living reality as well as the attempts at de-mythologizing political consciousness, found their common conceptual ground in psychiatric discourse.

Reference to the issues of social psychiatry was also justified by the theoretical tradition, which began with Freud and was further developed in various respects by Fromm, Horni, Marcuse, Delueze, Guatarri, Foucault and others. The capacity for social criticism of the Western left Freudianism and social anti-psychiatry fitted perfectly with the direction of the humanistic treatment of totalitarianism. However, beliefs in the universality and accountability of the psychiatric (or rather, anti-psychiatric) approach exploring the communist mentality and identity from a point of view of health sense turned into an oversimplification of the nature of the phenomena. According to the Russian sociologists Gozman and Etkind (1992: p.67), for example, the period of the 1960s in Soviet history can be interpreted easily with the help of the neurosis-catharsis model. Instead, the present day, post-communist transformation in the former USSR might be understandable within the concept of the Soviet syndrome. But, in a paradoxical way, the new conceptual schemes, elaborated on the basis of simplified social psychoanalysis reflected the types of consciousness which were subjected to their criticism, inasmuch as, the simplification of the world and reality was one of the main features of totalitarian consciousness and identity (Ibid.: p.18-21).

In fact, the traditional dichotomy, interpreted in another way lies at the base of large number of psychiatric, post-communist conceptualizations. The mechanical division between the normal and mad with respect to mass and individual consciousness in post-communist conditions is just another terminology for expressing the conventional thinking which generates such dichotomies as capitalist/socialist, traditional/modern, totalitarian/democratic and so on. In comparison with the latter, a theorist in psychiatric discourse relies on the role of an experienced psychoanalyst while society, (collective and individual consciousness as well as identity) are depicted as the patient needing an urgent treatment. Such an approach restores a classic behaviourist disposition which is related to the traditional rational view of the social and was realised partly in the paternalist and authoritarian model of the communist organization of social life.

However, in spite of all its shortcomings, 'social psychiatry' also represents in its own way a new humanistic orientation in the reflection on post-communist changes focusing upon, above all, human consciousness and psychology as both an object and a subject of these changes. Psychiatric discourse reveals the nature of post-communist reflexivity as an altered state of mind in its between-ness, in which perception and reception of the new are subjected and interpreted within the isomorphic structures of traditional consciousness. The isomorphism of communist and post-communist consciousness is one of the distinctive features of post-communist identity faced with an increasing polymorphism of post-modernity. The presence of traditional structures of consciousness, as it appeared vividly in the patterns of post-communist institutional reflexivity and politics, makes possible a pre-determined selection of the new as well as its transformation and interpretation according to those traditional structures.

The paradigm of social constructionism in its post-communist representation constituted one of the most vivid examples of this isomorphism. The term social constructionism in my context combines at least two important meanings: 1) the conventional theoretical concept, and 2) a conceptual allusion to a particular social practice which is based on an equation of consciousness and reality and associated with a politics of planned design of social action and change. The paradigm of social constructionism is represented in the following patterns of post-communist institutional reflexivity and politics of identity representation: 1) an adherence to the dogmatic style of thinking and doxic constructs; 2) a teleological nature of reflexivity, oriented by a linear movement towards a hypothetical final result; 3) a post-communist hyper-activism manifested in the form of engineering social processes.

The dogmatic isomorphism of post-communist reflexivity can be found in its radical split between traditional adherence to communist doxa, on the one hand, and unconditional uncritical acceptance of the complex of ideas known as neoliberalism, on the other. Neoliberal cliché - the post-modern remake of the *laissez-faire* liberalism - became a new common ideological and political credo of the eastern-European reformist movement. Its standard recipe includes an encouragement of entrepreneurial activity, a restriction on social protectionist policy and tough monetary control. However, blind and dogmatic application of this unified scheme to countries with different cultural traditions and economics levels and in the process of political construction of market economy appeared quite unsuccessful.

The second pattern in the isomorphic nature of post-communist institutional reflexivity - teleological orientation on a linear path towards a hypothetical final result - appeared in a proliferation in the terminology of post-communist transition. Teleologism is a characteristic consequence of traditional rationality which implied a notion of a linear dimension in historical time and space. This cognitive and rational bias is reflected, for example, in the Marxist concept of five-stage historical development of humankind - the so-called social-economic formations- passing from primitive to communist societies. The post-communist scheme of transition from communism to democracy and civil society is isomorphic to this ideology of ideal society, which has recently been represented in communist doctrine. Another post-communist representation of this isomorphism constituted itself in the patterns of catastrophical thinking. In a paradoxical way, pessimistic finalism is the particular case of inversion of the same teleological paradigm that is orientated to the ideal society.

And, finally, there is a post-communist hyper-activism formulated in the terms of engineering the social processes. The communist pattern of active life attitude (*aktivnaia zhiznenaia pozicia*) and the model of active builder of communism are partly restored in an the official post-communist discourse on the active building (or construction) of democracy and civil society. Although, the actual variations of post-communist activism at the level of day-to-day routine are represented in new types of consumerist behaviour and in the cultural scenarios of self-made-man and free riders, who are not restricted by any principles and norms and are oriented only to their pragmatic interests.

Post-communist isomorphic structures found their theoretical justification in a certain type of rationality and logic which might be characterised as traditional, or using Webers notion as *formal* rationality. Mamardashvili (1972: 37) terms this type of rationality as classic one. Its characteristic nature is an equation of consciousness and practice. Such a practical consciousness is associated strongly with the so-called industrial paradigm which presupposes a full autonomy for technological development without cultural or political consequences - in fact, a sociotechnology or social engineering. The essence of this paradigm is represented by its orientation to the macro-approach and to mega-mania and reflected in the mottoes the more, the better and progress at any cost. Thus human activity is subjected to the mechanical functions of the process, or in communist terminology, it plays the role of the nut and bolt. In fact, even a new thinking - a post-modern version of communist mentality - revealed the dominance of this approach in the expressions of post-communist institutional reflexivity. In this context the following revelation is remarkable: We only thought that we were driving, but in a reality the machine had not been going in the direction which was planned by the drivers (Gorbachev, 1988: p.18).

The post-Soviet social practice, which was legitimised with *perestroika,* continues to be realized in the frame of the social constructionist paradigm based on the tradition of formal rationality. At the same time, this process is unfolding in the new circumstances of cultural polyphony, fragmentation and plurality of partial truths. In the Ukrainian case this is a strange mixture consisting of the remains of former communist pattern, some elements of civil society in their embryonic form, post-colonial cultural milieu and global post-modern cultural values. The social alchemy of post-communist transformation is taking place in the context of this hybrid culture, the components of which have lost their original meanings and have become deformed. The post-communist reflexivity and identity constitute themselves as fragmental, unstable and hybridized insofar they take their forms in the context of that mixture.

Although, multiculturalism, pluralism and the open nature of post-communist transformations despite its side effects are the principal historical achievement of this period, the main algorithms of post-communist political practice coincide formally with the practice of communist social engineering. The societies have been turned into new building objects or, rather into live laboratories, where, under conditions of a natural experiment, (Iadov, 1944: p.38) civility, democracy and market economy have been modelled. The dominance of cognitive isomorphic structures in new forms of identity and self-reflexivity make possible an ideological manipulation by new macro-values such as the nation state, civil society and democracy. They acquire their priority by relation to individual micro-values.

The principal theoretical and practical issues which have arisen in this respect are how and in what form does the interpretation and transformation of values really occur? How are the emergence and the establishment of the new possible in post-communist isomorphic structures, whether the transformed social reality and identity are really different or reconstructed and restored old and whether the construction of new values is possible at all from the old fabrics of social meanings?

REFERENCES

Adam, B (1996) Detraditionalization and the Certainty of Uncertain Futures *in* Heelas P, Lash Sc, Morris P (eds.) *Detraditionalization: Critical Reflections on Authority and Identity* Oxford: Blackwell pp.134-148

Bauman, Z (1994) After the patronage state *in* Bryant Cr and Mokrzycki E *The new great transformation? Change and continuity in East-Central Europe* London: Routledge pp.14-35

Beck, U and Beck-Gernsheim, E (1996) Individualization and Precarious Freedoms: Perspectives and Controversies of a Subject-oriented Sociology *in* Heelas P, Lash Sc, Morris P (eds.) *Detraditionalization: Critical Reflections on Authority and Identity* Oxford: Blackwell pp.24-49

Bhabha, H (1996) Cultures In-Between *in* Hall St and Du Gay P *Questions of Cultural Identity* London: SAGE Publications pp.53-61

Bryant, Cr and E.Mokrzycki, eds. (1994) *The new great transformation? Change and continuity in East-Central Europe* London: Routledge

Clifford, J (1986) Introduction: Partial Truths *in* Clifford J and Marcus G E (eds.) *Writing Culture. The Poetics and Politics of Ethnography.* Berkeley: University of California Press pp 1-26

Drabadze, T (1987) Fieldwork at home: the USSR *in* Jackson A (ed.) *Anthropology at Home* pp. 154-168

Gellner, E (1987) *Culture, Identity, and Politics* Cambridge: University Press

Giddens, A (1991) *Modernity and Self-Identity. Self and Society in the Late Modern Age* Cambridge: Polity Press

Giddens, A (1994) Living in a Post-traditional society *in* Beck, U Giddens, A Lash, Sc *Reflexive Modernization: Politics, Traditions and Aesthetics in the Modern Social Order* Cambridge: Polity Press pp. 56-110

Golovakha, E and Panina, N (1994) *Sotsialnoie bezumiie (The social madness)* Kiev:Abris

Heelas, P (1996) Introduction: Detraditionalization and its Rivals *in* Heelas P, Lash Sc, Morris P (eds) *Detraditionalization: Critical Reflections on Authority and Identity* Oxford: Blackwell pp.1-21

Gorbachev, M (1988) *Perestroika i novoie myshleniie (Perestroika and new thinking)* Moscow: Politizdat

Gozman, L and Etkind, A (1992) *The Psychology of Post-totalitarianism in Russia* London: The Centre for research into communist economies

Iadov, V (1994) Sotsialnaia identifikatsiia v krizisnom obshchestve (Social Identification in a Crisis-Ridden Society) *Sotsiologicheskii zhurnal* No1 pp.35-52

Lash, Sc (1994) Reflexivity and its Doubles: Structure, Aesthetic and Community *in* Beck, U Giddens,A Lash, Sc *Reflexive Modernization: Politics, Traditions and Aesthetics in the Modern Social Order* Cambridge: Polity Press pp. 110-174

Levada, Iu ed. (1993) *Sovetskii prostoi chelovek: opyt sotsialnogo portreta na rubezhe 90-kh. (The soviet ordinary man: the social portrait by the beginning of 1990s)* Moscow: Mirovoi Okean

Mamardashvili, M et al (1972) Klassika i sovremennost: dve epokhi v razvitii burzhuaznoi filosofii (The classic and contemporarety: two epoches in the development of western philosophy*) in Filosofiia v sovremennom mire (Philosophy in contemporary world)* Moscow: Nauka

Polokhalo, V, ed (1995) *The Political Analysis of Postcommunism* Kyiv: Political Thought

Schoplin, G (1993) *Politics in Eastern Europe 1945-1992* Oxford:Blackwell

Unrully Child. A survey of Ukraine (1994) *The Economist* May 7th pp 3-18

Whitefield, St, ed. (1993) *The New Institutional Architecture of Eastern Europe* New York: St. Martins Press, Inc.

CHAPTER 2

ECONOMIC-SECURITY NEXUS IN EAST-CENTRAL EUROPE

DENIS KRIVOSHEEV
Minsk, Belarus; Manchester, UK

INTRODUCTION

After the Cold War, national security remains as problematic for countries in all parts of the world, as it was before. The post-communist Europe has emerged as a vastly heterogeneous and insecure sub-region. While most of the former Soviet states find themselves increasingly isolated and helpless in questions of security and economic and political development, countries of East-Central Europe (ECE)[1] at the moment are actively engaged in regional security, political and economic arrangements, such as NATO and EU enlargement. Their experience and consequent performance will be crucial for their eastern neighbors. In case of their general, and first of all economic success, it is plausible to expect that the governments in Eastern Europe, first of all in Ukraine, Belarus and Russia, will be experiencing a growing pressure from their public to pursue policies similar to those in the ECE countries. However, those East Europeans who are critical of their governments for being slow and irresolute on the path of reforms and who look west for a remedy for their hardships, have to ask a question about the meaning of the processes that take place west of their countries' borders.

The prospect of NATO enlargement have shaken stability in Eastern Europe on both international and domestic level, and have already put the above question in a subtle way. Security arrangements in ECE point to broader considerations of their proponents. Starting our analysis with the eastern enlargement of NATO, we come across a single body of problems. Attempting to find a solution to these problems takes us out of the area of proper security pro-occupations. We may start with the questions of to what extent the ECE countries feel insecure, and to what extent their membership of NATO can be helpful in tackling this problem. These questions are worthy of many debates, given that the North Atlantic nations - who are believed to be the victors in the Cold War - surprisingly enough

1 The notion of ECE applies to Poland, the Czech Republic, Slovakia and Hungary, while by Eastern Europe I mean the European part of the former Soviet Union.

may claim that they face serious security problems as well (Huntington, 1996; 1993), and work actively for a new regional and, as I will argue further, global security re-settlement.

There were many attempts to re-conceptualize security during the Cold War, both in the West and East (for example, see Waever, 1989). The end of this tense global conflict has contributed greatly to this process, urging re-thinking both of security as a concept, security on various levels (national, individual, international), and the security agenda for each of them. It has also prompted to intertwine security studies with various other debates - those concerning questions of international political economy, global governance, human rights and international law. The universal nature of problems in the contemporary interdependent world drives all policies towards a complex approach.

I will argue that security discourse and policies of the post-communist governments' in ECE, as well as more general debates about security, suggest that the question of national, collective and international security should be studied from a much broader perspective - that of the current structural adjustments of global power. I will undertake to show that the logic of geopolitics currently predominates in international relations, bringing closely together various issues, most notably the economic and security ones. The structure of this system can be described in terms of the centre-periphery model, as it was suggested by Wallerstein (1991), although other models may as well be helpful. The important question to be elucidated is the continuity and novelty of the place of the former "Second World" in this system. This will point to the essential analytical link in the analysis of the new global and regional (European) security system, and to the important analytical perspectives for further investigation.

My initial interest in East-Central European security arrangements is caused by the strategic position of ECE in relation to the former Soviet states, and their crucial influence upon the politics in Eastern Europe. More generally, the importance of ECE for an international security analysis is determined by the fact that it is, nowadays, obviously a missing link in many serious discourses on security from a global perspective. As I will argue, its contemporary role is most significant from the point of view of the global, not only regional, power-security structure. While conflicts and other threats to the "centre" that exist in what is called South can be "fenced off or resolved" by a major powers' concert, as some analysts suggest (Tickner, 1995: p. 184), those in Central, Southern and Eastern Europe cannot, at least not so easily. This vision is dictated by the physical proximity of ECE to Western Europe and to the major contender of the new North-Atlantic security arrangements, Russia. Preoccupations with the vulnerability of eastern "frontier" of the West[2] are reinforced by the unprecedented economic and social costs of the process of transition in the post-communist Europe (Andor, 1996: p. 216). The West has acknowledged the fact that ECE is a key to its security in the military and in a broader sense, as I will show later, and has involved ECE in a bigger game - a game which is played against the rebel social movements, potential geostrategic contenders (Russia and other parts of the former USSR - semi-periphery) and the rest of the world ("periphery" or South, not to distinguish between its diverse parts).

---

2 In this essay I use it as a synonym for "centre".

The complex nature of security in the contemporary world requires a multi-dimensional approach (Mack, 1993: pp. 5-6) where economic considerations are of a primary importance. The key to national security problematic is what Buzan (1991: p. 261) calls economic nationalism. This notion applies equally well to the Western and East-European societies. The West, being economically, politically, militarily and ideologically predominant, is interested in securing its position. With the collapse of state-socialist models in Europe and proliferation of free market-based neo-liberal models, the West's privileged position has been enhanced. However, maintaining its high standards of living (previously often achieved at the expense of less privileged parts of the "world capitalist system") under the conditions of growing economic competitiveness and global trends towards liberal economy, and responding to the growing pressure from the periphery and semi-periphery who are experiencing the most painful effects of the global structural adjustment to the victorious free market, determines the quest for firm security guarantees. These include not only prevention of conflicts and peace-keeping in the strategic areas (oil fields of the Middle East, geographically adjacent territories (Bosnia), regions demonstrating economic dynamism (Cambodia), etc.), and support of key partners elsewhere, but also ideological domination which supplements global proliferation of market-responsive political regimes and open economies.

The understanding of such a necessity is prompted by the broadening of contemporary security agenda advocated by various scholars in the West (Buzan, 1991: pp. 19,20). The logic of reformulated comprehensive security unambiguously shows that the referent object will not be secure unless the threats are minimized in every sphere of its vital activity. In the contemporary international system such an object is the state (or regionalised group of states), and the vital spheres are the political, economic, societal, and ecological ones (Buzan, 1991)[3].

NEW PRIORITIES OF EAST-CENTRAL EUROPE AFTER THE COLD WAR

The Cold War ended with the failure of the state-socialist model in Europe. Socialism has been seriously discredited in various ways, with the most decisive stroke being the defeat in economic competition with the West (Dunn, 1992: pp. 1,2; Andor, 1996: pp. 211-2). So far, it has been the most obvious link between the economy and security for the countries of the region. The collapse of the state-socialist model has contributed greatly to the body of myths about a possibility of a rapid economic improvement after a relatively short period of structural adjustment - under the conditions of liberal democracy and with the adoption of liberal economic policies. In the beginning, this has created a consensus in the post-state socialist societies about the necessity and direction of transformation, and this consensus has been more enduring in the more developed countries of the northern tier (Lewis, 1997: p. 411). Despite several difficulties, and return to power of the ex-communist forces, for

3 However, it may be argued further who are the real benefactors of this "national" security (Falk, 1997; Halliday, 1993).

example in Poland, the elite, and probably general public commitment to reforms is unchallenged.

The process of transition in ECE countries is often perceived by their populations as a "return to the West". Practically, it is actualized as a pursuit of new identity and joining the "Western club" - European economic and North-Atlantic military-political structures. The desire to enter EU has clear economic motivation and cannot be misunderstood. The rationale for joining NATO, however, can be questioned on various grounds. The major problem is the absence of an obvious threat, at least for ECE countries, which would justify their desperate will to join a military alliance. Worst of all, it has become an issue of serious diplomatic battles between the parties concerned and an actively hostile Russia. The arguments of both sides are presented at length elsewhere (CFDP, 1996; NATO, 1995). However, the real meaning of NATO enlargement, as I will argue, is disguised by them.

NATO enlargement is suggested as a security arrangement that would benefit all member countries and harm no one. Taken formally, as a collective security mechanism which (at the moment) is not directed against anyone, it should not create problems. However, both the fact that Russia, the most influential state in Eastern Europe and "occasionally" former antagonist, is understood to be precluded from the North-Atlantic Alliance in any foreseeable future (CFDP, 1996) and the obvious neglect and marginalising of other security structures where the countries concerned are already present (OSCE, UN, etc.), suggests that something different than collectively maintained military security is at stake.

Unpacking of this problem (which, I believe, genuinely is not about security of ECE proper) requires some further analysis in the areas of (1) contemporary security discourse, (2) inter-relatedness between security and other areas, primarily, the economic-security nexus, and particularly the Western perspective on this issue; (3) priorities of ECE countries in the transition period, and (4) the objectives of the West that make it sensitive to aspirations of the latter.

POST-COLD WAR SECURITY DISCOURSE AND POLICIES

Most of contemporary security debates revolve around the realist analysis of the nature of international relations, according to which states are the major - self-interested - actors, with security being their highest end. This logic prompts the view that states cannot rely on mutuality of interests and must pursue an increase in their relative power. Economic power is crucial as long as it contributes to the state's general capabilities (Waltz, 1979: pp. 126,105).

The global conflict of the Cold War, based on this logic, resulted at its paramount in a stalemate, and put the peoples of the two conflicting blocs and the whole humankind under a constant threat. This has provoked questioning of the realist assumptions about the possibility of achieving security through constant accent on power and capabilities, the legitimacy of the state as the principal recipient of security - at the expense of the insecurity of its citizens, and the utility of military means (Tickner, 1995).

Alternative thinkers present security as an indivisible phenomenon, and suggest a focus on commonality of interests as a means of achieving *common security* (Mack, 1993: pp. 2-3). However, fixing on commonality of interests soon elucidated that the real scope of threats vastly exceeds that perceived within the military-political agenda. The idea of *comprehensive security* was suggested to accommodate this new vision (Mack, 1993: p. 3).

This broadening agenda of security studies and policies has raised a crucial question about the referent object of security. Among other things would be, variously suggested, the quality of life (see Buzan, 1993: p. 19; Tickner, 1995: pp. 179-81). Therefore, security cannot be understood only as prevention of war. Another important insight of security studies into the nature of security is that comprehensive security should be maintained through combination of various means (Buzan, 1991: pp. 19-20). The significant point for my argument is that maintaining economic well being has to be reassured by military, but not only military, means.

Almost inseparably from the criticism of realist thinking and the language of division associated it (Tickner, 1995: p. 189), criticism of policies congruent with it and with the North-Atlantic vision of security started to be developed. For example, Tickner (1995: pp. 179-81) presents several alternative approaches as a "vision of security from the South" that "turns" the realist assumption about boundaries between anarchy and order "on its head" and clearly illustrate that most of the world has not in the least been comfortable in spite of the absence of any direct conflict between the superpowers during the relatively "peaceful" period of the human history after the World War II. There was, and still is no peace in many countries of the so-called South, and the world nowadays is an immensely insecure place, even in the narrow military sense.

For various reasons, such as political, military and economic predominance, the West has assumed responsibility for maintaining peace and security in the post-Cold War world. Understanding this task in the narrow traditional sense, as minimalisation of conflicts and turbulence, it has approached it in a rather traditional way too. The proposed "new" instruments - conflict prevention, peace-keeping, peace-making - are in fact based on military-political power, but this time legitimized through representative international organisations (UN, OSCE). To reassure the current absence of military threats, multilateral policies of non-proliferation are also implemented. NATO, an enormous Cold-War time military defense mechanism, has been made an instrument of peacekeeping, which in military terms means facilitation of offense.

However, as I have indicated above, security is understood today not only as absence of wars and military conflicts. Through the notions of states as self-interested actors, and of quality of life as an important compound of comprehensive security, we can elucidate the rationale behind the West's global security endeavour. Contemporary "reformulated" realism (Tickner, 1995) has adopted this logic about comprehensive security too. Buzan warns about the economic threats to domestic stability. "These occur when states pursue economic strategies based on maximization of wealth through extensive trade. Over time, such policies result in high levels of dependence on trade in order to sustain the social structures that have grown up with increasing prosperity" (Buzan, 1991: p. 128). Obviously, in this sense the Western nations must feel more insecure than many others. Besides, this logic points to the global scale of contemporary economic life, universal interdependence, fragility and fragmentation (when one's own national/ local interests have priority over those of others).

Buzan emphasises vulnerability of every participant in the world economy today, which is essential for the operation of free market (1991: p. 235). However, this sense of constant relative insecurity varies, according to the place which the economic unit occupies in the system. "Uneven development refers to the way in which the market distributes wealth, and in a broader sense development, unevenly through the system" (Buzan, 1991: p. 255). No doubt, maintaining a privileged economic position in this system is the state's important end, because "economic capability is the crucial foundation on which the relative status of great powers in the system rests" (Buzan, 1991: p. 127). According to the realist logic, such a status can only be maintained in a relative sense - vis-à-vis other states' lesser capabilities (Waltz, 1979: p. 105).

This sense of constant economic and general insecurity - both through the rising international competitiveness and vulnerability of vital economic links, but also the quest for alternative economic models - is echoed in the works of various Western authors. Huntington (1993; 1996) tries to ascribe to it some power of symbolism to the Western preoccupations - the "clash of civilizations". Huntington's (1993: p. 23) words suggest that this may take a form of struggle against the global structural inequality, where "the peoples and governments of non-Western civilizations [would] no longer remain the objects of history as targets of Western colonialism but [would] join the West as movers and shapers of history". Huntington also reveals the West's attempts to give legitimacy to its actions: "The very phrase "the world community" has been the euphemistic collective noun (replacing "the Free World") to give global legitimacy to actions reflecting the interests of the United States and other Western powers" (Huntington, 1993: p. 39). Buzan tries to explain this phenomenon in less provocative words, noting that power of strong states "project beyond their boundaries" (1991: p. 197).

Huntington's reasoning brings us back to NATO expansion and other questions related to ECE. "The West in effect is using international institutions, military power and economic resources to run the world in ways that will maintain Western predominance, protect Western interests and promote Western political and economic values" (Huntington, 1993: p. 40). He suggests that there are three alternatives for the non-Western countries to take: (1) self-isolationism; (2) to merge with the West; (3) balance: "to modernize but not to Westernize" (1993: p. 41), of which ECE has already taken the second one. He adds that it is in the West's interests "to incorporate" these countries (1993: pp. 48-9; 1996: p. 161).

This reasoning underpins Tickner who argues that many contemporary security discourses follow the traditional realist notion of national security - this time "through a new and modified Pax Americana" (1995: p. 181). A new global power structure is emerging where the US, with its continued strong military capabilities and the help of its Cold War alliance partners, is seen as that of a guarantor of global security - security in the interests of the West and understood as absence of dangerous conflicts and turbulence[4]. This situation, in

[4] This tendency looks quite evident, despite the backlash among "America first"/ nationalist thinkers and policy-makers who argue for the primacy of domestic interests over international ones (Bienen, 1993).

my opinion, is best described by the "concert of powers" model (see Camilleri, 1993: pp. 86-8) which grants significance to all (not only the US) Western powers. One of the possible depiction and explanation of the mechanisms of uneven global capitalist development is suggested by Halliday (1993). A critical analysis of the recent global security arrangements also brings us to the question about the economic and social forces that stand behind them[5]. "Security policy as associated with globalization from above is preoccupied with the protection of market forces and the perceived interests of geopolitical actors, that is strategic concerns of both global and regional scope" (Falk, 1995: p. 139).

To promote these objectives, a new mythology is being created. According to it, the world has entered a stage when the "old-fashioned aggression is of declining utility as an instrument of statecraft - at least in the more developed parts of the world" (Mack, 1993: pp. 3-4)[6]. At this peaceful stage conflicts become of concern to everyone and will be exterminated through joint efforts. Besides, promotion of global free trade, in a Western view, becomes synonymous with the promotion of peace[7].

In fact, understanding of economy and security as interdependent phenomena, perception of economic well being and social stability as mutually reinforcing, is common nowadays. However, promotion of free trade is not always equated with the promotion of prosperity, and hence the suggested economic conditions of security differ. Boutros-Ghali, for example, stresses the role of development (1995: p. 1), whereas the critical voices dispute developmental power of economic neo-liberalism (for example, Halliday, 1993; Falk, 1995; Tickner, 1995; Andor, 1996). On the other hand, opinions are less different on the fundamental sources of threats and insecurity. These are economic despair, social injustice and political oppression (see Boutros-Ghali, 1995: p. 43, or a generally recognised document of 1945 - the UN Charter), but they have hardly been so decisively addressed by a joint coalition as, say, Iraq's aggression against Kuwait. Instead, to legitimize their indefinite continuity, realists label them, in Buzan's words, "normal day-to-day consequences of life in a competitive international environment" (1991: pp. 114-117). It is of no surprise that critical writers like Falk argue that a "militarist, regressive view of security" continues to prevail in the North, and that today's geopolitics shifts its preoccupations from balance of power to those of world economic hegemony (1995: p. 145). Consequently, Falk note that "[t]here is no assurance that the role of war will be diminished during the transition. This prospect will depend on which social forces define and control the mechanisms of security at a global level" (1995: p. 135).

---

5 The importance of such an analysis is stressed by the models that do not overemphasise the hegemonic role of the US in post-Cold War world.

6 The latter part of this notion referring to the "more developed parts" is essential for the myth.

7 For example, "[p]rosperity and security go hand in hand. [...] Britain's vision of global free trade and open markets will both promote prosperity and enhance security" (FCO, 1996)

NEW ROLE FOR ECE IN THE NEW GLOBAL POWER STRUCTURE

As with any mythology, the global era mythology requires testimonies. In this section I will argue that providing such a testimony is the role assigned by the West to ECE. I have already indicated above that the process of transition (political and economic) in the post-socialist societies in ECE is directed by the commonly shared beliefs in the virtues of liberal democracy and market-led economy. It is largely driven by strong economic expectations and is supplemented by a pursuit of a new identity of ECE countries with the West (Western Europe). The latter, being generally reluctant to extend its economic structures towards impoverished East because of the inevitable costs, on the other hand, is compelled to accommodate ECE's expectations. The "moral" reasons for this are grounded in the Cold Wartime promise of well-being to the insurgents against communism. The more practical reason is the necessity to reassure against turbulence on its eastern borders (Falk, 1995: p. 135). Thirdly, the Western prosperity and unsurpassed superiority of its political and economic model suddenly became quite questionable (Falk, 1995: p. 139).

Political stability and economic performance of ECE at this stage gains strategic importance and has to be facilitated. It is meant to be the biggest political marketing operation in history to reassure confidence within (where turbulence also becomes possible, especially in the prospect of "embracing globalisation"), and to set the path for the rest of the as yet "unwesternised" world. This global political project has been depicted by Fukuyama, one of the most celebrated ideologues of westernisation, as the "end of civilization". He states that:

> "[a]ll countries undergoing economic modernization must increasingly resemble one another: they must unify nationally on the basis of a centralized state, urbanize, replace traditional forms of social organisation like tribe, sect, and family with economically rational ones based on function and efficiency, and provide for the universal of their citizens. Such societies have become increasingly linked with one another through global markets and the spread of a universal consumer culture." (Fukuyama, 1992: p. xiv)

As one can see from this passage, economic considerations are inescapable from any Western considerations. If fact, it is a system that is oriented towards universalisation of consumerism and marketisation.

ECE, from a certain point of view, is left at this stage without an alternative. Its previous socio-political constitution was based on a promise of future general prosperity, which has never been accomplished. Consumerism has become a superior ideology there. By the early 1990s its former affiliation to the USSR was completely abandoned not least because of impossibility of further free riding (Andor, 1996: p. 212) and the formers economic and political impotence. ECE has never been a region of its own significance in Europe[8], and it could hardly aspire to an independent identity and development. Such an attempt (Visegrad

---

[8] In fact, it emerged as a result of three empires' collapse early this century (Rupnik, 1994: p. 92).

arrangements) has been very weak (Dunn, 1992: p. 27), whereas the prolonged uncertainty had to be addressed quite radically, and the governments of the transition countries, quite naturally, have sought to do it by increased efforts to gain admission into the EU and NATO (Andor, 1996: p. 218).

Moreover, Western Europe is at the moment a well-established economic bloc (in the form of EU) which threatens to become a "fortress Europe" whose protectionism (especially in the areas crucial for ECE, for example agriculture) would be impenetrable from independent positions. Joining EU, by contrast, promises economic benefits and prestige. It gives ECE a chance to join the "better" - the richer and more secure - part of what Falk calls "global apartheid" (1995: p. 138). Complete identification with the West, however, is problematic[9]. However, it can have a different form: not as identification with the West, but identification against the rest (especially the former Soviet Eastern Europe, Russia). This discourse requires "construction of those outside as "other" and therefore dangerous" in order "to secure its identity and legitimization which depend on the promise of security for its citizens" (Tickner, 1995: p. 189). The ideas of joining NATO, from where Russia is precluded, and the rhetoric on political and economic instability east of ECE's borders (for example, Cimoszewicz, 1996: p. 3) perfectly illustrates this mechanism.

CONSEQUENCES OF NEO-LIBERAL ECONOMIC ADJUSTMENT IN EAST-CENTRAL EUROPE

The results of adopting liberal economic policies in ECE are contradictory. Partially, this is a result of the nature of liberal economic systems: "[l]iberalism may or may not strengthen the economy, depending on the state's position within the global market" (Buzan, 1991: p. 366). Under conditions of economic liberalism, even the citizens of the Western countries have to be persuaded that the corresponding policies are beneficial, as they may also be exposed to growing economic, social and ecological hardship (Falk, 1995: pp. 134, 138). As far as ECE is concerned, suspicions about the adequacy of neo-liberal economic policies should be much higher. It is hardly ever discussed that similar economic difficulties would be unsustainable in the richer countries (Andor, 1996: p. 216). The hardship of post-socialist reforms is high and lasting, while the compensation (sustainable economic growth and macro-economic stability) is still pending. As a result, the prolonged economic crisis of the mid-1990s is becoming a source of further instability in the region (Andor, 1996: pp. 211, 215). Even more disappointingly, as Andor witnesses, the ECE states have pursued their national economic fortunes individually "competing with each other for Western aid, investment, and praise". It has resulted in a "competitive devaluation encouraged by BWIs [Bretton Woods Institutions]", by the virtue of which "short-term sacrifices have turned out to have led to long-term losses" (Andor, 1996: pp. 218-9).

Democratisation, for which East European peoples so long aspired during the previous decades, is an indisputably positive development in ECE. Still, if we take its economic and

9 Even if the ECE countries join the EU, they will be its poorest part with very limited real influence upon its decisions.

security implications into consideration, certain reservations have to be made. Western "assistance" in promoting democratisation in ECE can be seen as part of its new global economic project, and not a benign end in itself. As Andor points out:

> "[w]estern pressure for democratization in ECE had a major objective, highlighted by political scientists employed by the World Bank. Haggard and Kaufman, among others, argued that adjustment policies can be much more successfully implemented in "democratic" circumstances, where economic and social distress questions the legitimacy of the government, but not the entire regime." (Andor, 1996: p. 216)

The replies to this may be different, varying from hypocritical notions on "mistakes" of East-Central Europeans[10] to sad admission that "[w]hether the focus is Britain or globe, liberty without economic status is propaganda" (Booth, 1991: p. 322).

CONCLUSION

The inferences from this discourse cannot be optimistic. Analysing contemporary security arrangements in ECE brings us to broader discussions on security, and shows that the latter are inescapably linked to economic issues. In fact, it is economic nationalism that drives equally the policies of the ECE countries and those of the Western powers in the field. All actors in the international system are self-interested, with the strongest parts trying to institutionalise their advantage and use it for its economic, political and ideological purposes. ECE, having been urged to reformulate its economic and security identity, attempts to join the privileged "Western club". As a result, policies of the ECE governments in fact juxtapose their countries to their eastern neighbours. This creates additional tension in the region, promotes its heterogenisation and precludes sustainable and commonly acceptable solutions to the regional economic and security problems in the future. Boldly put, ECE rush into the Western sphere of "economic prosperity" giving the West additional political, economic and ideological leverage and leaving their eastern neighbours less chances for equal participation in the world economic and security system. The West, while experiencing difficulties in the era of adjustment to globalisation, willfully adheres to the logic of geopolitics, having its major preoccupations shifted from the balance of power to world economic hegemony (Falk, 1995: p. 145). Therefore I argue that it has opted to use ECE in its global security-economic project.

What is true when we speak of the effects that these developments on the Eastern Europe, is also true of the whole world. The nascent global power structure will affect negatively practically every country, seriously impeding the prospects for genuine international security, and complicate the economic positions of "the rest" (as opposed to the West and, possibly, ECE as its new "member").

---

[10] For example, an opinion expressed at one of the Wilton Park conferences: "East-central Europeans made their first mistake with democracy before they had even attained it. Most saw democracy as the exact opposite of their own Marxist-Leninist order, as another ideology, whose implementation would guarantee prosperity and stability" (Dunn, 1992: p. 6).

REFERENCES

Andor, L. (1996) "Economic Transformation and Political Stability in East-Central Europe", *Security Dialogue* Vol. 27, No. 2, pp. 207-225

Beinen, H, (1993), "America: The firsters, the decliners, and the searchers for a new American foreign policy", in Leaver, R. & Richardson, J. (eds) *Charting the Post-Cold War Order* (Boulder CO: Westview Press)

Booth, K. (1991) "Security and Emancipation", *Review of International Studies*, Vol. 17, No. 3, pp. 313-26

Boutros-Ghali, B. (1995) *An Agenda for Peace* (2nd ed.) (New York: UN)

Buzan, B (1991) *People, States and Fear* (2nd ed.) (New York: Harvester Wheatsheaf)

CFDP (1996) "Russia and NATO: Theses of the Council on Foreign and Defense Policy", *Comparative Strategy*, Vol. 15, No, 1, pp. 91-102

Camilleri, J. (1993) "Alliances and the Emerging Post-Cold War Security System", in Leaver, R. & Richardson, J. (eds) *Charting the Post-Cold War Order* (Boulder CO: Westview Press)

Cimoszewicz, W. (1996) "Building Poland's security: Membership of NATO a key objective", *NATO Review*, N3 (May), pp. 3-7

Dunn, J. (1992) *East-Central Europe: The Challenge of Freedom*, Whilton Park Papers 50, Jan. (London: HMSO)

Falk, R. (1997) "State of Siege: Will globalisation win out?", *International Affairs*, Vol. 73, No. 10 (January), pp. 123-36

Falk, R. (1995) *On Human Governance: Towards a new global politics* (Cambridge: Polity Press)

FCO (Foreign and Commonwealth Office) (1996) *Global Free Trade and Foreign Policy* (http://www.open.gov.uk/index.htm)

Fukuyama, F. (1992) *The End of History and the Last Man* (London: Hamish Hamilton)

Halliday, F. (1993) "The Cold War and Its Conclusion: Consequences for International Relations Theory", in Leaver, R. & Richardson, J. (eds.), *Charting the Post-Cold War Order* (Oxford: Westview Press)

Huntington, S. (1996) *The Clash of Civilizations and the Remaking of World Order* (New York: Simon & Schuster)

Huntington, S. (1993) "The Clash of Civilizations", *Foreign Affairs*, Vol. 72, No. 3 (Summer), pp. 22-50

Lewis, P. (1997) "Democratization in Eastern Europe", in Potter, D. et al (eds.) *Democratization* (Cambridge: Polity Press), pp. 399-420

Mack, A. (1993) *Concepts of Security in the Post-Cold War*, Working Paper 8, (Department of International Relations, A.N.U.)

NATO (1995) *Study on NATO enlargement* (http://www.nato.int/docu/basictxt/enl-9501.htm)

Rupnic, J. (1994) Europe's New Frontiers: Remapping Europe", *Daedalus*, Vol. 123, No. 3, pp. 91-114

Tickner, A. (1995) "Re-visioning Security", in Ken Booth and Steve Smith (eds.) *International Relations Theory Today* (Cornwall: Polity Press), pp. 175-97

Waever, O., Lemaitre, P. & Tromer, E. (eds.) (1989) *European Polyphony: Perspectives beyond East-West confrontation* (London: Macmillan)

Wallerstein, I. (1991) *Geopolitics and Geoculture: Essays on the changing world system* (Cambridge: Cambridge University Press)

Waltz, K. (1979) *Theory of International Politics* (Reading, Mass.: Addison-Wesley)

CHAPTER 3

MONETARY TRANSMISSION IN RUSSIA: THE ROLE OF INTERENTERPRISE ARREARS

IRINA A. DENISOVA
Moscow, Russia - Manchester, UK

Market-oriented economic reforms, started in Russia in 1992, pave the way to the country's higher involvement in international economy. Many economic processes are similar to those in transition economies of Eastern Europe. At the same time the depth and the length of output decline which accompanies the transformation in Russia (in 1995 real GDP was only 60% of 1991 level, with industrial production contraction of 50%), together with persistently high inflation, provide a challenge for economists.

The process of passing from the central planning principles of government budget formation to the market principles, complicated by exchange rate significant appreciation and servicing large external debt, is believed to underlie the upsurge of inflation at the early stages of transition in Russia (Ickes (1995)). Given the infant stage of private economy development and the large share of state ownership, the degree of flexibility in changing fiscal policy parameters, i.e. taxes and budget spending, is very limited at the early stages of transition, meaning chronically large budget deficits and making monetary policy the main instrument of output and inflation stabilization for the period.

With the general agreement that monetary policy propagation in transition economies is complicated by financial underdevelopment, there is no agreement about trade-off between disinflationary policy of monetary tightening in 1992-1995 and output decline, and particularly about the role of inter-enterprise arrears. There are authors who exclude tight money as a factor of dramatic decline, believing instead that wide-spread inter-enterprise trade credit was a normal substitution for banking credit and there is no specific arrears problem; so that it is relative price change together with drastic demand decline and systemic change shock that are responsible for the depth of output fall (Alfandari and Schaffer (1996), Koen and Phillips (1993)). At the same time it is stressed by many (Calvo (1991), Calvo and Coricelli (1993), Ickes and Ryterman (1993), Polterovich (1995)) that strict monetary policy which did not take into account the specific financial environment of transition economies, and the lack of developed credit markets in particular, made the condition of covering costs out of current cash flow excessively tight, especially given the additional expenditures imposed by the systemic shock accommodation, therefore making even viable in the long run firms currently loss-making and adversely affecting output.

It is difficult to conclude whether the monetary policy during the period was too tight and therefore has contributed to the output decline without investigating possible channels of monetary impulse propagation. The latter is the topic of the paper.

There are four main parts in the paper. General indicators of monetary policy in Russia in 1992-1995 are analyzed in the first part. Possible monetary transmission channels are discussed in the second part, and both banks' and enterprises' sides of the lending channel get special attention. Empirical analysis, based on industrial sectoral data, comprises the third part. The fourth part concludes.

MONETARY POLICY

The Central bank of Russia (CBR) pursued direct quantitative targeting in 1992-1995 and controlled money supply through credit ceilings and restrictive refinance policies. From Summer 1995, after the exchange rate corridor introduction, money supply became endogenous, though the crawling peg adoption since 1996 allows a certain degree of control.

The upsurge of inflation following price liberalization, together with the huge monetary overhang on the eve of reforms and the necessity to impose hard budget constraint on enterprises, requested strict monetary policy. The necessity to prove credibility of the economic reforms, especially acute in the context of changing political regime, provided additional rationale for tight monetary and credit policy. At the same time, the difficulty of demand for money estimation at the early stages of transition, stemming from ongoing structural changes, including substantial shifts in relative prices, and high inflation environment, increase the probability of money supply mistargeting, and excessive monetary contraction in particular, with severe consequences for efficiency and growth (Calvo and Coricelli (1993), Hilbers (1993), Bofinger et. al. (1995)).

Both broad money (M2 aggregate) and monetary base in real terms experienced a pronounced contraction throughout 1993 and seem to stabilize by the end of 1994 - beginning of 1995, with broad money on average being only 55 % of beginning of 1992 level. If compared with earlier years, the reduction in money supply is even more striking. Indeed, M2 to GDP ratio has experienced more than a fourfold reduction as compared with the middle of the 1980s level (Table 1).

The depth of broad money decline in 1992-1994, together with systematically reported cash shortages[1], appear to suggest that the adopted monetary policy aimed at fighting inflation turned out to be excessively restrictive (Calvo and Coricelli (1993),

1 Wage and other payments' arrears are widespread and are especially heavy in the public sector thus undermining the general payment discipline in the economy.

Table 1. *Money Aggregates as Percentage of GDP Dynamics and Velocity.*

	1986	**1987**	**1988**	**1989**	**1990**	**1991**	**1992**	**1993**	**1994**	**1995**
M0 as percent of GDP	9.1	9.4	9.8	10.7	12.8	9.7	5.2	4.6	3.8	
M2 as percent of GDP	49.2	53.2	57.4	61.3	69.2	57.7	22.6	14.1	11.7	9.3
M0 velocity	6.0	5.8	5.7	5.6	5.3	6.0	7.5	10.3	15.1	
M2 velocity	2.0	1.9	1.7	1.6	1.4	1.7	4.4	7.1	8.5	10.8

Source: (Illarionov (1995): Table 3, p.24-5); Goskomstat and author's calculations for 1995.
Note: 1986-1990 refer to the USSR, 1991-1995 refer to Russia.

Polterovich (1995)). Naturally, one should be careful comparing the M2/GDP ratio for the middle of the eighties and after 1992, because, as is stressed by many (Illarionov (1995), e.g.), the former is likely to include a large monetary overhang component. Before price liberalization estimations of the price increase necessary to delete the monetary overhang were on the order of 50 per cent (Ofer (1993): p.554). Even if the post-1991 ratios are adjusted to eliminate the overhang component and to take into account the increased desired velocity in the context of high inflationary expectations, the hypothesis that the observed M2/GDP decline was too dramatic and monetary policy which caused it excessively restricted can not be ruled out. The widely acknowledged fact that the actual inflation in 1992 far exceeded the expected one suggests that the dramatic reduction of real money balances were not supposed.

It is likely that excessive reduction in broad money supply, mainly via credit contraction, pushed money market into disequilibrium by creating liquidity shortage in the economy which resulted in sharp real interest rate increase and aggravated recession. The widespread payment arrears in general and interenterprise overdue trade credit in particular seem to be evidence in favor of this line of reasoning, though it is contestable (Koen and Marrese (1995), Alfandari and Schaffer (1996), Polterovich (1995)).

Table 2. *Monetary survey data of selected countries, 1995**
(end of period, per cent of GDP)

	Russia	Estonia	Czech Republic	Poland	Ukraine	Canada	Fin-land	UK	USA
Domestic credit	22.3	12.8	88.6	34.8	24.1	74.2	68.4	124.2	78.2
Net claims on central government**	10.2	-4.1	5.8	10.9	7.6	13.0	3.7	5.1	13.1
Claims on nonfinancial public enterprises	3.8	2.3	18.8	12.8	11.9	-	-	-	-
Claims on private sector	8.2	14.6	64.0	11.1	4.6	61.2	64.7	118.3	65.2
Money (M1)	9.3	19.8	34.4	13.3	15.4	17.3	32.2		16.8
Money +quasi-money (M2)	16.9	25.2	86.7	32.3	26.7	61.4	58.6	104.2	58.5
Total trade credit***	31		...	35		30	43	39	31
Trade credit extended	17		50	19		16	20	20	17
incl. overdue	9		18	10		...	9	12	...
Trade credit received	14		...	16		14	23	19	14
incl. overdue	8			6					

Source: Author's calculations based on (International Financial Statistics (1997): pp.572-5) for Russia and (International Financial Statistics (1996): pp. 166, 222, 254, 506, 638, 642) for the rest of the countries. Trade credit data is from (Alfandari and Schaffer (1996): pp.104-5).

Note: * Data for Ukraine is for 1994.

** General government for Russia, Poland and Ukraine; central and local governments for Canada; central government and official entities for the UK; central, state and local governments for the USA.

*** 1994 for Russia, 1993 for Poland, 1994 for Czech Republic, 1993 for the rest of the countries; trade credit data is over annualized GDP.

International comparisons appear to affirm our hypothesis: the share of domestic credit to GDP in general, and credit to non-government in particular, is rather small on international scale even for transition economies (Table 2). In 1995 domestic credit to non-government (the sum of claims on nonfinancial public enterprises and on private sector) was 23% of GDP in Poland, 82.8% of GDP in the Czech Republic and only 12 % of GDP in Russia. The lowest levels of both M1 and M2 to GDP ratios were observed again in Russia.

It is often argued that the observed low levels of money aggregates are compensated by higher velocity, implying that it is velocity that distinguishes the Russian economy from many other economies in transition. At the same time as most of the economies in transition started reforms with roughly the same financial system characteristics, as well as the level of inflationary expectations, desired (by economic agents) velocity of money is unlikely to vary significantly across the sample. It is rather actual (observed) velocity that could be different reflecting different monetary policy. Therefore, the aforementioned line of reasoning appears to implicitly assume that money supply meets demand for money, while supply mistargeting[2] is very probable given large shocks to demand for liquid assets and financial sector underdevelopment.

It is hardly possible to judge whether the credit policy in Russia was too tight and therefore has caused real costs without proper understanding of monetary transmission mechanism.

TRANSMISSION MECHANISM

It is generally accepted that monetary policy can have a significant influence on real economic variables in the short run, whereas propagation mechanisms of a monetary impulse are debatable. There are four major types of monetary channels recognized in literature (see e.g., Mishkin (1995), for a review):

1. The interest rate channel, originally associated with the basic Keynesian (IS-LM) model: monetary tightening (reduction in money supply) leads to excess demand for real money balances; economic agents, seeking ways to increase their money holdings, sell their financial assets (bonds); enhanced supply of bonds results in their price reduction and interest rate increase, which in turn pushes investment spending' and housing and consumer durable expenditures' to contract. In the short run, the aggregate demand decrease is transmitted into output fall and price increase, whereas in the long run the monetary impulse is accommodated by price adjustment.
2. Growing internationalization of economic development raised the importance of the exchange rate channel operating through net exports: contractionary monetary policy, increasing interest rate in the aforementioned manner, makes domestic currency denominated deposits more attractive relative to foreign currency deposits, therefore leading to domestic currency appreciation; given price stability, the real exchange rate also appreciates, meaning the loss of domestic goods' competitiveness; net exports decline; to adjust to the aggregate demand fall, output diminishes, while prices increase.
3. The so called other asset price effects constitute the third possible channel. Money supply reduction, leading to excess demand for real money balances, forces economic agents to cut their spending, including spending for equities (and/or land

2 Broad money multiplier, calculated as the ratio of M2 aggregate to base money (i.e the sum of currency outside the CBR and reserves), experienced substantial fluctuations in 1992-1996.

and property, as in (Meltzer (1995))).[3] Demand for equities diminishes, resulting in lower equity price, and therefore decreasing market price of firms relative to the replacement cost of capital (Tobin's q). As a result, investment spending fall, and so do aggregate demand and output. On the other hand, equity price (and/or land and property valuation) fall causes economic agents' financial wealth depreciation, which, through life-cycle model argument, decreases consumption, which adds to the aggregate demand and output reduction.

4. The credit channel (Kashyap et.al. (1993), Bernanke and Blinder (1992)) stresses the influence of imperfect information on financial markets, and in particular, the fact that informational asymmetries result in equilibrium credit rationing. Two types of propagation mechanisms are emphasized: bank lending and the balance-sheet channels. The bank lending channel is supposed to work as follows: contractionary monetary policy, through Central Bank open market sales, for example, drains reserves and hence deposits from the banking system, and therefore, limits the supply of bank loans by reducing banks' ability to access loanable funds[4]. It is argued in (Bernanke and Blinder (1988)) that this effect, transmitted through the level and composition of bank assets, is over and above the traditional (IS-LM) money supply and interest rate effects reflected in declining bank liabilities. The decreased supply of loans affects equilibrium credit rationing making more firms rationed. Firms are not homogenous in respect to their ability to access external finance sources: large firms can raise funds through stock and bond markets, whereas small firms are likely to be "bank-dependent". Having no, or little, substitutes for bank credit and scarce cash resources, small firms face lack of working capital in periods of monetary tightening and have to reduce production. In (Gertler and Gilchrist (1994)) it was shown that there are striking differences in behavior between large and small firms in periods of monetary policy tightening in respect to their short-term debt and inventories accumulation.

It is generally accepted that financial infrastructure affects the way a monetary impulse is propagated. Most of financial institutions in Russia are new, therefore typically lacking both reputation and experience so important for financial system reliability. The financial system is dominated by the banking sector, while the short-term money market lacks depth, and medium- and long-term capital markets, including equity and bond markets, are at the early stages of development.

Given the infant period of stock market development in Russia, the lending channel of monetary policy transmission appears to be dominant at the initial stages of transition, whereas interest rate and exchange rate channels are likely to become significant only in 1995-1996 after government treasury bonds' (GKO) market has developed; the so-called other asset price and balance sheet effects are hardly observable at all.

---

3 Incorporating interest rate channel, one may add that interest rate increase makes bonds more attractive than equities.

The sharp growth of foreign currency denominated deposits[5] of both households and enterprises, which, in the absence of securities' market, served as a major means of inflationary hedges, complicated monetary control, not to mention the large seigniorage losses from the sizable foreign currency exposure of the banking system. Changes in exchange rate expectations, and the consequent substitution between domestic and foreign currency deposits, appear to result in significant short-run shifts in the demand for domestic currency assets. Some of the changes in exchange rate expectations and actual values may be attributed to monetary policy variation, meaning the traditional exchange rate channel transformation in high inflation/negative real interest rate context.

It was only in 1995 that ruble deposits' yield exceeded dollar deposits' return, which, being put on a sustained basis in the environment of pegged exchange rate system, is likely to diminish the source of money demand instability. At the same time, after the crawling peg was introduced in 1996 and inflation diminished substantially, the possibility of employing traditional exchange rate channel of monetary policy transmission appeared: monetary tightening, for example, which is likely to result, via GKO market, in increased interest rates, may cause a shift into domestic currency denominated deposits, leading to real exchange rate appreciation and net exports decline.

The enhanced role of GKO market in the economy, together with the sharp reduction of inflation, is likely to lay down grounds for traditional interest rate channel of monetary transmission: monetary tightening/expansion may have a significant impact on the T-bills secondary market interest rate, which in turn, would affect the whole system of interest rates in the economy. With the increased interest rate sensitivity of private investment, it could result in aggregate demand and consequently, output changes.

The lending channel, which is likely to stay the main channel at initial stages of transition, is significantly modified in comparison with traditional, both on demand for loans and supply of loans side, since the credit extenders and recipients are quite different.

Banking side.

The structure of the banking industry was shaped principally during institutional reforms at the end of the 1980s -beginning 1990s, which has lead to the emergence of a two-tiered - Central bank-commercial banks - system. Domestic commercial banks can be divided into two basic categories: banking institutions based on the former state specialized banks account for approximately one-third of all banks, with the remaining two-thirds being newly established banks. Even the largest (by domestic standards) commercial banks are small by international standards: the average size of assets per bank in the sample of 577 Moscow banks was $0.032bn in the end of 1994 against $27.7bn in the UK and $3.9bn in Germany in 1993 (Dmitriev (1996): p.3). Credit

4 Loanable funds and securities are not perfect substitutes in bank portfolio, and banks do not absorb deposit losses completely by reducing securities holdings.

5 Foreign currency denominated deposits increased from 19% of total deposits in January 1992 to 43% in June 1993 and 30% in August 1993. The ratio of hard currency to (M2+hard currency denominated deposits) increased from 15% in March 1992 to 29% in December 1993 (Granville (1995): p.42).

organizations are generally poorly capitalized: in January 1996 the share of credit organizations with statutory capital of more than Rb30bn (approximately $6mn) was only 2.8%, whereas the major group (36.6%) falls into Rb1-5bn (less than $1mn) interval (Vestnik Bankovskoi Statistiki (1996): p.38). Underdeveloped financial infrastructure makes credit market highly segmented. Regional differences are substantial: the share of the Central region in banking credit in January 1996 was 31%, with Moscow and the Moscow region accounting for 28% (Vestnik Bankovskoi Statistiki (1996): p.45).

The movement from monobank system, characterized by an uneven distribution of deposits and credits among banks and former specialized banks' dominance[6], resulted in a large dependence of most banks, particularly the new ones, on the Central bank of Russia (CBR) refinance. Similar processes were observed in Czechoslovakia, Poland, Hungary and other transition economies (Sundararajan (1990)). That made the CBR not only the anchor of the banking system, but the system's major source of credit, especially during the first years of transition: it provided refinance resources for small banks and channeled credit funds through large banks. Directed state credit funded by the CBR or the budget amounted to 48% of total bank credit in 1992 and was reduced to 29% and 23% of total bank credit in 1993 and 1994 respectively (Koen and Marrese (1995): p.58).

Given the dependence, refinance ceilings have an impact on credit that is similar to credit ceilings: refinance policies, although in principle an indirect instrument, have more of a direct character, as limiting the amount of refinance directly restricts bank lending. The CBR refinance rate and the method of distributing aggregate refinance among banks affect both the effectiveness of monetary control and the evolution of the interbank and credit markets. In the period of 1992-1995 the refinance rate was the key interest rate in the economy, influencing the deposit and lending rates. With the banking system development and refinance interest rate increase, the share of CBR refinance resources in commercial banks' liabilities diminished (Table 3).

The structure of Russian commercial banks' assets and liabilities differs substantially from that in developed countries (Table 4). On the liability side the share of demand deposits is relatively higher, at the expense of time deposits mainly, implying relatively cheaper resources. On the asset side reserves are rather high, making less funds available for lending; also credit to the government accounts for a significant portion of credit. The difference is even more striking according to the survey of 577 Moscow commercial banks reported in (Dmitriev (1996): pp.3-4): the share of "interest-free" obligations, i.e. those on which banks do not pay interest or pay interest much less than on time deposits,

6 About 75% of private savings are handled by Sberbank - the largest bank historically dealing with household deposits, which has a broad network of local branches throughout the country and is backed by state warranties.

Table 3. *Russian deposit money banks' balance sheet structure** *(% of total assets, end of period).*

Assets	1993	1994	1995	1996
Reserves	13.1	11.7	10.7	11.4
Foreign assets	26.2	23.9	13.5	13.3
Claims on general** government	1.3	5.1	18.3	22.1
Claims on nonfinance public enterprises	25.9	23.3	18.2	17.7
Claims on private sector	33.5	35.9	39.1	35.1
Claims on other financial institutions	-	-	0.2	0.3

Liabilities	1993	1994	1995	1996
Demand deposits	20.7	15.8	20.3	17.9
Time, saving and foreign currency dep.	28.3	29.6	36.4	33.0
incl. foreign currency deposits	*20.0*	*18.1*	*16.1*	*14.0*
Money market instr.	0.3	1.7	3.5	3.2
Foreign liabilities	7.8	7.0	8.7	11.8
General government deposits	3.5	3.3	2.8	2.4
Credit from monetary authorities***	14.0	8.3	2.3	2.5
Capital accounts	19.9	12.7	19.5	24.2
Other items (net)	5.3	21	6.5	5.1

Source: Author's calculations based on International Financial Statistics (1997), pp.572-5

Note: * Consolidated accounts of the commercial banks (including branches of foreign banks), the Savings Bank (Sberbank), and Vneshekonombank. All data include both ruble- and foreign currency denominated accounts. Data before June 1995 were compiled by the IMF using basic accounting data and other information provided by the authorities prior to establishment of regular data reporting.

** General government comprises central and local government units and their extra budgetary funds.

*** Credit from monetary authorities is consolidated credit from the CBR and from the central government conducting monetary authority functions.

was about 70% of total assets in 1994, and non-working assets (mainly reserves, including excess, and monetary assets) were 51% of total assets.

High credit risks, underdeveloped payment system with large size and variability of payments float[7], preventing from effective liquidity management are likely to explain

7 The term float refers to amounts that have been debited from a payer's account before the corresponding credit entry has been posted in a payee's account, and vice versa (amounts that have been credited to a payees account before the corresponding debit entry has been posted in a payer's account). It reflects differences in timing between crediting and debiting of accounts caused by delays in the transmission of

Table 4. *Balance sheet structure of deposit money banks in selected countries in 1995*
(% of total assets, end of period)

Assets								
	Russia	**Poland**	**Czech Republic**	**Estonia**	**Finland**	**UK**	**Canada**	**USA**
Reserves	10.7	12.9*	10.8	10.2	8.5	0.4	0.7	1.8
Foreign assets	13.5	13.5	6.7	29.2	19.5	49.4	12.6	0.8
Claims on general government***								
Claims on non-finance public enterprises	18.3	30.0	13.0	5.1	7.0	1.6	14.7	10.1
Claims on private sector								
	18.2	15.5	15.7	7.6	-	-	-	-
Claims on other financial institutions								
	39.1	28.0	53.7	47.8	65.0	48.5	72.0	87.3
	0.2							

Table 4. *Balance sheet structure of deposit money banks in selected countries in 1995 (% of total assets, end of period) (cont'd)*

Liabilities	**Russia**	**Poland**	**Czech Republic**	**Estonia**	**Finland**	**UK**	**Canada**	**USA**
Demand deposits	20.3	13.6	20.8	34.8	30.4	41.5**	16.6	19.3
Time, saving and foreign currency deposits	36.4	51.1	40.3	17.7	26.5		51.9	40.3
incl. foreign cur. dep.								
Money market instrum.	*16.1*		*3.8*	*12.8*				10.6
Bonds								
Foreign liabilities	3.5	3.9	3.1	26	23.7	50.7	14.8	4.4
General government deposits ****								
Credit from monetary authorities	8.7	4.2	11.5	0.7	3.5		0.9	8.2
	2.8	5.9	6.2		1.6			0.5
	2.3		6.2					0.0
Capital accounts	19.5	9.9	13.1	14.5				
Other items (net)	6.5	11.3	0.0	-6.5	14.4	7.8	15.8	16.7

Source: Author's calculations based on International Financial Statistics (1997), pp.572-5 for Russia and International Financial Statistics (1996), pp. 166, 222, 254, 506, 638 and 642 for the rest of the countries

Note:
* includes nonreserve claims on monetary authorities.

** includes demand, time, savings and foreign currency deposits.

*** include claims on central and local governments and on National Property Fund for the Czech Republic; claims on central government for Estonia and Finland; claims on general government for Poland and Russia; claims on central and local governments for Canada; claims on central, state and local governments for the USA; claims on central government (net) and official entities for the UK.

****include deposits of central and local governments and of National Property Fund for the Czech Republic; deposits of central government, counterpart funds and government lending funds for Estonia; deposits of central government and government lending funds for Finland; deposits of general government for Poland and Russia; deposits of central government for Canada and the USA.

holding excess reserves, whereas high profitability of short-term foreign exchange operations in chronically high inflation/Ruble depreciation environment stimulated holding non-working foreign currency assets (Granville (1995), Balino et.al. (1994)).

Exchange rate corridor introduction in July 1995 decreased profitability of foreign exchange operations. Together with the high return on GKO in the context of massive government borrowing, this resulted in the shift in commercial banks' assets from foreign exchange operations to credit to the government (Table 3). Government borrowing is likely to crowd out non-government credit, which decreased from 59% of assets in 1993-1994 to 53% in 1996.

Decreased inflation augmented time and saving deposits' portion in liabilities. At the same time continued strict monetary policy revealed itself in the diminished share of credit from monetary authorities. The overall share of resources from the government and monetary authorities is rather low as compared with other transition economies (Table 4): in 1995 it was only 5.1% of total assets in Russia, while it amounted to 10.1% and 12.4% in Poland and the Czech Republic respectively. Given the banking system underdevelopment discussed above, this is likely to adversely affect supply of credit.

Overall, the banking system's weakness at the initial stages of transition reflected in the lack of private loanable funds, together with the absence of substantial securities counterpart in banking assets caused by capital market underdevelopment, impede substitution for reduced centralized loanable funds and appear to reinforce the impact of tight monetary policy on banking credit supply. In periods of monetary contraction, either via direct CBR resources rationing or via refinance interest rate policies, credit supply to the economy in real terms was reduced, whereas, for example, the CBR nominal refinance interest rate decline in the period of April 1994 - September 1994 was accompanied by practically immediate credit in real terms enlargement.

Moreover, a high degree of economy-wide systemic risk stemming from large structural changes, which can not be fully diversified in the environment of underdeveloped capital markets, deteriorated the quality of loan portfolios, reduced the number of profitable investment opportunities for private banks and resulted in high excess reserves, increasing the chance that potentially viable enterprises could face a credit crunch because of credit ceilings and high interest rates. The high inflation context also contributed to resource allocation distortion, since banking assets were devoted to exploiting financial opportunities (foreign currency exchange and interbank credit market operations), rather than invested in real sector. Massive government borrowing on domestic money market (GKO sales) diverts banking sector resources from real sector to budget deficit finance, thereby aggravating credit rationing of the former.

In addition, there appears to be another possible channel of monetary tightening transmission into lower banking credit supply, affecting mostly small banks: strict refinance policy of the CBR together with the decreased profitability of foreign exchange operations after the corridor introduction, which resulted in banking sector liquidity crises in Summer 1995, is likely to impair banks' capital, therefore, meaning low "collateral" value for banking operations, including raising loanable funds[8].

All these factors are likely to adversely affect both the willingness and the ability of banks to provide adequate funding to enterprises, meaning that in the short-run a reduction in state credit is unlikely to be matched by an expansion of private credit, which may have severe consequences for investment and growth.

> "Eventually, private credit may emerge full bloom, but there is likely to be a period of credit shortage during the transition that is not trivial. The duration of this transition is likely to depend on the pace, breadth and depth of the financial reform."
>
> (Calvo (1991): p.201)

Enterprises' side.

Enterprises' side (demand for loans) also has some distinguishing features. Most enterprises are "transitional" by character, since they are already not socialist enterprises but at the same time they are not firms yet. Ickes and Ryterman (Ickes and Ryterman (1993)) call them survival-oriented enterprises, as the main motive for them in the period is to survive in the changing environment.

Transformation shock, incorporating significant relative price change following price and foreign trade liberalization together with demand contraction after the CMEA[9] and the USSR collapse and systemic shock of moving from planning system to market organized economy, adversely affected the profitability of most enterprises. Adjustment requires substantial financial resources. Directors of the industrial enterprises in the survey of 151 industrial enterprises in Moscow, St. Petersburg, Voronezh, Krasnoyarsk, Novosibirsk, Stavropol and Kostroma oblast in August-September 1993 (Strategiya vizhivaniya (1994)), reported financial problems to be the most difficult, with the main reasons being high taxes (74% of respondents), material prices increases (48%), Ruble depreciation (30%), break-down of inter-enterprise commercial relations and technological chains (40%). Money balances were named as the most deficit resources by 79% of respondents, raw materials and investment by 31%, while labor and equipment were mentioned by only 12% of respondents.

Most enterprises do not have enough internal funds, and therefore, have to rely upon external finance, which is in line with most developing countries experience: the average 1980-1988 share of external finance in net investment expenditure of nonfinancial enterprises was 65% in India, 79% in Korea, 82% in Turkey (Calvo and Kumar (1993): Appendix Table 2, p.30). What seem to distinguish transition economies is the limited ability to raise funds through equity emission in the environment of not fully defined property rights and difficulties with exercising control rights given the role of insiders.

---

8 The fact that after the banking crises in 1995 interbank credit lost its significance as the source of liquid funds for small banks testifies in favor of the argument.

9 Council for Mutual Economic Assistance.

And equity finance accounted for rather large portion of net investment expenditure of nonfinancial enterprises in developing countries: 44% in Korea, 61% in Turkey (Calvo and Kumar (1993): Appendix Table 2, p.30). This makes banking credit and financial transfers from the government the main sources of external finance for transition enterprises, leaving trade credit aside.

Total federal government financial transfers to the enterprise sector were reduced substantially during the reforms: they amounted to more than 30% of GDP in 1992 and were cut to about 6-7% of GDP in 1994, according to the World Bank estimations (Alfandari, Fan and Freikman (1996): p.166). Besides, government financial transfers are reported (Ibid.) to be small by average size, and thereby not enough to provide finance for enterprises' adjustment, allowing to cover only part of operational costs. They are also highly concentrated in energy sector.

In a developed financial system, potentially viable enterprises would be able to raise funds through banking credit or equity finance. But financial markets' underdevelopment and the aforementioned property rights difficulties practically eliminated the stock market opportunities of gaining funds and, together with the lack of retained earnings, increased enterprises' dependence on banking credit.

Government financial transfers reduction together with the limited availability of banking credit due to credit rationing in 1992-1993 and high interest rates since 1994, both reflecting the CBR monetary policy tightening, contributed to the widespread of inter-enterprise trade credit to finance working capital investment. The specificity of trade credit in transition economy, characterized by rapid inflation, high systemic risk of default and incomplete public financial information, is that enterprises extend credit to other enterprises at negative[10] real interest rates and with uncertain prospects of repayment. There are two main reasons for such a behavior:

1. Survival motive: systemic changes during transition require time, in particular, the replacement of the old planning system of direct inputs' distribution for a new market-style wholesale trade and acquiring marketing skills is time consuming, especially given the lack of appropriate infrastructure and product market regional segmentation; in the meanwhile period it was optimal for enterprises to stick to their traditional suppliers and customers, and providing them with trade credit served to guarantee from the failure of an important supplier or a customer, which was crucial for survival of an enterprise itself (Ickes and Ryterman (1993)).
2. Another obvious reason for inter-enterprise credit rapid growth is the lack of finance for current operations: with an underdeveloped financial system, the scope for borrowing against future income is severely limited.

10 It is likely that as time goes enterprises start taking into account the expected inflation and probability of non-payment when determining prices.

Inter-enterprise trade credit became the dominant source of short-term finance of industrial enterprises[11]. Payables to suppliers accounted for almost 50% of total industrial enterprises' liabilities in 1993-1995, with about half being overdue, whereas banking credit and internal financial resources (real money balances and securities' holdings) were on the order of 15% of total liabilities each (Table 5).

It is difficult to evaluate what is a "normal " level of trade credit, and particularly, overdue trade credit, for an economy in transition. Total trade credit (receivables and payables) in Russia in 1994-1995 was on the order of 25% of annualized GDP, with overdue trade credit about 12%, that is not exceptional according to international standards (Alfandari and Schaffer (1996)). But trade credit is only the fourth source of finance, after internal resources, banking loans and securities, in most developed countries (Table 6). Banking loans' share in gross financing varies from 13% in Canada to more than 40% in France and Japan. Total trade credit to GDP ratio in Russia is at least twice as much as total banking credit to GDP share, which is likely to be not only a sign of a general financial system underdevelopment but an indication of excessively tight monetary policy as well. Besides, a large part of the stock reflects uncollectible receivables from firms which will never pay, and tradable value of a Russian receivable is much lower than in an economy with developed capital market. Hence, is hardly possible to call the corporate financing pattern in Russia "normal".

There is no clear understanding of the role of inter-enterprise arrears in monetary transmission in transition economy. Brought to life by strict monetary policy and the lack of banking credit, the arrears provided an alternative source of short-term finance. At the same time the low-liquid quasi-money (creditories and debitories) are unlikely to provide a perfect substitute for normal credit. The wide spread of trade credit arrears, making enterprises involved in the network without their will, slows down structural changes in the economy, deteriorates public financial informational and prevents viable enterprises from being distinguished from non-viable. The overall impact is contestable.

EMPIRICAL ANALYSIS

Enterprises are not passive in respect to the level of trade credit arrears they hold: naturally, they choose the level of payables; they are also reported to control the level of receivables with a variety of formal and informal methods (Alfandari and Schaffer (1996)). In what follows we will try to determine the factors that govern arrears-to-production ratios[12], with the stress on banking credit accessibility indicators, and to find out whether liquid assets structure affects real output.

11 Total industry accounts for more than 70% of receivables and payables of industry, agriculture, transport and construction.

12 It is natural to think that sectors decide upon the levels of arrears/output ratio.

Table 5. *Short-term (Liquid) Assets and Liabilities of Industrial Enterprises (% of total short-term liabilities, end of month)*

Assets	**Nov-93**	**Nov-94**	**Nov-95**	***Liabilities***	**Nov-93**	**Nov-94**	**Nov-95**
Total Industry							
Total debtors	74.3	70.3	61.8	Total creditors	83.7	79.9	82.3
incl. in arrears	*30.2*	*38.3*	*29.0*	*incl. in arrears*	*29.2*	*42.7*	*41.8*
Receivables from customers	60.7	57.0	48.0	Payables to suppliers	52.3	48.7	43.3
incl. overdue	*26.1*	*33.0*	*24.9*	*incl. overdue*	*21.3*	*27.6*	*19.8*
Cash and bank deposits	11.2	6.8	3.1	Payables to the budget	11.1	14.4	17.6
Financial investment	2.4	5.3	7.6	*incl. overdue*	*3.7*	*8.9*	*11.6*
				Total bank credit	16.3	20.1	17.7
				incl. overdue	*1.2*	*2.4*	*2.0*
Energy Sector							
Total debtors	80.2	86.5	77.2	Total creditors	95.0	93.8	92.1
incl. in arrears	*33.2*	*54.3*	*43.0*	*incl. in arrears*	*30.0*	*56.9*	*54.1*
Receivables from customers	63.9	72.0	63.7	Payables to suppliers	55.5	57.9	49.4
incl. overdue	*28.1*	*47.0*	*37.5*	*incl. overdue*	*20.6*	*35.8*	*25.8*
Cash and bank deposits	16.9	10.7	2.7	Payables to the budget	19.6	21.4	23.1
Financial investment	2.5	6.7	9.6	*incl. overdue*	*6.4*	*14.9*	*17.2*
				Total bank credit	4.9	6.2	7.9
				incl. overdue	*0.2*	*0.5*	*0.5*
Manufacturing Sector							
Total debtors	70.2	60.7	52.9	Total creditors	78.2	71.8	76.9
incl. in arrears	*28.5*	*29.1*	*21.0*	*incl. in arrears*	*28.5*	*33.4*	*35.2*
Receivables from customers	58.1	47.9	40.3	Payables to suppliers	48.4	42.7	39.1
incl. overdue	*24.9*	*25.0*	*17.7*	*incl. overdue*	*21.3*	*21.7*	*16.3*
Cash and bank deposits	7.8	4.4	3.3	Payables to the budget	6.7	10.6	14.8
Financial investment	2.3	4.6	6.6	*incl. overdue*	*2.3*	*5.6*	*8.6*
				Total bank credit	21.8	28.2	23.1
				incl. overdue	*1.7*	*3.6*	*2.9*

Source: Author's calculations based on Goskomstat data

Note: The energy sector is defined as electricity and fuel (i.e. gas, coal, oil and oil refining) industries. The manufacturing sector is then defined to consist of ferrous metallurgy, non-ferrous metallurgy, chemicals and petrochemicals, machinery and metal processing, forestry, timber processing, pulp and paper, construction materials, light and food industries (eight industries altogether).

Table 6. *Average Gross Financing of Nonfinancial Enterprises: Large Industrial Countries, 1970-1985 average,(percent of total financing)*

	Canada	**Finland**	**France**	**Germany**	**Italy**	**Japan**	**United Kingdom**	**United States**
Internal finance	54.2	42.1	44.1	55.2	38.5	33.7	72.0	66.9
External finance	45.8	57.9	55.9	44.8	61.5	66.3	28.0	33.1
Loans	*12.8*	*27.2*	*41.5*	*21.1*	*38.6*	*40.7*	*21.4*	*23.1*
Trade credit	*8.6*	*17.2*	*4.7*	*2.2*	-	*18.3*	*2.8*	*8.4*
Bonds	*6.1*	*1.8*	*2.3*	*0.7*	*2.4*	*3.1*	*0.8*	*9.7*
Short-term securities	*1.4*	*2.5*	-	-	*0.1*	-	*2.3*	*1.4*
Equities	*11.9*	*5.6*	*10.6*	*2.1*	*10.8*	*3.5*	*4.9*	*0.8*
Other	*4.9*	*3.6*	*-3.3*	*18.6*	*9.6*	*0.7*	*-4.2*	*-10.1*

Source: (Calvo and Kumar (1993): Appendix Table 1, p.30; Mayer C. (1991): Table 12. 3, p.312)

Industrial sectors are not homogenous. The depth of output decline is less in energy industries. Energy sector[13] appears to benefit from the relative price changes which occurred after 1992, and, being the main exporting sector, to experience smaller trade shocks following the CMEA break up and the USSR dissolution. At the same time, energy prices are still subjected to regulation, though government financial transfers[14] seem to provide partial compensation for this. The distinction is likely to be translated into different financing pattern of the sector (Table 5): cash and bank deposits and financial investment account for a larger share of assets; total creditors in arrears (both payables to suppliers and to the budget) are a larger portion of liabilities. The substitution from arrears' financing to bank credit, noticeable in both sectors, is stable in the energy one, possibly suggesting better ability to access bank credit, that is not surprising if one notice that the portion of overdue bank credit is much lower in the energy sector than in manufacturing.

Therefore, it seems reasonable to distinguish between the energy and the manufacturing sectors in regression analysis. One should mention that well-known problems with available statistics on transition economies in general, and on the Russian economy in particular, preclude the application of certain sophisticated econometric methods demanding long time series (co-integration analysis being an example). Moreover, many statistical methodologies inherited by the State Statistical Office (Goskomstat) from the central planning system appear to be not suitable for the new

13 The energy sector is defined as electricity and fuel (i.e. gas, coal, oil and oil refining) industries. The manufacturing sector is then defined to consist of ferrous metallurgy, non-ferrous metallurgy, chemicals and petrochemicals, machinery and metal processing, forestry, timber processing, pulp and paper, construction materials, light and food industries (eight industries altogether).

14 As it was already mentioned, government financial transfers are highly concentrated in energy sector.

market-oriented economy, therefore limiting the scope for econometric analysis. The on-going process of adopting modern statistical methodology results in time series reconsideration, making some of the series incompatible with collected earlier and hence too short for analysis. Altogether, statistical problems limit the scope for standard regression analysis.

Industrial data are the most reliable and complete in comparison with other economic sectors' data. Goskomstat monthly data on industrial, total and by sectors[15], production, trade credit extended and received, money balances (i.e. cash and both Ruble and hard currency bank deposits) and industrial price indices in 1994 - 1996 are used. Unfortunately, with the exception of price indices, there is only fragmentary data on the aforementioned series for 1992-1993.

Testing factors determining arrears' ratios.

The ratio of overdue payables to suppliers over total material costs[16] of a sector appears to be a good proxy for the arrears' ratio of the sector, whereas the proportion of overdue receivables of an industry from customers to its production is an analogue of the probability of nonpayment for the sector's product. The former is denoted $(1-\gamma)$ for the energy and $(1-\beta)$ for the manufacturing sector; $(1-\hat{\beta})$ and $(1-\hat{\gamma})$ stand for the latter.

The series used in the regressions below were converted to logarithmic scale and equations were estimated in first difference form[17]. AR(n) and MA(m) are autoregressive and moving average correction terms of orders *n* and *m* respectively[18]. t-statistics are in parenthesis under the respective coefficients, while diagnostic checking of regressions' residuals with Box-Pierce test statistic is presented after the coefficient of determination and Durbin-Watson statistic, with the probability of the residuals being random given in parenthesis next to the statistic.

To take into account the change in the energy sector liquid assets structure (the substitution from money balances to financial investment) following the increased

---

15 Nominal variables associated with the energy and manufacturing sectors are obtained by summation across respective industries, and real variables are obtained by dividing the nominal variables by the respective industrial price index (IPI). Energy sector IPI is calculated according to the formula: *Energy sector IPI* = (Nominal output in Electroenergy + Nominal output in Fuel sector)/ (Real output in Electroenergy + Real output in Fuel sector). Manufacturing sector IPI is obtained as: *Manufacturing sector IPI* = Sum of Nominal output in the eight industrial sectors / Sum of Real output in the eight industrial sectors. Real output is calculated as nominal output divided by the according IPI. Interest rates and monetary aggregates come from the Central bank of Russia statistics. Real interest rate is obtained by the formula $\mathbf{r=(1+R)/(1+\pi)-1}$, where R is monthly nominal interest rate (= annual /12), and π is industrial IPI changes.

16 Material costs data available is quarterly; monthly data is obtained by assuming that the ratio of material costs in production is constant within a quarter.

17 Testing the series with augmented Dickey-Fuller test for unit roots suggested that the series were integrated of order one, therefore regression equations were estimated in first-difference form to eliminate the fixed effects.

18 Inclusion of an ARMA(n, m) term means suggesting that a regression disturbance follows a process of the form: $u_t = \phi_1 u_{t-1} + ... + \phi_n u_{t-n} + \varepsilon_t + \theta_1 \varepsilon_{t-1} + ... + \theta_m \varepsilon_{t-m}$. The terms are included to take into account seasonal effects and to fight serial correlation (Harvey (1981): pp.203-4, 211).

profitability of GKO obligations and real interest rate on Ruble three-month deposits decline in Autumn 1994, it is reasonable to introduce a dummy variable to take into account the structural change. The dummy used takes zero prior to December 1994 and becomes one thereafter. Both the differential intercept and differential slope coefficients turned out to be statistically insignificant in regressions for arrears ratio (so that regressions with the dummy are not reported in Table 7). At the same time the dummy variable introduction in energy sector production regressions (Table 8) appears to be significant.

The same kind of substitution is observed in the manufacturing sector as well, though on much less scale, which possibly reflects different financial situations of the sectors. The fact that the main changes in energy sector money balances stem from "rich" electricity and oil-extracting industries, whereas oil-refining, gas and coal industries' patterns stay roughly the same, appears to support the last argument.

Table 7 contains the results of explaining energy and manufacturing sectors' arrears ratio behavior. As is seen from the table, overdue commercial receivables over sectoral production ratio is statistically the most significant factor in all the regressions. The elasticity is between 0.93 and 1.04 for the energy sector and about 0.7 for the manufacturing sector, meaning that a one per cent increase in the arrears from customers ratio is immediately translated into 0.93-1.04 per cent and 0.7 per cent increase[19] in arrears to suppliers ratio in energy and manufacturing sectors respectively. The positive dependence and approximately unit elasticity is agreeable with the reported enterprises' strategy of balancing overdue payables with overdue receivables.

Real money balances are statistically significant and negative in the regressions, which is intuitively correct and in agreement with (Alfandari and Schaffer (1996): p.110), who established that arrears are highly correlated with liquidity. According to our regressions, a one per cent decrease in a sector real money balances contribute on average to 0.14 - 0.22 per cent and 0.37 per cent increase in energy and manufacturing sectors non-payment ratios respectively.

To estimate the influence of credit conditions in the economy on enterprises' behavior, real bank credit to the sectors and real interest rate were introduced. The CBR real refinance interest rate is used in the regressions as the most influential rate for the period under consideration, and also as the most reliable series among other interest rate series available. As regressions two, three and five in Table 7 show, the real interest rate is statistically significant in energy sector regressions and insignificant in manufacturing sector ones. According to our results, a one per cent increase in the real refinance interest[20] rate translates into 1.1- 1.7 per cent increase in energy sector arrears' ratio, implying interest rate sensitivity.

---

19 On average and holding all other variables constant.

20 Real refinance interest rate series is presented as (1+r), i.e. gross interest.

Table 7. *Energy and manufacturing sectors arrears ratio estimation*

Dependent variable *Explanatory variables*	**D(log (1-γ))**	**D(log (1-γ))**	**D(log (1-γ))**	**D(log (1-γ))**	**D(log (1-β))**	**D(log (1-β))**
Constant term	**-0.0206** (-1.42)	**-0.0054** (-0.71)	**-0.0182** (-2.11)	**-0.0139** (-1.31)	**-0.0199** (-1.60)	**-0.0179** (-1.63)
D(log(1-$\hat{\beta}$))	**0.9320*** (12.12)	**1.0217*** (15.01)	**1.0399*** (13.44)	**1.0151*** (13.29)		
D(log(1-$\hat{\gamma}$))					**0.6559*** (7.04)	**0.7430*** (9.07)
D(log(Energy sector real money balances)$_{-1}$)	**-0.1433**** (-2.91)		**-0.2227*** (-4.56)	**-0.0977****** (-2.02)		
D(log(Manufacturing sector real money balances))					**-0.3692**** (-3.34)	**-0.2918**** (-1.67)
D(log(Real banking credit to energy sector)$_{-2}$)				**0.0406** (0.42)		
D(log(Real banking credit to energy sector)$_{-1}$)						**-0.2443******* (-1.67)
D(log(Real refinance interest rate))		**1.6695**** (3.28)	**1.1151****** (2.09)			
D(log(Real refinance interest rate)$_{-1}$)					**-0.1645** (-0.33)	
AR(n)	n=3; 0.1659 (0.81)	n=1; -0.6179 (-1.78)	n=2; - 0.3905 (-1.82)	n=1; - 0.1952 (-1.05)		
MA(m)	m=5; 0.8841 (13.27)	m=1; 0.3759 (0.96)	m=3; 0.8975 (17.75)	m=5; -0.8751 (-11.38)	m=5; -0.9472 (-27.08)	m=5; -0.9601 (-22.44)
R^2 adjusted	**0.9088**	**0.8176**	**0.8937**	**0.8954**	**0.9011**	**0.9242**
DW	**2.4435**	**2.0004**	**2.0786**	**2.0302**	**1.7733**	**1.6528**
Box-Pierce Q-Statistic	1.90 (probab. 0.9291)	1.62 (probab. 0.9514)	2.11 (probab. 0.9090)	2.54 (probab. 0.8643)	0.83 (probab. 0.9912)	1.25 (probab. 0.9743)
Sample range Number of observations	1994.06 - 1996.01 20	1994.03 - 1996.07 29	1994.05 - 1996.01 21	1994.05 - 1996.01 21	1994.03 - 1995.12 22	1994.03 - 1995.12 22

Note: Ordinary least squares (OLS) estimators;* - significant at 0.1% level ;** - significant at 0.5% level;*** - significant at 1% level;**** - significant at 5% level; ***** - significant at 10% level.

At the same time the quantity of real bank credit is statistically (weak) significant in the manufacturing sector regression (a one per cent increase leads to almost 0.25 per cent decrease in the arrears' ratio the next period) and insignificant in the energy sector one. This is likely to suggest that the manufacturing sector is credit rationed, i.e. the quantity of credit extended to the sector is less than the sector's demand for it at the prevailing interest rate. The energy sector's decisions are regulated by interest rate.

Overall, the two sectors turn out to be asymmetric: the receivables' ratio elasticity is significantly less, while real money balances elasticity is larger, in the regression for manufacturing sector compared with energy sector regressions. In addition, the real refinance interest rate is statistically insignificant in explaining manufacturing sector arrears' pattern, whereas energy sector arrears' ratio is rather interest sensitive. The differences are likely to reflect distinctions in external finance, and banking credit in particular, along with sectoral idiosyncrasies. Banks are typically more reluctant to lend to manufacturing sector enterprises, which are much less competitive on the world market than energy sector companies.

The lack of external finance substitutes makes the manufacturing sector more dependent on real money balances, and, hence, more sensitive to demand shocks reflected in retained earnings dynamics. This relatively higher exposure of the manufacturing sector production to falling demand is likely to explain the observed less elastic response of the sector to overdue receivables ratio change: the response is likely to be restricted by the danger of losing customers. It may also be expected to affect the production pattern: it is likely that arrears will have more influence on manufacturing sector production dynamics than on energy sector since the latter is able to hold balance in arrears' ratios.

Testing factors determining sectoral output.

As it was shown by the analysis above, overdue commercial receivables and payables[21] are closely interrelated, implying that the use of both series simultaneously as regressors would cause multicollinearity problems. Therefore, in what follows, only one of the variables was used, while the other is left aside. The results are summarized in Table 8.

As regressions 5-8 in Table 8 show, real enterprises' money holdings are statistically significant in determining manufacturing sector output, with the average elasticity being about 0.5. Trade credit (overdue payables to suppliers) is also significant and positive, reflecting the buffer function of trade credit in periods of liquidity shortages. The

---

21 We have to substitute the payment ratios for overdue commercial receivables and payables in real terms. As it was already mentioned, material costs series are quarterly, and, since the sample period is too short to run regressions using quarterly data, a proxy for monthly material costs was obtained using monthly output series and assuming that the proportion of material costs in production did not change within a quarter. The proxy was then used to obtain (1-γ) and (1-β) series. The technique used, though natural, put some restrictions on further analysis, and, in particular, implies that one can not use the series as explanatory variables in equations for sectoral output, because that would mean that our regressors include an endogenous variable, therefore violating exogenuity assumption of OLS regressors.

elasticity is between 0.3 and 0.4 on average. Real interest rate is weakly significant, though has predicted signs: a one per cent increase in the real interest rate is likely to lead on average to a 1.2 per cent decrease in manufacturing sector production a month later,

The two sectors are substantially asymmetric: trade credit arrears are likely to have little effect on energy sector production, whereas they are statistically significant in manufacturing sector regression. As already mentioned, this might be a consequence of energy sector ability to hold balance in arrears' ratios, given its relatively lower exposure to falling demand in comparison with manufacturing sector.

Energy sector production is less elastic with respect to real money balances than manufacturing sector: the elasticity is 0.3 against 0.5. The dummy variable introduction in energy sector production regressions appears to be significant: differential slope coefficient is about 0.03, meaning that the aforementioned change in energy sector liquid assets structure resulted in the real money balances elasticity of production increase on 0.03. Inflation appears to be statistically insignificant regressor.

At the same time, energy sector production appears to be rather interest sensitive: a one per cent increase in the real interest rate leads to almost 3.1-3.5 per cent decrease in production two months later. Regressing energy sector output against the interest rate only allows to explain 32% of its variation. The difference is likely to stem from different access of the two sectors to banking credit and external finance in general, along with sectoral idiosyncrasies.

One of the factors that typically determine sectoral output is the relative price ratio. In 1992 there was an immense increase in energy sector to manufacturing sector relative price with substantial fluctuations in 1993 - beginning of 1994 and subsequent stabilization. By the end of 1994 relative prices seemed to stabilize. Since the middle of 1994 and during 1995-middle 1996 the ratio of energy to manufacturing sector prices was approximately constant and near 1. Regression analysis supports the guess that the ratio should not have a significant impact on the industrial sectors output in 1994 -1996: energy IPI/manufacturing IPI ratio turns out to be statistically insignificant in regressions for both sectors. Real exchange rate is also found to be statistically insignificant, implying that export quotas restrictions in operation are binding.

Overall, using only "monetary" variables as regressors allow to explain a large fraction of output variance (about fifty and forty per cent in manufacturing and energy sector equations respectively) which seems to be a good support for the hypothesis that monetary policy issues, and liquid assets availability in particular, along with trade, post-

Table 8. *Energy and manufacturing sectors production estimation*

Dependent variable *Explanatory variables*	**D(log(Real energy sector production))**	**D(log(Real energy sector production))**	**D(log(Real energy sector production))**	**D(log(Real energy sector production))**	**D(log(Real manufacturing sector production))**	**D(log(Real manufacturing sector production))**	**D(log(Real manufacturing sector production))**
Constant term	**-0.0076** (-0.42)	**-0.0219** (-0.53)	**-0.0285** (-0.69)	**0.0359** (0.68)	**0.0139** (0.89)	**0.0136** (0.88)	**0.0157** (0.73)
D(log(Overdue energy sector payables to suppliers in real terms))		**0.3363** (0.92)	**0.2270** (0.61)				
D(log(Overdue manufacturing sector payables to suppliers in real terms))					**0.3138***** (1.77)	**0.3356***** (1.97)	**0.3379***** (1.81)
D(log(Energy sector real money balances))		**0.2794****** (1.65)	**0.3441***** (1.97)	**0.3115***** (1.80)			
Dummy variable (=0 for Jan-94 -Nov-94; =1 starting Dec-95)		**0.0629** (1.08)	**0.0698** (1.22)	**-0.0011** (-0.02)			
D(log(Energy sector real money balances)* Dummy variable)		**0.0361****** (1.37)	**0.0424****** (1.61)	**0.0376****** (1.41)			
D(log(Manufacturing sector real money balances))					**0.4968**** (2.64)	**0.4699**** (2.59)	**0.5526**** (3.04)
D(log(Real banking credit to energy sector)$_{-1}$)			**0.2342** (1.24)				
D(log(Real banking credit to manufacturing sector)$_{-1}$)							**-0.4444** (-1.32)

Table 8. *Energy and manufacturing sectors production estimation(continued.)*

D(log(Real exchange rate))				**0.3536** (1.15)			
D(log (Energy IPI/Manufacturing IPI)$_{-1}$)				**-0.4574** (-0.42)			
D(log(Real refinance interest rate)$_{-1}$)						**-1.2055****** (-1.35)	
D(log(Real refinance interest rate)$_{-2}$)	**-3.1275*** (-3.79)	**-3.5339*** (-3.66)	**-3.6179*** (-3.80)	**-3.5546*** (-3.54)			
AR(n)					n=1; -0.5520 (-2.67)	n=1; -0.4966 (-1.35)	
MA(m)							m=1; -0.8582 (-3.69)
R^2 adjusted	**0.3229**	**0.4254**	**0.4450**	**0.4078**	**0.4652**	**0.5433**	**0.5384**
DW	**2.0881**	**2.3146**	**2.3103**	**2.2165**	**1.8544**	**2.2391**	**1.6792**
Box-Pierce Q-Statistic	0.80 (probab. 0.9922)	1.75 (probab. 0.9412)	1.96 (probab. 0.9233)	1.00 (probab. 0.9856)	3.12 (probab. 0.7938)	2.19 (probab. 0.9016)	2.59 (probab. 0.8583)
Sample range Number of observations	1994.04 - 1996.08 29	1994.04 - 1995.12 21	1994.04 - 1995.12 21	1994.04 - 1995.12 21	1994.02- 1995.12 22	1994.04- 1995.12 21	1994.03 - 1995.12 22

Note: Ordinary least squares (OLS) estimators;
* - significant at 0.1% level;
** - significant at 1% level;
*** - significant at 5% level;
**** - significant at 10% level

Cold-War and systemic transformation shocks[22], are likely to affect industrial output pattern.

CONCLUSION

General underdevelopment of financial markets in transition economies, and money and credit markets in particular, together with widespread inter-enterprise arrears, are likely to perplex monetary transmission mechanism and, if not taken into account, make it unreliable and policies less effective. The lending channel of monetary policy transmission, being major in the Russian economy, appears to be intensified by weak private banking system and the absence of substitutes for the CBR loanable funds - on supply side, and the lack of other than trade credit substitutes for banking credit - on demand side.

In this case tight monetary policy could have added to the output losses not caused by efficiency considerations, as potentially viable and profitable firms were unable to follow optimal financing pattern given. Massive government borrowing on domestic money market (GKO sales) diverted banking sector resources from real sector to budget deficit finance, thereby aggravating credit rationing of the former.

The empirical analysis indicates that there is a substantial asymmetry in financing patterns between industrial sectors: the energy sector behavior regarding bank credit is governed by the real interest rate, whereas the manufacturing sector appears to be credit rationed; overdue trade credit is likely to exert little influence on the energy sector output dynamics, while it is important for the manufacturing sector. Along with other factors (the relative price change and different exposure to demand shocks), different banking credit availability to the two sectors which resulted in different patterns of short-term finance may have contributed to the variance in output decline across the sectors.

Trade credit arrears, providing an alternative source of short-term finance, compensated, in part, the financial system imperfections and dampened adverse output effects of monetary tightening in financially underdeveloped system with weak private banking. On the other hand, the network of inter-enterprise arrears increases the risk that firm-specific shocks may be spread across enterprises and transformed into economy-wide shocks. This has a negative impact on the quality of financial information in the system, and therefore the ability of both financial institutions and government to assess enterprises' creditworthiness (liquid position) and distinguish between potentially viable and not-viable enterprises (net worth), hence making bankruptcy and liquidation procedures very costly, complicating hard budget constraint imposition and undermining long-term investment and privatization programs.

---

22 Trade shock stems mainly from the loss of former Soviet Union and Eastern European markets, post-Cold-War shock means the necessity of the economy's demilitarization on a large scale; systemic transformation shock involves the issues of transition from a centrally planned to a market economy.

REFERENCES

Alfandari, Gilles and Mark E. Schaffer (1996), ""Arrears" in the Russian Enterprise Sector" in *Enterprise Restructuring and Economic Policy in Russia*, ed. by Simon Commander, Qimiao Fan and Mark E.Schaffer, EDI Development Studies (Washington D.C.: World Bank), pp.87-139.

Alfandari, Gilles, Qimiao Fan and Lev Freinkman (1996), "Government Financial Transfers to Industrial Enterprises and Restructuring" in *Enterprise Restructuring and Economic Policy in Russia*, ed. by Simon Commander, Qimiao Fan and Mark E.Schaffer, EDI Development Studies (Washington D.C.: World Bank), pp.166-202.

Balino, Tomas J.T., Juhi Dhawan and V. Sundararajan (1994), "Payment System Reforms and Monetary Policy in Emerging Market Economies in Central and Eastern Europe", *Staff Papers,* International Monetary Fund, Vol.41, No.3 (September), pp.383-410.

Bernanke, Ben, and Alan Blinder (1988), "Credit, Money, and Aggregate Demand", *American Economic Review,* (Papers and Proceedings), Vol. 78 (May), pp.435-9.

Bernanke, Ben, and Alan Blinder (1992), "The Federal Funds Rate and the Channels of Monetary Transmission", *American Economic Review,* Vol. 82(September), pp.901-21.

Bofinger P., G. Flassbeck and L. Hoffman (1995), "Ekonomika Ortodoksalnoi Monetarnoi Stabilizatzii: Primer Rossii, Ukraini i Kazakhstana" (Economics of Orthodox Monetary Stabilization: the Case of Russia, Ukraine and Kazakhstan), *Voprosi Ekonomiki,* N12 (December), 1995, pp.26-44.

Calvo, Guillermo A. (1991), "Are High Interest Rates Effective for Stopping High Inflation?" in *Managing Inflation in Socialist Economies in Transition*, ed by Simon Commander (Washington D.C.: World Bank), pp.247-60.

Calvo, Guillermo A., and Fabrizio Coricelli (1993), "Output Collapse in Eastern Europe. The Role of Credit", *Staff Papers,* International Monetary Fund, Vol.40, No.1 (March), pp.32-52.

Calvo, Guillermo A., and Manmohan S. Kumar (1994), "Money Demand, Bank Credit, and Economic Performance in Former Socialist Economies", *Staff Papers,* International Monetary Fund, Vol.41, No.2 (June), pp.314-49.

________ (1993), "Financial Markets and Intermediation" in *Financial Sector Reforms and Exchange Arrangements in Eastern Europe,* IMF Occasional Paper No. 102 (Washington D.C.: International Monetary Fund), pp.3-33.

Fan, Qimiao, Une J. Lee and Mark E. Schaffer (1996), "Firms, Banks, and Credit in Russia" in *Enterprise Restructuring and Economic Policy in Russia*, ed. by Simon Commander, Qimiao Fan and Mark E.Schaffer, EDI Development Studies (Washington D.C.: World Bank), pp.140-65.

Gertler, Mark, and Simon Gilchrist (1994), "Monetary Policy, Business Cycles, and the Behavior of Small Manufacturing Firms", *Quarterly Journal of Economics,* No. 109, pp.309-40

Granville, Brigitte (1995), "Inflyatziya: Visokaya Tzena i Nikakoi Otdachi" (Inflation: High Costs and No Return), *Voprosi Ekonomiki,* No.3 (March), pp.34-44.

Harvey, Andrew C. (1981), *The Econometric Analysis of Time Series* (Oxford: Philip Allan Publishers Limited)

Hilbers, Paul (1993), "Monetary Instruments and Their Use During the Transition from a Centrally Planned to a Market Economy", *IMF Working Paper 93/87* (Washington D.C.: International Monetary Fund, Monetary and Exchange Affairs Department)

Ickes, Barry W., and Randi Ryterman (1993), "Roadblock to Economic Reform: Inter-Enterprise Debt and the Transition to Markets ", *Post-Soviet Affairs,* Vol. 9, No.3 (July-September), pp.231-53

Illarionov, Andrei (1995), "Popitki Provedeniya politiki Finansovoi Stabilizatzii v SSSR i v Rossii" (Financial Stabilization Attempts in the USSR and Russia), *Voprosi Ekonomiki,* No.7 (July), pp.4-37

International Financial Statistics (1996), Vol.XLIX, No.12 (Washington D.C.: International Monetary Fund)

________ (1996), Vol.L, No.5 (Washington D.C.: International Monetary Fund)

Kashyap, Anil K., Jeremy C. Stein and David W. Wilcox (1993), "Monetary Policy and Credit Conditions: Evidence from the Composition of External Finance", *American Economic Review,* Vol. 83, No.1, pp.78-98

Koen, Vincent, and Maurice Marrese (1995), "Stabilization and Structural change in Russia, 1992-4", in *IMF Occasional paper No. 127* (Washington D.C.: International Monetary Fund), pp.53-65

Koen, Vincent, and Steven Phillips (1993), "Price Liberalization in Russia: Behavior of Price, Household Incomes, and Consumption During the First Year", *IMF Occasional paper No. 104* (Washington D.C.: International Monetary Fund)

Dmitriev M.E. (1996), "The Financial Position of Moscow Banks During a Period of Financial Stabilization" - Paper presented at the Conference 'Government in Economic Transition', (Moscow: New Economic School, September 4-6)

Mayer, Collin (1988), "New Issues in Corporate Finance", *European Economic Review,* No.32, pp.1167-88

Meltzer, Allan H. (1995), "Monetary, Credit (and Other) Transmission Processes: A Monetarist Perspective", *Journal of Economic Perspectives,* Vol. 9, No. 4, pp.48-72

Mishkin, Frederic S. (1995), "Symposium on the Monetary Transmission Mechanism", *Journal of Economic Perspectives,* Vol. 9, No. 4, pp.3-10

Ofer, Gur (1993), "Makroekonomicheskaya Stabilizatziya i Strukturnye Izmeneniya: Ortodoksiya, Geterodoksiya, ili Inache?" (Macroeconomic Stabilization and Structural Change: Orthodoxy, Heterodoxy, or Otherwise?), *Economics and Mathematical Methods*, Vol. 29, No.4, pp.548-62

Polterovich, Viktor (1995), "Ratzionirovanie Kredita, Inflyatziya i Transformatzionnii Spad" (Credit rationing, inflation and transformational recession), *Economics and Mathematical Methods*, Vol. 31, No.3, pp.50-62

Strategiya Vizhivaniya Gosudarstvennikh i Privatizirovannikh Predpriyatii Promishlennosti v Perekhodni Period (Survival Strategy for State and Privatized Industrial Enterprises in Transition) (1994), (Moscow: Izdatelstvo Visshei Shkoli Ekonomiki)

Sundararajan V. (1990), "Financial Sector Reforms and Central Banking in Centrally Planned Economies", *IMF Working Paper 90/120,* (Washington D.C.: International Monetary Fund)

Vestnik Bankovskoi Statistiki (1996), No. 6 (Moscow: Central Bank of Russia)

CHAPTER 4

EMPOWERMENT THROUGH BUSINESS, CRIME AND POLITICS AMONG YOUNG PEOPLE IN THE FORMER SOVIET UNION[1]

KENNETH ROBERTS
University of Liverpool

AHARON ADIBEKIAN
Independent Sociological Centre, Yerevan

GRIGORY NEMIRIA
University of Donetsk

LEVAN TARKHNISHVILI
Change Management Support Unit, Tbilisi

JOCHEN THOLEN
University of Bremen

Abstract

This paper is based on interviews with a total of 469 young people, aged up to 30, in three countries of the former Soviet Union - Armenia, Georgia and Ukraine. The analysis focuses on those who were self-employed and experiencing reasonable success, and political activists, and the links between these groups, mostly forged in the countries' substantial shadow economies. The course of transformation in the former Soviet Union is contrasted with experiences in East-Central Europe. It is argued that the business and political elites that consolidate their positions in the former countries are most likely to remain very different from, though not necessarily unacceptable to, their Western counterparts.

---

[1]The research reported in this paper was supported by INTAS grant 93-2693 and ACE/TACIS grant T94-1034R. The authors would like to acknowledge the contributions of their colleagues, S C Clark, C Wallace, N Chernysh, A Romanjuk and E Stadnik, and all the other research workers who took part in the project.

BACKGROUND

In 1991 the Soviet Union ended and its republics became new independent countries. Before long they had regrouped as the Commonwealth of Independent States (CIS). There had been reform and independence movements in all the European/Christian countries in the late-1980s. *Glasnost* had permitted freedom of expression and association but there had been little real *perestroika* (restructuring). The Soviet economy was sliding into deeper trouble, and the reform movements were more a symptom than a cause of the mounting crisis in Soviet communism. In Ukraine, Georgia and Armenia, the three countries in this research, the late-1980s saw an explosion of political activity in which young people were prominent, especially those in higher education. However, the countries became independent not through the strength of their own reform movements but because Yeltsin's Russia quit the USSR. Suddenly the reformers in other Soviet Republics had everything that they had demanded - national independence, the freedom to form political parties and fight elections, and to trade and sell their labour on the market. The independence celebrations were intense but short-lived. Before long all the countries of the former Soviet Union were in crisis. It mattered little whether, as in Ukraine, the former rulers retained office having retitled themselves as nationalists and democrats, or whether the nation split into warring factions as in Georgia (see Aves, 1991, 1992). All the governments were disempowered as the countries' economies collapsed. The people learnt quickly that the vote empowers electors only if those who they elect have real power.

The countries' economies folded not under the deliberate shock therapy of market reforms but through the almost total disintegration of the trading relationships that had linked enterprises throughout the USSR and, to a lesser extent, in central Europe (International Monetary Fund, 1991, 1992; International Labour Office, 1995). Businesses lost suppliers and customers, and virtually all enterprises were affected. Basic services of gas, water and electricity were disrupted. In some countries including Armenia and Georgia the economic collapse was exacerbated by military conflicts. Enterprises that could offer no work or, even if so, no wages, did not usually dismiss their workforces in any of the countries in this study. People stayed officially employed and registered unemployment remained extremely low. To this extent the depth of the crisis was hidden. However, the governments were disempowered by the economic crisis. Their own incomes shrivelled. The armed forces and police were often unpaid, and cash for schools, hospitals, pensions and unemployment benefits was a lower priority. A consequence was that economic and social life were subjected to extreme and rapid deregulation. In the former communist countries of central Europe the crisis period was relatively short-lived whereas in much of the former Soviet Union in 1996 there was still no end in sight. It was misleading to speak of reform in these countries since this suggests that someone is implementing a known programme. Talk of transition has been equally misleading with its implication of a known destination. 'Transformation' has become the preferred expression (see Bryant and Mokrzycki, 1994). In the early 1990s the societies were changing radically into uncharted territory. There were no post-Soviet precedents.

Young people were left with no routes beyond education. In all the countries education itself was maintained. Enrolments actually expanded even though the schools and colleges were starved of cash. Young people were remaining in education for longer because there was nowhere else for them to proceed to immediately, though no-one knew where their educational programmes would lead. Later in their lives, looking back, the first post-communist generations will be able to explain their biographies, as will sociologists, but looking ahead in the early 1990s they could not know what positions would exist for them to occupy as adults let alone how to reach them.

An option that remained open for most young people in Ukraine, Armenia and Georgia was to take state sector jobs even though there might be no work or wages, or, in the event of any being paid, the amounts would be trivial; around 10 USA$ a month for a school-teacher in Georgia for example. Ukraine was the most prosperous of the three countries: its teachers could expect $50 or even more. Young people could take such jobs and hope that things would improve. Those who were doing so explained to us that there was no better alternative. Young (and older) people could try to trade (see below) but the chances were that they would be unable to make themselves independent of their generally impoverished families. Whether the new independent countries' young people have been an advantaged or disadvantaged age group will become known only as their lives unfold. In the early 1990s their elders had homes and possessions. On the other hand, young people had no careers to lose and plenty of lifetime in which to recover.

THE RESEARCH

Up to now there have been no tried and tested methods for researching young people in circumstances such as arose in the former USSR in the early 1990s. When it has been possible to map Western concepts onto their situations the impressions may have misled. It has been possible to find examples of individualisation and polarisation but the similarities with the Western situations have been limited. When exploring the experience of unemployment it has been necessary to take account of this not really being the same predicament as joblessness in the West. Since the 1980s it has made little sense to ask whether post-Soviet youth have been resisting or accommodating. These responses were possible under the old system whereas by the early 1990s there was no clear object to embrace or resist. It was obvious to young people in Ukraine, Georgia and Armenia that the old predictors of life chances in their countries were no longer working. Success in general (academic) education no longer guaranteed an intelligentsia position. Some families that had been powerful and privileged under the old system had been able to convert their assets into advantages under the new conditions, but others had experienced long-range and rapid socio-economic demotion. A common perception among young people in the post-Soviet countries, echoed by some of their researchers (for example see, Bruno, 1996), has been the heightened importance of the 'self', specifically individuals' ability and willingness to be pro-active in reading and responding to problems and opportunities.

The following passages focus on such pro-active groups who had developed or found empowerment strategies under the new conditions. They were doing this in politics, through crime or in business. In all three countries such young people were highly untypical of their age group and we must make it clear from the outset that those who were succeeding did not represent all political activists, everyone who was trying to do business, or with experience in the criminal arts. However, for some young people these were proving to be means of empowerment. There was nothing comparable among the bulk of the young people who we studied who were students, employees, peasants, housewives, war refugees or trying to make livings as artists.

The investigators from outside and within the countries had considerable prior experience of researching young people. The Armenia, Georgia and Ukraine research groups were familiar with, and indeed had contributed to the state of the art in their respective countries. Eventually the intention was and remains to conduct quantitative surveys with sufficiently large and representative samples to answer, 'How many?' and 'Which young people?' questions, but prior to embarking on such enquiries it seemed necessary to undertake quite extensive qualitative fieldwork to gain a firmer grasp of the issues, and young people's own experiences and perspectives, in the countries. We therefore conducted interviews with selected groups of young people, 15-65 per group, and between 149 and 170 in total in each country (see Table I).

One of the largest groups of interviewees comprised young people who were 'doing business' as a main and, as far as they could foresee, permanent occupation. The attention that we paid to this group was due to them appearing to epitomise the post-Soviet condition. Many young people were being obliged to try to work on their own accounts due to the absence of proper paid jobs. Very few had aimed to start businesses when they were at school. Most had been driven into business because the jobs for which they had been prepared had become low paid and devoid of prospects. For most business was a survival tactic. Meanwhile, for much smaller numbers

Table I The respondents

	Armenia	Georgia	Ukraine	Total
Students	45	--	40	85
Post-graduates	19	--	--	19
Artists	--	20	--	20
Workers	20	--	39	59
Self-employed	48	65	50	163
Peasants	18	--	--	18
Unemployed	20	--	--	20
Political activists	--	15	20	35
War veterans/servicemen	--	15	--	15
Refugees	--	20	--	20
Housewives	--	15	--	15
	170	**150**	**149**	**469**

business was proving a fast track to wealth and status. Other groups of young people were targeted for interview according to the conditions and the investigators' particular interests in each country, but always with the aim of encompassing a wide span of backgrounds and experience. Most respondents were aged between 18 and 30 but some were older, up to 34. They were not all 'young people' in the usual sense of this term in Britain and North America, but in the communist world 'youth' had been the age group organised by the Komsomol (14-28) and in the countries concerned this cultural frame had survived communism. More to the point, the ages of the subjects matched the aim of the research which was to explore young people's experiences through all their main transitions into adulthood from entering their secondary schools, usually when aged 14-16, through entering the labour market to marrying and becoming parents, and from the years immediately prior to, then throughout the period since their countries became post-communist. All the fieldwork was conducted during 1995 and 1996.

The respondents were not selected so as to ensure that each group would be statistically representative of any larger population but to guarantee a wide spread of experience. 'Snowballing' was used in most of the groups but within guidelines which insisted, for example, that the political activists should be from a range of parties and movements, that the self-employed should be engaged in different kinds of businesses, that the employees should be from different kinds of enterprises, and so on. Wherever possible there were similar numbers of males and females in each group but when one sex was predominant our subjects inevitably reflected this. So the groups on which the following passages focus - political activists, business people, and persons with military experience - were entirely male in the latter case and predominantly so in the others.

Within each country the samples were drawn from two regions: Lviv and Donetsk which are in the western (mainly Ukrainian) and eastern (mainly Russian) regions of Ukraine respectively, and Tbilisi and Telavi in Georgia, and Yerevan and Armavir in Armenia, the capital and a provincial town in each of these countries.

There was no uniform interview schedule. Although some quantification of the responses was possible the interviews were basically open-ended except that certain topics were always covered. These were the young people's experiences in education, of earning money, politics and religion, peer relationships, leisure and family life. The fieldwork was conducted by postgraduates who interviewed a target group then interpreted their own findings. The evidence from each country was subsequently blended into an overall country by the principal country investigator, and these reports, plus specimen interview material, were translated into English. The following passages are a collaborative attempt to make sense of some of the evidence. They generalise across the three countries, and focus on groups of young people for whom the transformation was proving a more positive experience than for the majority of their contemporaries.

POLITICS

Levels of political interest and activity among all the groups except the political activists were extremely low, even by Western standards. Only minorities expressed even support for any political party. The young people had demobilised in the 1990's just as rapidly as they had been politicised in the late-1980's. A few years on they had little favourable to say about any politicians. A typical view was that politicians' main concern was their own betterment. When exceptions were named these were usually the countries' presidents. Political parties were regarded as weak and ineffective. They were not blamed for the economic conditions but their inability to find solutions had lowered their esteem. Some respondents had realised that the fates of their countries depended more on the policies of the World Bank, the International Monetary Fund, Russia, the European Union and the West more generally than their own national governments. Many resented how quickly their countries appeared to have dropped to Third World status. Even those who wished to retain national independence (majorities everywhere) sometimes had fond recollections of the time when they had been proud to be citizens of the Soviet Union, a world power. The young people were inclined to dismiss their countries' national assemblies as talking shops. Some favoured the installation of a 'democratic dictatorship' which, they hoped, would get to grips with the country's problems. This was a minority demand, but all the political parties represented minorities.

Rather than being empowered, young people in general had been politically disempowered by the end of communism. Under the old system many would have joined the Komsomol. Membership had been more or less routine for students in secondary and higher education. They had been expected to become involved, and to display loyalty and gratitude to their countries' leaders. Maybe the majority of young people had been cynical but they had been able to express their feelings through their political inactivity or by adopting Western styles of dress and musical tastes though by the 1980's this type of non-conformity had been normalised. The changes had conferred the right to be politically active in a party of one's choice, but had simultaneously removed most of the former incentives. Under the old system compliant political activity, within the one legitimate party, had been a reliable route to career advantages. Young people's new freedom was to be openly cynical, indifferent and non-participant, but such behaviour had ceased to be defiant and challenging. In the early stages of the transformation it had been difficult for anyone to align with broad political movements because no-one was sure what the main interest groups in the new conditions would be, let alone which they would belong to (see Kolarska-Bobinska, 1994). Under the prevailing conditions the best strategy seemed to be to seek private solutions to one's problems.

The political activists who were deliberately sought for interview in Ukraine and Georgia were very small minorities in their age group. In fact it was difficult to reach the target numbers (20 per city). Some parties in the cities where the research was conducted explained that they had no active members aged under 25. What set the activists apart from the rest of their age group was not that they had definite views on how their countries' problems should be addressed (see below), or the nature of their views, but that they were interested in careers in politics. Some had definitely decided to make politics their vocation. Others regarded this as just a possibility. Most of the activists had received, or were currently in higher education, typically studying social sciences. They tended to be from intelligentsia families so many had parents who had been Communist Party members, but it is necessary to stress that the majority of such children, and higher education students in general, were politically inactive. The parties that the activists had joined were all groups gathered around national leaders rather than mass organisations, so the activists' political careers depended much more on their standing vis-a-vis other activists and, in particular, the party leaders, than any popular appeal. A carry-over from the old system was that all the activists regarded it as simply normal for party workers to be rewarded (paid) for their efforts. The fact that most of the parties were unable to pay their workers in the mid-1990s was usually regarded as a feature of the continuing economic crisis rather than a normal state of affairs. Most of the activists hoped, in time, to gain elected office, and one of our Georgian respondents was in fact elected to the national assembly during the course of the research. Some activists' ultimate hope, needless to say, was to be in government. Alternatively they expected to be appointed to positions in government departments, or agencies, or in state or joint-venture enterprises. These were not unrealistic hopes. Such rewards were in fact being offered by party leaders in order to attract followers. This was viewed as normal politics, not corruption, though it was the reason why most young people regarded politicians as people who were concerned primarily for their own careers. They were correct in so far as the political activists who were interviewed did have personal ambitions, though they also had ideological motivations which had determined their choices of party and, indeed, were necessary to sustain their participation.

Everyone recognised that politics could be a rewarding career. This had applied under communism. The difference was that the empowerment strategy had become more risky; its success depended on one's party achieving power. Another change was that political activists no longer commanded even outward public respect. These were among the reasons why politics did not attract the majority, though an over-riding reason was that few expected any party that they might have joined to prove efficacious in pursuit of its policy objectives.

In the countries that we investigated the official salaries of elected representatives, and even government ministers, were extremely modest, but additional forms of self-aggrandizement were available (see below). Already some of the young activists were benefiting from their political connections and their ability to 'open doors', as well as travel within their countries and sometimes elsewhere as members of party delegations. All this, of course, had happened under the old system. The change, as already mentioned, was that there were now many rather than just one party to join. Individual activists' prospects depended on the fortunes of their parties. But since most of the parties were new the young activists had real if hazardous prospects of rapid personal promotion. There were incentives but, in the meantime, for most of the activists, politics was an unpaid or, at best, very modestly rewarded full-time or substantial part-time occupation.

Most of the young people spoke scathingly about party politics, but post-communism was proving fertile ground for the development of strong political convictions. These motivated the activists and were shared by many inactive young people. Their inactivity was more a reflection of their lack of confidence in all the parties' ability to deliver than indifference to the condition of their countries. Also, some knew that their own convictions could be dangerous and were afraid of the consequences. This was a reason why their politics were often discussed only with friends and family members. Given the conditions under which they lived, often described as not just 'difficult' but 'heavy', it would have been amazing if any of the groups that were studied had held no views about the state of their countries and what should be done.

There were in fact three highly emotive and contentious issues in each of the countries. One was whether to return to the old system or to persist with the development of the market economy. It was a minority view, but the minority was far from trivial among each country's young workers, unemployed and peasants, that collective farms should be restored and the governments should re-assume overall responsibility for economic planning and trading relationships. Some of the young people had become impatient with democracy. It was they who favoured some kind of dictatorship. They knew that there had been corruption and a black market under communism but, some argued, these had been nowhere near as widespread as since independence. Whatever complaints young people had against the former communist leaders, they could point out that at least they had been effective. Needless to say, restoring the past was completely unacceptable to other groups. None may have regarded themselves as extremists, but many held views which were extremely unacceptable to others.

A second divisive issue was relationships with Russia. There were those who wanted a stronger relationship - the restoration of the USSR in some cases or, more often, the development of the CIS into some type of confederation. The Russian minorities, roughly a fifth of the population in Ukraine but much smaller in Georgia and Armenia, were pre-disposed towards a closer relationship. Apart from those who had family and national ties with Russia, it was possible to argue that the countries' own histories had been closely entwined with Russia's, and that the neighbour to the north was their main trading partner and most likely to remain so. Talk of any closer ties was anathema to other citizens who regarded Russia as their historic oppressor and feared a return to Russian domination.

Nationalism was the third, related emotive issue. Throughout the former communist world the nationalities question had been re-opened. This issue was regarded as dangerous in all the countries that we investigated. In Ukraine the mainly Russian and mainly Ukrainian regions were represented by almost entirely different sets of political parties. Armenia had a simmering armed conflict with Azerbaijan over the status of Nagorno Karabakh (see Walker, 1991). At the time of this research Armenia proper contained thousands of refugees from the disputed territory. Georgia had experienced two civil wars over the aspirations for autonomy of the majority populations in the Abkhazia and South Ossetia regions.

None of the young people who were interviewed expressed hatred towards any other national group. In general the young people were exemplars of national and religious tolerance. Their aspiration was not to destroy or dominate any other people but for national self-determination in what they considered to be their homelands. Everywhere the nationalists' priority was the independence of their country, certainly from Russia, but often also from the West and the European Union. They felt strongly about the national language, the display of national symbols and school curricula. Some of the nationalist parties were so dedicated to the defence of independence that they had formed armed militias. Some such Georgian groups had participated in the wars inside Georgia, and outside their own country in the case of certain Ukrainian nationalist groups who had acted on the conviction, in Chechnya for instance, that any enemy of Russia was an ally of their's. In Armenia all military action was by the official army. Everywhere the military activity was experienced as threatening by national minorities. For example, Russians in west Ukraine complained that they were being made to feel strangers in what, having been born there, they had always considered their homeland. The minorities feared the more strident nationalist parties achieving power. Such parties had only minority support among the majority populations but, as already pointed out, this applied to all the other political parties.

CRIME

One of the Georgian businessmen had become a partner in a 'bank' having raised his share of the start-up capital through a robbery. It is unlikely that anyone in the CIS would be surprised by this story. Except in Armenia where the government, police and military remained in firm control, crime had rocketed following independence, which was another indication of the disempowerment of state apparatuses. In conditions where there were few legitimate ways of getting ahead or even earning enough to live independently, crime became a quite important avenue of socio-economic ascent.

Young males were most likely to learn relevant skills and acquire useful equipment while serving in the military. All the countries operated conscription for males. Avoiding it was a pre-occupation for many, as in other former communist countries (see Vlachova and Stanek, 1992). They feared the hard conditions and the brutal relationships between new recruits and senior ranks. From all accounts conditions had not changed in this respect since the break-up of the Soviet army, though one improvement for Georgian and Armenian conscripts was that they no longer feared discrimination and violence against their national groups. Another improvement was that conscripts could no longer be posted to distant republics. Against this, the chances of being involved in military action had risen. The Georgian army had fought two civil wars while Armenian conscripts knew that they would serve part of their time in Nagorno Karabakh. None of the young males who were still eligible was looking forward to military service. The best said by those who had served was that it had not been as bad as they had expected. Needless to say, many veterans wanted to preserve conscription because, in their experience, it made men out of boys.

None of the ex-soldiers who had experienced combat had found the experience glorious or heroic even in retrospect. They had all been traumatised. They had seen close comrades killed or gravely wounded. Some had been permanently maimed themselves. Some explained that they were still coping with sleeping and eating difficulties. Many felt unable to re-settle in civilian life. However, the wars that had been fought had not consisted entirely of battles between opposing armies. There had been more military action against civilian populations - dispossessing people of their homes and property if not their lives. Military action had created opportunities for looting. This was one reason why the ex-servicemen had not returned to civilian life as heroes. Too many people knew someone who had profited from the wars. It was one way in which young men had raised the capital to start themselves in businesses. Irrespective of whether they acquired any loot, they all returned to civilian life with military skills. They knew how to use weapons. Some returned home with their military equipment. This became widely available throughout the former USSR when the Soviet army was broken-up. The militias that were attached to some of the nationalist parties had no difficulty in obtaining supplies. This is not suggest that most former soldiers became armed gangsters. However, in situations where hardly anyone could obtain a proper job and earn sufficient to live legitimately, where policing had become ineffective in some districts, and where there was more private property and trading taking place, and a growing demand for protection, it seemed almost inevitable that some would turn to crime and use the skills and equipment to which they had access.

BUSINESS

While the state sectors were contracting all the countries in this research had booming private economies. Private sector growth by no means fully compensated for public sector decline. For most households, up to the mid-1990's, the transformation had entailed a substantial drop in living standards, impoverishment in many cases. Meanwhile, however, a minority had become wealthy through private enterprise and many more had eased their circumstances through work in the second economies.

There has been general agreement among previous researchers (for example Kusa and Tirpakova, 1993; Ray, 1994), and our informants in this enquiry concurred, that the leading players in the private economies were most likely to be people who had made money under or during the breakdown of the old economies and political regimes. People who had been making money in the second, then well-hidden, economies under communism were able to emerge as legitimate businessmen. State and Party officials who had used their positions for personal gain, maybe deposited in foreign banks, were able to create or buy into private enterprises. Managers of potentially profitable state enterprises were sometimes able to arrange privatisation into their own ownership. Alternatively they could run the businesses at a loss to the state but for their personal profit. These were the people who were driving Mercedes and building mansions. Much private enterprise in the 1990's was in the second economies, unrecorded in official company ledgers, undisclosed to the authorities and therefore untaxed. Small businesses could be wholly second economy. More substantial enterprises had to be legally constituted but could still transact some of their business off the record. There were advantages in being legitimate. '*One day the police walked in and asked for money so we decided to register.*' However, becoming registered could be costly. '*The registration and state authorities will be permanently finding faults, trifling cavils, with registration documents. They will keep delaying registration until you pay from $500 up to $2500 depending on the character and size of your businesses. You can hire middlemen, consulting firms, pay them the money, and have them register you quickly.*'

Young people could try to join the business elite. Becoming employees in private businesses could lift individuals out of poverty but it was not a route to riches. This had to be by doing independent business. The most common type of business in which young people could gain a foothold, and which most members of all the groups in this study had done at least occasionally, was buying and selling. Households facing impoverishment often sold some of their possessions on the streets. Families with any land could grow and sell produce. However, to make good money from trade people needed to be able to deal in larger quantities. Those with sufficient start-up capital could go on 'shopping tours' to countries where goods were cheaper than at home. Their starting capital could be self-generated, or borrowed from family members or close friends. If traders, or the operators of any other businesses could amass sufficient capital they might become 'bankers', never to the general public but always to their own people - family, close friends or members of the same 'clan'.

The capital sums needed to launch what could rapidly become quite substantial businesses could be quite modest. A Tbilisi street kiosk with an annual turnover of $24,000 in 1995 had been opened with a family's savings in 1992. A jewelry business with a similar turnover had been set up in 1994 by three friends who pooled sufficient capital to begin purchasing items that other citizens could no longer afford to keep. Some families had been able to invest more considerable sums. The nine founder partners of a Georgian bank had each put in between $17,000 and $220,000. Business partners were always previously known and trusted. If they were not from the same family they would be from the same 'clan' - people with specific national, regional or other links. New 'clans' could be formed. In the 1990's the former nomenklatura were becoming such a group.

In practice debts could not be enforced or recovered through legal processes. All business had to be on the basis of fear or trust. The latter was invariably preferred. So business networks tended to follow kin and 'clan' relationships. 'Bankers' who had shown that they could invest wisely could be asked to act for other wealthy individuals. One of our Georgian businessmen was investing funds raised by associates in Moscow. Business was not confined to, though the main activity was trading. There were also profits to be made in food and drink manufacture, and, in the cities, from taxis, restaurants and entertainment. Anyone with a skill - motor or computer repairs, or foreign languages - could operate in the second economy. But the keys to becoming wealthy were obtaining start-up capital, an entrepreneurial spirit, an ability to do unofficial deals, and not making bad business judgements. People who began *de novo* were always likely to find, if their trading became established, that they needed to liaise with, and in practice come under the auspices of, larger established businesses. Young businessmen thereby became part of wider business networks which always, to some extent, competed with other networks.

Very few of the businessmen who were interviewed had visions of gradually developing their enterprises, one day obtaining capital from a modern banking system and launching their firms as public companies. Their projects were nearly always much shorter term. Few were committed to particular lines of business. They would be trading in electrical goods one year, maybe running a transport business, a publishing house, a building firm, a hotel, a bank or a night club by the next. In fact many of the young entrepreneurs who were interviewed were in several types of business simultaneously. The exceptions included the rare cases where individuals had become self-employed in the fields for which they had trained - as lawyers, doctors or hairdressers for example. Any venture had to be able to show a profit quickly. When loans were arranged interest was charged by the day. Lenders wanted to be repaid as quickly as possible after which they would invest in some new venture. A general feeling among the young people who were doing business was that they needed to succeed quickly. As they saw the situation, the end of communism had created opportunities but before long the window would close: the economy would become dominated by large companies and small enterprises would be squeezed, or the government would regain command. In fact the 'window' was closing all the time. The early starters had the advantage. Later arrivals were attempting to muscle into markets where there were already established players.

Those who were succeeding in business could enjoy a good standard of living, relative to other citizens in their countries, but they were rarely spending large sums by Western standards. Most were taking $400-600 per month from the businesses. The businesses' additional earnings would be ploughed back. The private business culture was one of 'make quickly and make again' rather than 'make and spend'.

Staying in business, wholly or partly in the second economy, required at least tacit support from numerous officials. After all, the second economy was not exactly secret. It escaped government attention and taxation only while the relevant state departments chose not to look. Businesses required the co-operation of the police, tax and customs officials, and licensing authorities. They needed to be free from repeated state surveillance and interference. This could be bought for cash or favours, but preferably from members of a trusted group. Political figures who were able to appoint officials in national or local government departments were particularly useful allies. This was why the material rewards from a successful political career were likely to be far in excess of the official salary.

The businessmen who were interviewed had routinely made payments to officials in state departments to have their enterprises registered, to rent premises, to have repairs to their buildings and telephone connections arranged. The co-operation of state departments always had a price.

> *'The tax office is chaotic. There are no definite rules. It all depends on personal relationships. The system is basically corrupt and very powerful.'*

> *'The entire tax system is corrupt. The officers visit companies and demand money - always more than companies should pay according to the law. We pay for two reasons. First, we do not know the law. Second, the Soviet heritage of fear of state representatives.'*

It was common knowledge that, '*It's impossible to practice business honestly. It's not profitable.*' The tacit consent of officialdom had to be obtained, but beyond this businesses had to organise their own security. For this they could not depend on the police and courts. Property had to be self-protected. When goods moved the cargo had to be guarded. Business was always in cash and the places and persons with whom this was deposited had to be secure. This was where persons who could offer protection entered the business scene (see Varese, 1994). Robbery was not a long-term career. The main danger was not from the police but from other protectors. People who used violence as a means of empowerment needed to work with, not against, business and political actors, and their aim would nearly always be to build up capital and contacts so as to become business players in their own right.

> *'In this (office) building there is an official guard system which is paid for through the owner by the tenants. But in order to get proper protection we have to pay additionally for the protection system. So the official security system has a dual existence. On the one hand it is a legitimate business and, on the other, it is mafia.'*

The more established business networks became, the more difficult it was becoming for newcomers to break in without sponsorship from someone who was already aboard. This organisation of the private sector economies was the reason why, if asked who ran anything - enterprises or government departments - outsiders were most likely to answer, 'the mafia'.

AWAITING NORMALITY

The young people who were 'making it' were small minorities of their age group in Ukraine, Armenia and Georgia, and could in no way be described as representing their entire generation. They were acting in their own interests, and collaborating with other age groups in doing so. The political activists were mostly from intelligentsia families but the business people and their strong arm associates were from all backgrounds except that there were hardly any females among them. Females were not excluded by glass ceilings or panels. The barriers were overt. Politics, business and crime were regarded as male activities. The young women who were interviewed nearly all shared this assumption. Their principal roles were domestic. By their early 20s the majority of those who had not entered higher education were married and becoming mothers. In all three countries the role of the housewife had been resurrected. In so far as women were present in the public sphere - in business, politics and crime - this was usually via their relationships with men. It was much the same in the Moscow sub-cultural youth groups studied by Hilary Pilkington (1994, 1996).

The majority of young people in Ukraine, Georgia and Armenia were not 'getting on' but, if they were lucky, they were 'getting by', surviving physically, socially and psychologically. They were extending their education, taking such jobs as were available, engaging in small-time opportunistic trading, and were nearly always remaining dependent on their families unless their parents were sufficiently prosperous or influential to obtain independent accommodation for their children. Except in Ukraine, where the decline in the birth rate had become a matter of official concern, economic collapse had not arrested the vital processes of growing up, marrying and having children. Most of those who were 'getting by' did not feel oppressed, and they tended to be optimistic rather than depressed about their future prospects. The conditions under which they lived - where formal employment and living standards had collapsed, where politics was a place for people who were interested primarily in their own careers, where crime had often risen dramatically, where businesses were run by men seeking fast bucks, and where space was secured by undercover deals or the threat and use of force - will almost certainly lack appeal to Western audiences. These conditions were repugnant to most citizens in the countries, old and young. Georgia and Armenia had both lost around a fifth of their populations through emigration since independence.Yet most of the young people who remained felt that, in the long run, the destruction of the old systems would prove beneficial. They had lost the guaranteed futures that communism would have delivered but the majority preferred the new uncertainties. They expected that, at some point, the governments would restore order, the economies would grow, standards of living would rise and life generally would improve. The chances were that these expectations would be fulfilled.

The central European countries' economies also plunged in the 'wild east' conditions which followed the initial shock therapy market reforms, but within a few years their economies had begun to recover. These countries were not destabilised by the 'nationalities question' even though Czechoslovakia split. The 'window of opportunity' during which people came from nowhere to make fortunes using dubious methods opened but briefly. In the former Soviet Union the destructuration lasted longer but the countries were dynamic; new political parties and embryonic business elites were being created. Even so, these new independent states were never likely to follow exactly the same transformation routes as Poland, the Czech Republic and Hungary. These latter countries had pre-communist histories of industrial capitalism and political democracy. Under communism their industries became more productive than in the countries further east. After the collapse of communism it was possible to privatise much of the public sector in the central European countries - to foreign investors when the governments allowed this, as in Hungary. By the mid-1990's the central European countries were attracting significant inflows of Western money from tourists and exports. This helped to create a core of legitimate businesses, surrounded by legitimate smaller enterprises, all with stakes in the new economic order and vested interests in eliminating the remaining 'cowboys'. Street trading is soon regulated and squeezed once private enterprise is running the adjacent stores. By the mid-1990's the governments in central Europe were able to raise revenue from profitable businesses and their employees, and finance state services. The ex-communists had developed into moderate parties of the left and all the main political parties had begun to represent interests other than those of the politicians.

The countries of the former Soviet Union are unlikely to follow suite. Some, of course, are more likely than others to follow the course taken by the transformation in central Europe. Among the countries in this study such a course was most likely in Ukraine. It had a stronger economy than Armenia and Georgia, a border with Poland, Ukraine's western region had a pre-communist history as part of Hapsburg Empire and subsequently Poland, and in the 1990's it benefited from more Western aid and investment than the other countries in this research. However, even in Ukraine conditions in the aftermath of independence became distinctly post-Soviet in too many ways to make a longer-term central European transformation likely rather than just possible. Some CIS countries may eventually revert to authoritarian rule imposed by ascendant political factions with the support of the military. These are most likely to assume power, if they do so, on a platform of restoring order and imposing effective regulation on private and state enterprises. In the countries that we studied such a course of events looked most likely in Armenia. Elsewhere any attempt to impose an allegedly 'democratic dictatorship' was more likely to lead to civil war.

The countries might be Westernised through a sufficient inflow of aid, loans and investment thereby creating a legitimate non-governmental business sector with enough leverage to reshape the economies, politics and societies. In practice, however, conditions in the countries are more likely to repel investment. The Western projects that are initiated are most likely to be absorbed into post-Soviet realities, relying on 'the mafia' for protection for example. Moscow and St Petersburg, unlike Prague, Budapest and Warsaw, have not been Westernised.

The most likely course of events in countries such as Ukraine, Armenia and Georgia is that the empowered groups of young people that we have identified will become their countries' political elites and legitimate business communities, and be recognised as such within and beyond their own countries. Most of the business people who we interviewed wanted to become fully legitimate. They were all in favour of private enterprise and a market economy but stressed that it should be 'with rules... organised .... not totally free'. The conditions in which they were doing business were not of their own choice or making. If they manage to stay in business long enough the chances are that their hopes of legitimacy will be fulfilled. Within a decade their origins - how they made their first steps - could be as irrelevant as the British aristocracy's. The outcome will not be Western capitalism or democracy but post-Soviet versions. Nevertheless, for the West such a development will probably be the best of all the genuine possibilities. This is why the new elites will gain international respectability. If this future comes true, the young people featured in earlier passages will be members of their countries' future elites with whom Western politicians and enterprises will be happy to do business.

REFERENCES

J Aves (1991), *Path to National Independence in Georgia*, School of Slavonic and East European Studies, London.

J Aves (1992), 'The rise and fall of the Georgian nationalist movement, 1987-91', in G A Hosking, J Aves and P J S Rucam, *The Road to Post-Communism*, Pinter, London.

M Bruno (1996), 'Employment strategies and the formation of new identities in the service sector in Moscow', in H Pilkington, ed, *Gender, Generation and Identity in Contemporary Russia*, Routledge, London.

C G A Bryant and E Mokrzycki, eds (1994), *The Great New Transformation?* Routledge, London.

M M J Fischer and S Grigorian (1993), 'Six to eight characters in search of Armenian civil society amidst the carnivalisation of history', in G E Marcus, ed, *Perilous States*, University of Chicago Press, Chicago.

International Labour Office (1995), *The Ukrainian Challenge*, Central European University Press, Budapest.

International Monetary Fund (1991), *Armenia*, Washington.

International Monetary Fund (1992), *Economic Review - Georgia*, Washington.

L Kolarska-Bobinska (1994), 'Social interests and their representation: Poland in transition', *British Journal of Sociology*, 45, 109-126.

Z Kusa and Z Tirpakova (1993), 'On making decision for the career of private businessman', *Sociologia*, 25, 73-75.

H Pilkington (1994), *Russia's Youth and its Culture*, Routledge, London.

H Pilkington, ed (1996), *Gender, Generation and Identity in Contemporary Russia*, Routledge, London.

L Ray (1994), 'The collapse of Soviet socialism: legitimation, regulation and the new state', in P Brown and R Crompton, eds, *Economic Restructuring and Social Exclusion*, UCL Press, London.

F Varese (1994), 'Is Sicily the future of Russia? Private protection and the rise of the Russian mafia', *Archives of European Sociology*, 35, 224-258.

M Vlachova and M Stanek (1992), 'Young men's value orientations and its relation to their attitudes towards the Czechoslovak military', *Sociologia*, 24, 47-48.

C J Walker (1991), *Armenia: the Survival of a Nation*, Routledge, London.

CHAPTER 5

THE POLITICAL ORIENTATIONS AND SOCIO-ECONOMIC EXPERIENCES OF YOUNG PEOPLE IN ARMENIA, GEORGIA AND UKRAINE IN THE 1990'S[1]

KENNETH ROBERTS, AHARON ADIBEKIAN, GRIGORY NEMIRIA, AND LEVAN TARKHNISHVILI

ABSTRACT

This paper arises from open-ended interviews in 1995 with selected groups totalling 341 young people from major cities in Armenia, Georgia and Ukraine. The young people were questioned about their personal hopes and ambitions, their political views, and their personal experiences in education and the labour market, of military affairs, and family and peer group life since the early-1990's. The collapse of the planned economies, exacerbated by military conflicts in Armenia and Georgia, had made it impossible for most young people to obtain orthodox jobs. Living standards had been reduced to basics. War veterans and refugees had been traumatised by their experiences. However, the young people's appetites for education had strengthened, as had family and peer relationships. The majority had found ways of making money in the expanding private economies. There was widespread distrust of all politicians but most of the young people held strong political views. A minority wanted to restore the old systems. Another minority were staunch nationalists. But the majority wanted

[1] The research reported in this paper was supported by INTAS grant 93-2693. The authors would like to acknowledge the contributions of their colleagues, S C Clark, J Tholen and C Wallace, N Chernysh, A Romanjuk and E Stadnik, and all the other research workers who took part in the project.

their countries to press ahead with reform towards a Western way of life. Most of the young people were optimistic as regards their own, and their countries' futures. They believed they had shown that they could cope with adversity and preferred the current uncertainties to the old guarantees. Provided there was no reversal of the reforms, the majority were confident of their ability to build worthwhile futures for themselves and their children.

Aims and Methods

This is study of young people's experiences from 1991 to 1995, the first years of post-Soviet independence in Ukraine, Georgia and Armenia, three of the states that were formed when the Soviet Union ended. Our reasons for conducting the research were basic: very little was known about the experiences and outlooks of the countries' young people yet they were likely to prove a crucial generation. We expected to find that they were experiencing the full force of the macro-changes that were taking place, in the labour markets for example, and we believed that their opinions were likely to be good guides to the kinds of adult populations that the countries were producing.

The investigators from outside and within the countries where this research was conducted had considerable prior experience of researching young people. The Armenian, Georgian and Ukrainian research groups were familiar with, and had indeed contributed to the 'state of the art' in their respective countries. The Western participants had conducted earlier research among young people in Britain, Germany and Poland, and believed that broadly comparable methods would be appropriate and applicable in Armenia, Georgia and Ukraine. This is not to say that anyone had firm views even on what questions the research should ask or how these should be addressed, let alone clear expectations as to what the research would discover. Applying 'broadly comparable' methods meant, firstly, that the research in Armenia, Georgia and Ukraine would be collaborative, a combination of local knowledge and expertise and outsiders' perspectives. Second, it meant studying young people in selected localities where it would be possible to trace connections between the economic, political and housing conditions, for example, and the experiences of particular groups. In Armenia and Georgia the young people who were studied were mostly in the capital cities, Yerevan and Tbilisi, while in Ukraine the fieldwork was split between Donetsk which lies in the heavily industrialised east where the population is mainly Russian speaking, and Lviv which lies in the west of the country which was part of the Hapsburg Empire then Poland before 1939, and is populated overwhelmingly by people of Ukrainian nationality. Third, it meant designing the research so that the experiences of all the main social groups of young people would be captured. Fourth, it meant giving the research a longitudinal perspective which would relate the young people's biographies to the macro-changes that were in process in their countries. Fifth, it meant using a combination of quantitative and qualitative methods.

It was always our eventual intention to conduct quantitative surveys with sufficiently large and representative samples to answer, 'How many?' and 'Which young people?'

questions, but prior to embarking on such enquiries it seemed necessary to undertake smaller-scale qualitative fieldwork in order to gain a firmer grasp of the issues, and young people's own perspectives in each of the countries. We therefore conducted interviews with selected groups of young people, 15-45 per group, and between 99 and 142 in total, in each country (see Table I).

The groups that were targeted varied according to the conditions and the investigators' special interests in each country but always with the aim of encompassing a wide span of backgrounds and experiences, and ensuring that both males and females were adequately represented. Most respondents were aged between 22 and 25 but some were aged up to 30. They were not all 'young people' in the usual sense of this term in Britain and North America, but in the communist world 'youth' had been the age group organised by the Komsomol (16-28) and in the countries concerned this cultural frame had survived communism. More to the point, the ages of the subjects matched the aim

Table I The respondents

	Armenia	**Georgia**	**Ukraine**	**Total**
Students	45	--	40	85
Post-graduates	19	--	--	19
Artists	--	20	--	20
Workers	20	--	39	59
Self-employed	20	15	--	35
Peasants	18	--	--	18
Unemployed	20	--	--	20
Political activists	--	15	20	35
War veterans/ servicemen	--	15	--	15
Refugees	--	20	--	20
Housewives	--	15	--	15
	142	**100**	**99**	**341**

of the research which was to explore young people's experiences through all their main transitions to adulthood - from entering their secondary schools, usually when aged 14-16, through entering the labour markets, marrying and becoming parents - and from the period immediately prior to, then throughout the years since their countries became independent in 1991. All the fieldwork was conducted during 1995.

The respondents were not selected so as to ensure that each group would be statistically representative of any larger population but to guarantee a wide span of experience. 'Snowballing' was used in most of the groups but with guidelines that insisted, for example, that the political activists should be from a range of parties and movements, that the self-employed should be engaged in different kinds of businesses, that the workers should be from different kinds of enterprises, and that the students should be from a range of departments and institutions. Wherever possible there were similar numbers of males and females in each group but where one sex was predominant, as in the cases of political activists and the self-employed, or completely unrepresented as with housewives and military veterans, our subjects inevitably reflected this.

There was no uniform interview schedule. Although some quantification of the responses was possible the interviews were basically open-ended except that certain topics were always covered. These were the young people's experiences in education, of earning money, politics and religion, military affairs, peer relationships, leisure and family life. The fieldwork was conducted by post-graduates who interviewed a target group and interpreted the findings. The findings from all the groups in each country were then combined into country reports by the principal country investigators. These reports, and some specimen fieldwork material, were translated in English. The following passages draw from this evidence and are a collaborative attempt to note similarities and differences between and within each of the countries.

It may be worth stressing that with the exception of the peasants in Armenia and the internally displaced persons (war refugees) in Georgia, all the young people had spent their most of their lives in major cities. This was deliberate. The research's chosen method was to focus on young people in known local contexts. Our assumption was that within each country young people's (and adults') experiences were likely to vary considerably depending on where they lived. Eventually, in larger-scale quantitative surveys, these intra-country contrasts will be addressed. In the meantime our findings should be read as arising from the accounts of young people who were nearly all from major cities in Ukraine, Georgia and Armenia.

As is normally the case, we embarked on the research hoping that our eventual findings would be useful, but especially when conducting exploratory studies it is impossible to forecast what the eventual findings and their uses might be. We hoped that, in the West, the findings would offer new perspectives on the modern world and its youth. In the new independent states we hoped that the enquiries would stimulate interest and further research, and help to inform policies affecting young people. In these countries our research could hardly avoid being a substantial contribution to knowledge. In Soviet times, in some parts of the Union, there were regular, large-scale quantitative surveys of young people. Armenia was one such country and such enquiries continued, albeit on a less regular basis, after 1991 (see

Adibekian, 1985, 1986, 1987, 1991, 1992, 1995). In Ukraine such surveys began only following independence (see Academpress, 1994, A L D Publishers, 1995). In Georgia there had been no similar youth research. Qualitative enquiries among young people had no history in any of the countries. Nor, as far as we are aware, have there been any similar parallel studies. When other information has been available, mostly from surveys conducted in Armenia and Ukraine, this has been taken into account in interpreting our own findings which allow young people themselves to speak. Needless to say, they were not single-minded but their most common cries were of current discomfort combined with hope for the future. They were experiencing the costs of change but most were prepared to accept this as a necessary price. They did not want their countries to step backwards. Their overwhelming vote, if a referendum had been held, would have been to press ahead with reform to give them the chance to experience the benefits.

ECONOMIC LIFE

In all the relevant countries, not just the three covered in our research, the formal abandonment of communism was followed by sharp contractions in the public sector economies which were usually more or less co-terminous with the formal economies in which establishments provided regular employment. There were various reasons for this contraction, all of which applied in every post-communist country but to differing extents. One was the breakdown of the trading relationships that had linked enterprises throughout the communist bloc and especially within the Soviet Union (see International Monetary Fund, 1991, 1992). During the 1980's the communist economies had been encountering increasingly serious difficulties which became causes and effects of the weakening of the political regimes. When communist power structures were finally dismantled there was an almost total collapse of inter-country trading relationships. Businesses lost customers and suppliers of raw materials, sometimes because they were unable to pay in acceptable currencies and sometimes because a plant's suppliers' own supplies had been disrupted. Munitions factories in Ukraine and Armenia that had equipped the Soviet army lost their main customer (International Labour Office, 1995). In all the countries, supplies of oil, electricity and gas became less reliable. The net result was a domino collapse that affected virtually every enterprise in every country. Governments were always seriously affected because enterprises became unable to pay taxes. In some countries 'shock therapy' market reforms contributed to the contraction of the public sectors. This was a major catalyst in Central Europe. In Ukraine, Georgia and Armenia, however, the main shocks were administered not as deliberate acts of government policy but because the cash starved governments were unable to continue to subsidise enterprises, and by the general breakdown of trading relationships.

Whether enterprises continued to operate depended partly on their managers' skills, and also on their political leverage. The coal miners in Donetsk had to be kept in employment, and paid, for strategic economic and political reasons, whereas by 1995 the bus and television assembly plants in Lviv that were also visited in the course of this research were virtually at a standstill. Armenia's economic problems had been heightened by its armed dispute with Azerbaijan which was continuing the country's history of almost perpetual war (Walker, 1991), and the resulting economic blockade imposed by all its Muslim neighbours. Civil wars had exacerbated Georgia's economic problems (see Aves, 1991, 1992).

The post-communist governments in Central Europe were better able to prepare enterprises for privatisation. They had the more developed economies to begin with and as soon as reforms commenced the countries began to attract Western money from tourists, investors and customers. These inflows were much lower in Ukraine, and virtually non-existent in Georgia and Armenia.

The contraction of the state sector economies had not always led to a commensurate decline in employment and a rise in unemployment. It had been government policy in all three countries in this study to keep people in employment, temporarily laid off if necessary, and thereby prevent unemployment levels and benefit payments soaring (International Labour Office, 1995; Yaremenko and Komarova, 1995). Enterprises with labour surpluses did not always stop recruiting. It was usually possible for school-leavers to obtain state sector jobs, if they wanted them. The drawbacks were that there might be little work for them to do, and no money to pay them. This was why, in the countries where groups of young workers were interviewed (Ukraine and Armenia) it proved rather difficult to obtain the required numbers. Enterprises that were visited would be stopped, or most of their staff would be laid off. The young workers who were contacted often explained that they had not been paid for months and some described the pay that they did receive as 'symbolic', as low as $5 per month in some cases. 'We're paid when there are orders. No money at the moment though.' In Armenia there was a salary ceiling of $25 in most public sector occupations. Workers in Lviv were rather better paid, and in Donetsk they were generally much better paid (up to $70 in the public sector). Why did any young people take jobs when the pay was abysmal and irregular? Most were in fact declining to enter such employment. Those who had done so explained that they had no better alternatives. 'There's no choice. I would not be able to obtain a better job.' Even if there was no regular work, and salary payments were unreliable or symbolic, employees could hope that things would improve. And their jobs gave the young people positions in their countries and established their entitlement to welfare benefits (in the event of the governments being able to offer any). In Georgia and Armenia in particular the young people had been most likely to feel that public sector jobs were simply not worth taking. The young unemployed were not difficult to locate in these countries. They were numerous, but those who were interviewed had rarely registered at the Labour Offices. Most would not have survived the 'availability for work' test (see below). In any case, the benefits that they might have received would have been trivial, around $2 a month (see Boeri, 1993; Cybul'nyk et al, 1994; Komarova, 1993).

Needless to say, it was not only young people who were suffering from the collapse of the state sector economies. Their parents were equally affected. Living standards had plunged. Families were short of money and even of basic services - gas, electricity and water supplies had been severely disrupted throughout Georgia and Armenia, and in parts of Ukraine. Public transport had deteriorated everywhere. So had conditions in schools and hospitals. In Georgia and Armenia living conditions were described as not just difficult but 'heavy'. The cities were unlit. Roads were becoming hazardous through lack of repairs.

People in the West may wonder how households could survive on the incomes described above. 'Survive' is probably the most appropriate word. Locally produced goods, such as were available, cost much less than in the West but this did not apply to imports. In all three countries, but especially in Georgia and Armenia, most households' ways of life had been reduced to basics. 'We live from salary to salary... We have to use money sparingly.' People were benefiting, in a sense, from the communist countries never having become as 'monetarised' as Western societies (see Ashwin, 1996). Young people had never been able to lose the art of passing time together without spending money. Under communism, even when people had cash, the state shops did not necessarily have the goods they wished to purchase. Employees were often paid partly 'in kind' with goods supplied to their enterprises through barter arrangements, and this was continuing, on a reduced scale, in the 1990's. So when they were not being paid salaries employees might receive a share from a consignment of foodstuffs, clothing, household durables or even vodka. Under communism people had also been accustomed to self-servicing - making and mending in their homes, and for friends and neighbours. In the harder times of the 1990's households had survival strategies to fall back on. No one starved. Neither Armenia, Georgia nor Ukraine was short of food and in the cities where our research was based, with the exception of Donetsk, most households had family connections with the countryside. The former growth of the cities had been reversed; in the 1990's some families were returning to farm the land. Many had this option. Others had no choice but to remain in the cities, but these families were not at risk of eviction from their homes merely because they were unable to pay the charges. That said, life had become grim and heavy. Western visitors were sometimes surprised by the acquiescence of the local populations. Why were they not demanding action from local and national politicians and officials? Part of the answer is that poverty is normally debilitating, but, in any case, people in Armenia, Georgia and Ukraine knew that their governments had neither the money nor the power to solve their countries' problems in the short run.

Another part of the explanation of how households were surviving is that while the state economies had declined the private sectors had boomed. Although there had been steep overall declines in output and incomes in all the countries, with 30 percent or more ripped from people's living standards - devastation comparable to the effects of a major war - conditions were unlike in a recession in an established market economy. During such recessions business slows in all sectors, albeit to different extents. This was not the case in the post-communist societies. Their public sector economies declined but their private economies began to expand rapidly (see Konings et al, 1995; Roberts and Kurzynowski, 1996). Some people were able to take advantage of these new opportunities and young people were particularly likely to be among them. In some post-communist countries, but not in Armenia, Georgia or Ukraine, the private sectors soon began to grow as a result of the privatisation of state enterprises. In most regions of the former Soviet Union enterprises were in no condition to attract private purchasers. Such privatisation as occurred was often to the managers or all the workers in an enterprise which never led to injections of new capital and usually left the work regimes intact. In some countries new jobs were created as Western businesses and other organisations opened offices and plants. There were some such jobs in Ukraine, Georgia and Armenia, but very few, and nearly all of these were in the capital cities. Those fortunate enough to obtain such jobs could be paid $200 a month or more. This was among the dreams of the young people in this study (see also Cybul'nyk, 1994). It was unlikely to come true. Most of the private sector growth was due to businesses starting *de novo*, sometimes emerging from the second economies, and own account working, usually 'trading'. This was the most common way in which young people earned money.

Trading could be in locally produced goods. It could take place on the street or, as traders became better established, from kiosks or even shops. Instead of obtaining goods locally, traders could join 'shopping tours' to countries where products were available at lower prices. In all the countries in this research 'doing business' had become young people's main hope of earning decent money. They were as likely to regard trading as a necessity as their preferred occupation, though 'management' and 'business' had quickly become the new prestige professions (see also Adibekian, 1985, 1992). Most young people, the males at any rate, had first become involved when they were students to help themselves get by, and they were likely to have continued after they left school instead of, or as well as obtaining proper jobs. The line between trading as a survival and as an enrichment strategy could be wafer thin. In Armenia 65 percent of the males in this study had been involved in some kind of business. A few had been spectacularly successful, as was the case in Georgia where one of the young people interviewed was a director of a private bank while another owned a bakery.

Trading was always risky business. It would invariably be wholly or partly in the second economy, beyond taxation and government statistics on economic activity. Business was not conducted within a framework of state enforced commercial law. It had to be done on a basis of fear or trust. None of the countries in this study had a reliable banking system. Business was usually on a cash basis. There was no bank credit, only person to person loans. People doing business had to be able to protect their pitches and property or pay someone else to do so. In all the countries there were frequent references to Mafia who could either be linked to the governments or state apparatuses, or independent (see Varese, 1994).

The expansion of private economic activity was promoting new attitudes to money. In Soviet times money had not been a prime value for most people but this was changing. All the countries had new, high profile, high status big spenders. With money it had become possible to buy anything, and making money had become respectable rather than disreputable. In all three countries the young people were clear that, although they did not necessarily aspire to riches, if possible they wanted to embark on working lives in which they would be able to earn decent money. Their societies could no longer guarantee even basic needs, so the people's desire for personal material security had strengthened (see Adibekian, 1985). And the role of the 'self' had been enlarged (see Adibekian, 1985). The young people in this study knew that they needed to make their own plans, build their own futures, and accept the consequences of their success or failure.

Everywhere the higher education graduates were proving better able than other young people to take advantage of the new, and to claim the better old jobs that remained. The graduates were by far the most likely to be obtaining state jobs in which the work and pay remained fairly regular if not generous, in health and education for example. They were also the young people who were being taken on as employees by Western based and linked, and locally owned businesses. In addition, they featured prominently among the more successful traders. However, the sharpest division among the young people within each country was not by educational level or family background but between those who were trying to hold on to the old employment opportunities that were fast disappearing and, when they remained, were becoming less attractive, and those whose aims and efforts were geared to the expanding market economies. A third group was simply passive, bemused, apparently content to remain dependent on their families with no ideas or even clear preferences as regards the adult lives that they would build. There were graduates and non-graduates in all these groups, though in different proportions, and the largest group was composed of young people who were engaging with the new opportunities.

The countries were not changing in an evolutionary manner. Economic life and social strata were being restructured on a revolutionary scale. Some families had been able to use their positions in the old systems to join their countries' new business classes (see Ray, 1994), but many formerly high status individuals had suffered rapid, long range socio-economic demotion. Meanwhile, some young people from workers' families with no more than basic secondary education were succeeding in business. Unemployment and other economic difficulties were not concentrated among young people from any particular kind of family background. New kinds of advantaged and disadvantaged positions were being created, and distributed in ways unlike those familiar in the West. Maybe this was just a transitional situation but while the countries remained in transition the reactions to given circumstances of young, and older people, seemed likely to flout predictions derived from Western social science.

EDUCATION

Education had not collapsed in any of the countries. The schools and universities were suffering from shortages of books and even paper, and the fabric was typically deteriorating. Teachers' salaries were not being paid regularly and had dropped to almost symbolic levels in Georgia and Armenia. But the numbers of pupils and students had not declined. There had been no flight from education. Quite the reverse: there was more pressure to stay in. The countries had been well-educated under communism by West European standards in terms of the years of schooling that young people received, and in the 1990's young people were becoming even better educated. The rush into the labour market that some commentators had forecast had not materialised (see Cranston, 1992).

All the communist countries had similar education systems. Young people received a common schooling up to age 14-16 after which they were split into academic, then a variety of professional and vocational streams. However, the non-academic tracks were less developed in the Soviet Union than in 'Germanic' Central Europe, and, especially in the former Soviet Union, when the state economies contracted the schools' former links with enterprises withered and general (academic) secondary schooling became the norm.

Although all secondary schools always had theoretically equal status some developed particularly strong academic reputations and selected students on the basis of entrance examinations for which ambitious parents would pay for their children to receive private coaching. There was the same need for extra tuition when students prepared for the university entrance examinations. Completion of any type of secondary education was, again in theory, a sufficient qualification for higher education but entry to the leading institutions was always fiercely competitive. Private teaching was a way in which teachers could augment their salaries. Those with commercially useful skills such as languages could do further work in the second economies. All these features of education not only survived, but had been strengthened in the 1990s in all three countries in this study. And as proper jobs became scarce young people had become more likely to complete general secondary education and try to proceed to higher education or, at any rate, to some kind of post-secondary schooling on either a full-time or part-time basis. This was compatible with earning money though trade, though to varying extents depending on the attendance requirements at different colleges. Some students complained that they had virtually no time for anything but their studies.

At the time of this research higher education in state institutions was free for students who passed the entrance exams. State maintenance grants were also awarded to such students in all three countries. However, the value of these grants had declined to nominal levels in Georgia and Armenia. The grants were more significant, around $100 a year, in Ukraine, but nowhere near to the individuals' living costs. The students complained that they were badly treated compared with their counterparts in Russia and Poland. In all three countries in this research students had to depend basically on their parents or their own private earning capacity, but this also applied to those who did not proceed to higher education. Young people who did not qualify for free places, and those studying part-time, were normally required to pay fees. Facilities in the universities were generally spartan. Teaching was formal, in large classes. There were few books let alone PCs or other advanced teaching aids but this was not stemming the inflow of students. They accepted the need for a fair measure of 'self-education' though many were critical of the standards of teaching and, in particular, that even courses which were supposed to offer professional qualifications were nearly all theory and
little practice.

Nevertheless, most of the young people who were interviewed, not just the higher education graduates, were keen to become as well educated and as well qualified as possible. Education per se was status conferring in these countries and, in addition to this, it was believed that the emerging market economies would need and reward the well educated and professionally qualified. The young people were sensitive to labour market signals and had a good grasp of the combinations of skills that would give them the best possible starts. They recognised the growing demand for foreign languages, especially Western languages, and that they needed to become acquainted with information technology and, if possible, to gain experience in commercial environments. In the major cities in all three countries private colleges and classes offering foreign languages and computer training had multiplied. Private universities, some with support from Western foundations, had opened. They charged fees of up to $800 per year and sufficient families were somehow finding the money to fill the classes. There was a stark contrast in all three countries between the highly educated young adults who were being produced and the surrounding decline to pre-modern living conditions.

Professional self-realisation was a common career aspiration among the young people irrespective of their educational levels. This value had been propagated under communism but it was never peculiar to the communist countries. It resonates equally throughout Germanic Central Europe, more so than in Anglo-American culture. Communism may have been unable to offer the prospect of riches but it was possible to motivate young people by urging them to seek and enter vocations in which they could develop and express their potential. By the 1980's there was a widespread feeling that communism obstructed rather than fostered professional self-realisation, and the reforms were surrounded by hopes that the value would become realisable for more young people. Professional self-realisation occurs when there is a fit between an individual's ideas about his or her own abilities and inclinations, the education and training that the person receives, and the occupation that he or she practises. In the 1990's most young people in the countries that we studied still subscribed to this ideal. It was being joined by another, sometimes more powerful value, making money, but the two were not necessarily incompatible.

In practice most young people's desire for professional self-realisation was being frustrated, as was their desire for money. As had always happened, many young people were finding that they were not really suited to the fields of work into which their secondary or higher education normally led. Some had chosen courses while still unsure about their own inclinations and longer-term aims, or had been influenced primarily by the prestige or location of a department, advice from parents or teachers, the ease of entry to a particular course, or the fact that military training which could be substituted for actual military service was provided in a college. Those who wanted to work in the fields for which they had been educated were often balked by the lack of opportunity. The applied to all the young artists who were interviewed in Georgia. Many felt that it would be necessary to emigrate if they were to practise their vocations properly and obtain reasonable financial rewards. The young workers who were interviewed at the bus and television plants in Lviv were frustrated not just because they were unable to work and earn regularly but also because, when they were at work, the lack of proper materials and equipment prevented them achieving commendable standards. The young people who were relying on trade as their main source of income were rarely using the knowledge acquired during their formal eduction. Some had defined business as their vocation, and had enrolled on courses related to their actual occupations, typically courses in management or business. The desire for professional self-realisation was not being abandoned but as the young people gained experience in the market economy they were learning that some of the most useful skills, languages and computing for example, were generic to many occupations, and that the best rewarded qualities included competitiveness and adaptability.

PRIVATE LIFE

This was important in all the communist countries. Families and networks of friends took on some of the roles performed by civil society, voluntary associations for example, in Western countries (see Wedel, 1988). In the 1990s in the post-communist countries private life became even more important and, simultaneously, was subjected to new restrictions and pressures. The young people in this study explained how, in the 1980s, friends had been for recreation, amusement and companionship. By the mid-1990s peer relationships were performing additional functions. They were important for business contacts. Also, the young people spoke of how, under the 'heavy' conditions, friends often acted as mutual psychotherapists. Yet peer group activities had been cut back to basics as had happened to living standards in general (see also Jung, 1994). Holidays and visits to theatres and cinemas had been eliminated from most young people's leisure. This is mainly for financial reasons, and it was why the young artists in Georgia were unable to earn livings from their professions. State support for the arts had disappeared and private customers lacked the means to pay. New commercial facilities - bars, restaurants and discos - were opening in the major cities in all three countries. They all had good quality establishments, charging Western prices, which were accessible only for the countries' new economic elite. There were also lower quality bars and cafes but even these were beyond the means of most young people.

In Armenia the respondents were asked a structured question about their leisure activities. Only three percent of the males and none of the females reported that they played any sport regularly. Only 20 percent listed listening to the radio or music, or watching television or videos, as normal uses of leisure. This was due to their homes having electricity for only a few hours each day. The young people's most common use of leisure was reported to be 'wasting time'. Spare time was typically being spent in or around the young people's homes where they talked or quarrelled with one another.

But life went on. The young people were still forming heterosexual relationships, marrying and becoming parents. Only in Ukraine had the marriage and fertility rates fallen, and divorce risen to a West European level (see Volynec et al, 1995). In all three countries in this study it was still normal for young women who did not enter higher education to marry and become parents by their early twenties. Higher education graduates normally experienced these life events a few years later. So nearly all the young people who were interviewed in this study were either already married and parents or were contemplating these events.

They were facing new complications. Some arose directly from the young people's economic circumstances. They did not have the levels or regularity of income to enable them to be financially independent. In all three countries most of the young people who were interviewed were wholly or partly dependent on their parents. Some faced the reverse problem: their families were dependent on them and the young people could see no way of escaping from these responsibilities. In all three countries there were exceptional young couples who had been able to move into independent accommodation. This had nearly always been achieved with substantial assistance from at least one set of parents. In some cases the families, and the young people themselves in rather fewer instances, had been sufficiently prosperous to purchase flats. More young people had been able to inherit relatives' tenancies. Obtaining independent accommodation had always been a problem for young people in the Soviet Union. It had often been necessary for young couples to live with one set of parents for many years before they qualified for their own flats or inherited the parents'. The new problem for many young people in the 1990s was that even by their mid-twenties they could not envisage how they would ever be able to live independently and self-sufficiently. Dependence on families had increased (see Komarova, 1993; Wallace, 1994).

Yet simultaneously the countries had become more open to, and the young people were being influenced by Western values and lifestyles. This meant, among other things, that their desire for independence was growing. In Georgia and Armenia this was creating serious inter-generational conflicts. In both countries the traditional ideal had been an extended family with three or more generations living together, all under the authority of the elder members. Very few of the young people who were interviewed subscribed to this ideal. Only 10 percent of the respondents in Armenia were prepared to continue to submit to their parents' authority. Yet the young people believed that their seniors continued to uphold traditional values. The elders were being disempowered by their lack of employment and income, but the young people, in most cases, had no alternative to staying with their parents which created situations in which quarrels about money and the young people's rights to self-determination were commonplace. Most of the young people who were in such situations seemed sanguine rather than bitter. 'It is nothing extraordinary. It is just a normal family situation. It has advantages and disadvantages.'

Another sign of Westernisation in Armenia and Georgia was the idea that sex life could properly begin prior to marriage. Where contrary beliefs persisted these were being challenged, and contraception was becoming the preferred method of fertility control. Up to the end of the 1980s Armenia and Georgia had not experienced even the Russia version, let alone the Western sexual revolution. The prevailing view remained that, for females at any rate, pre-marital sex was unacceptable. This ruled out cohabitation. Single parenthood was simply unthinkable. But by the mid-1990's values were changing, especially among young people, particularly those in the big cities and in higher education. Nevertheless, in Armenia 41 percent of the males and 51 percent of the females who were interviewed in this study stated that there were no circumstances in which it could be acceptable for a woman to have sex before marriage. Both sexes, but particularly the males, were more tolerant of male pre-marital sexual activity. In Ukraine pre-marital sex and cohabitation were acceptable in most sections of the population. The main obstacle to cohabitation was not morality but housing.

In all three countries abortion had been the normal method of fertility control during the Soviet years. In the 1990's young women were continuing to become mothers soon after they became sexually active, and were continuing to resort to abortion to control their fertility. In Georgia a half of the young women who were interviewed had already experienced at least one abortion. But contraception was becoming more widely available and preferred to abortion. Oral contraceptives and barrier devices were available in the drug stores in all three countries. The dilemma that most young women faced, apart from the cost, was whether to use oral contraceptives without medical advice and supervision.

The availability or oral contraceptives, and the growing acceptance of pre-marital sexual activity by both sexes, were giving young women more control over their lives. But overall the trends in the 1990's were not towards greater sex equality (see Watson, 1993). There was still a double standard; wide ranging sexual experience was considered less acceptable for a woman than for a man. In Armenia there were nearly as many young people who believed that the male should rule the family as considered that the responsibility should be shared equally with the wife. Business and politics were overwhelmingly male activities in all three countries and by the mid-1990's the role of the young housewife had been resurrected. The young women with housewife as their actual and self-defined main occupation did not complain of sex oppression. In most cases they saw it as a sensible choice. Some welcomed the opportunity to stay at home and concentrate on family care as a sign that their countries were becoming normal societies. However, this was in a context where most of the young women had been unable to obtain regularly paid jobs, where men dominated the world of business, where nurseries and kindergartens were being privatised and becoming expensive, and where daily breakdowns in electricity and water supplies were intensifying the labour involved in home and child care.

POLITICS

Making sense of young (and older) people's political responses to the situations in Armenia, Georgia and Ukraine in the 1990's requires a digression into how these situations arose. Reform in these countries did not occur as a result of sustained pressure from internal reform movements. It was unlike Poland and Czechoslovakia where, during the 1980s, Solidarity and Civic Forum respectively contributed to the breakdown of communism. At the end of the 1980s there were reform and independence movements in Ukraine, Georgia and Armenia but these movements were not so much a cause as a symptom of the mounting crisis in Soviet communism. Young people were heavily involved in these movements. Most of our respondents could recall their involvement, especially those who were in secondary schools or higher education between 1988 and 1991. They recalled that virtually everyone had then been active. There had been simultaneous religious revivals in all three countries (see Adibekian, 1986, 1987). People had celebrated their new freedom to express and practise their faiths openly. However, change came in 1991 not through the strength of these movements so much as because Russia made itself independent of the Soviet Union.

Suddenly the would-be reformers in the Union's other republics had everything that they had asked for - independence, freedom of expression and belief, and the freedom to work and trade in the market sectors of the economies.

When the Soviet Union ended the politicians who held office in Ukraine, Georgia and Armenia were not necessarily overthrown but mostly transformed themselves into nationalists, democrats, new communists or socialists, and splintered into a variety of parties none of which had mass memberships or even nationwide organisations (see Fischer and Grigorian, 1993). While this was happening the formal economies folded. The new governments were not the cause of this collapse but they were unable to prevent it. This was the context in which disillusionment spread and political interest evaporated. Young people demobilised politically just as rapidly as they had mobilised a few years earlier (see Korniyevs'kyi and Mishchenko, 1995; Tregubova, 1992). By the mid-1990s the same had happened to religious enthusiasm. In all three countries most of the young people who were interviewed were 'believers' but only a minority were practising and very few seemed to be basing their ways of life on a religious world view. In Armenia, where virtually everyone expressed allegiance to the Armenian church, only 24 percent were attending regularly whereas 50 percent thought that fortune telling was wholly or partly true. The young people seemed to have little regard for the statements of church leaders, and they appeared to have even lower opinions of their countries' politicians. All the countries had become low trust societies. Many politicians were believed to be more interested in their own betterment than the state of their countries. In any case, it was blatantly clear that the governments were not in charge of what was happening and had no solutions to the immense problems which people faced in their everyday lives.

Young political activists were interviewed in Georgia and Ukraine. They were an important group, not least as their countries' likely future leaders, but highly untypical of their age group in their political interest and activity. The young activists were having to adjust to a situation which some experienced as strange and abnormal where political parties lacked the resources to pay their active supporters. The young people were discovering that politics could no longer be the same kind of career as under communism.

Most of the respondents in all three countries were disappointed, highly concerned and sometimes angry about the prevailing circumstances, and dismissive towards politicians. 'This country (Ukraine) is in a deep crisis. Everything is going to the bottom. We seem to live in worse conditions than Third World countries... Everything is corrupt. The Mafia are everywhere. The ordinary person is unprotected... Politics is nothing more than a talking shop. There is no hope of changing anything. All the politicians want power just to become rich. They pay no heed to other people's interests, needs and hopes and do not represent them effectively. Politics is a theatre with its own company of actors but the actors are not professional. They should be professional in politics the same as everywhere else.'

Few of the young people were politically active but this was no barrier to them holding strong political opinions. A common strongly held view, as we have seen, was disdain for all politicians and their parties. Beyond this, however, most of the young people had definite ideas about the directions that their countries should take. Maybe none would have defined themselves as extremists but many had opinions that were extremely unacceptable to other groups. In all three countries there were nationalists to whom independence was the priority; they wanted their countries' futures to be based squarely on their own traditions and cultures. There was also (minority) support for restoring the old communist economy and the USSR; the latter proposition was, of course, anathema to the nationalists. Many young people felt that some parties ought to be banned. There was significant support for the installation of a strong leader, or a group of leaders, who would restore order and give a sense of direction. Very few of the young people referred to environmental issues. This applied even in Ukraine where Chernobyl had been superseded by more pressing problems (but see Hateniuk et al, 1994 for a contrasting view). By the mid-1990's cheap food from the contaminated region had been on open sale for several years. It was rather different issues that were stirring young people's passions at the time of our research.

> 'We must return to the rouble zone. We must restore the old regime and rejoin Russia.'
>
> 'The former communists have camouflaged themselves and returned to power as democrats. They must be ousted.'
>
> 'We do not need external help. We will revive through our own efforts. We must tell the world, "Don't help us but don't hinder us". It is better to die of hunger than to live on our knees as before.'
>
> 'The nationalists are sick people. They must be kept under control. These guys have guns and they're ready to shoot.'

In all three countries the majority of the young people who were interviewed wanted to retain the market economies and multi-party democratic politics, but none of the countries had parties which shared these aspirations firmly installed in government and opposition. Everywhere there was strong, albeit minority support for rejoining Russia and in some way rebuilding the old communist economy. Young people in rural areas, workers without post-secondary education, and the unemployed were particularly likely to express these opinions. And within all shades of opinion there was significant support for the view that some groups' politics were so unacceptable that the groups ought to be suppressed. None of the countries could be described as a stable democracy in 1995.

THE NATIONALITIES QUESTION

In all the countries in this research independence had re-opened an older nationalities question. Up to 1995 there had been no military action within Ukraine but the western region, with its mainly Ukrainian population, and the east with its Russian majority, were represented by almost entirely different sets of political parties. Armenia had been militarily involved in the dispute with Azerbaijan over the status of Nagorno Karabakh. In Georgia there had been civil wars in two regions which claimed autonomy, South Ossetia and Abkhazia, plus armed conflicts between different Georgian political factions (see Aves, 1991, 1992). Armed militia from some of western Ukraine's nationalist parties had participated in the wars in Abkhazia and Chechnya on the principle that anyone fighting the Russians was an ally of theirs.

All young males had been eligible for conscription in the Soviet army for up to two years. There had been various ways of claiming exception which had been a pre-occupation for some, but all the countries in this research had nationals in the Soviet army at the time of independence. Many returned to their home countries with their uniforms and guns at a time when the new states had still to create national armies. The young soldiers had sometimes allied themselves with their preferred political factions. In Armenia the existence of an external enemy accelerated the process whereby the state monopolised legitimate military power. The civil wars had a similar effect in Georgia. In both of these countries some of the young males who were interviewed had been directly involved in post-independence armed conflicts. Some had joined their countries' new independent armies with enthusiasm. The young people had been politicised during the reform movements and after independence there were national interests to defend. The countries manifestly needed their help. Apart from their roles as soldiers, many of the young males were otherwise unemployed. It was patriotic sentiment rather than hatred of another group that had made them willing soldiers. It was apparent in our interviews that none of the nationalities hated the others. Indeed, most of the young people were exemplars of national and religious tolerance. What they found unacceptable, and were often prepared to fight to resist, was their people becoming a dominated minority in what they considered their homeland.

None of the males who had fought had found the experience glorious. It had been traumatic. Some had been seriously and permanently wounded. They had all seen comrades maimed and killed. Even two or more years afterwards many were still suffering trauma, unable to sleep or settle in any situation. The young soldiers in Georgia and Armenia and not returned victorious. They had not been welcomed back into civilian life as heroes. They were widely suspected, with some justification as the ex-soldiers themselves acknowledged, of looting and using their positions for personal gain. Tbilisi and Yerevan both had refugees, Georgians and Armenians who had been displaced from the war zones. The displaced persons occupied hotels and sanatoria, or were living with friends. They had lost everything - family members in some cases, and usually all their belongings. Most were simply unable to settle in their new cities. They found it difficult to understand how and why their fellow nationals were allowing them to remain dispossessed.

None of the males who had been involved in battle wanted to repeat the experience. They all explained that, in the event of further emergencies, they would do everything possible to avoid enlistment. Conscription had not become popular in any of the independent countries (see also Tomchuk, 1994; Vlachova and Stanek, 1992). Most young males were still doing everything possible to claim exemption. They appeared even less keen than in the 1980s to place their lives at the service of their countries (see Adibekian, 1985). Those who expected to be conscripted sometimes hoped that the experience and any qualifications that they gained would help them in their subsequent civilian lives. Only 13 percent of the young Armenians who were interviewed named serving their country as one of their life goals. Of course, there were some, with and without personal military experience, who defended conscription for 'making real men out of boys' and 'giving them real life experience', but most of the young people spoke of military service in entirely different terms. 'It's total disorder... It's two years for nothing... The army is an unpaid workforce... My associations with the word "army" are rudeness, cruelty, dirt, violence and senselessness.'

Almost without exception the young people were opposed to war. They wanted political solutions to inter-national problems. At the same time, they lacked confidence in their countries' politicians delivering solutions. They wanted their countries reconstructed on the basis of civic responsibility, people respecting and caring for each other, rather than an aggressive nationalism. Yet many still believed that there could be circumstances in which it was necessary to fight to defend national interests. By the mid-1990s males who had fought in previous wars were explaining how, in combat situations, they had made real friends and how heroes had been separated from cowards. Their listeners included younger men without regular work or other definite roles in their societies. None of the countries had settled its nationalities questions. None had achieved internal political stability. Personal safety had become an issue everywhere. All the countries had experienced mounting problems of crime and lawlessness in the early 1990s but the empowerment of the governments and state apparatuses was rarely considered an ideal solution. A common view was that state power would be used primarily for the private interests of politicians and apparatchiks. The most common reaction to this situation among the young people was to debate politics only within their families and with personal friends, and to withdraw into private life and concentrate on private goals that might be achieved irrespective of the fates of the countries (see also Korniyevs'kyi and Lytvyn, 1994; Yevtukh et al, 1994).

AIMS AND HOPES

Given all the above it may come as a surprise that most of the young people were optimistic as regards their own if not their countries' futures. However, most believed that their countries would recover. Optimism appeared to be rising everywhere (Adibekian, 1986, 1995). A prevalent feeling was that the people had shown that they could cope with adversity, that conditions had hit the bottom and the countries would revive. Not everyone shared this optimism but even in Armenia where conditions were 'heaviest' only 16 percent of the young people expressed unqualified pessimism. In Armenia there was equal support for and opposition to emigration (when advising a hypothetical friend). Surveys among Armenian youth in the early 1990s which used identical questions had recorded much higher levels of pessimism and support for emigration (Adibekian, 1991, 1992, 1995).

Some of the young people would have welcomed a restoration of the old systems, but they were a minority in each country (see also Korniyevs'kyi and Mishchenko, 1995). If the young people in this study were typical, ex-communists would have stood no chance of elected power in any of the countries had the vote been restricted to the under-30s. The young people knew that they had lost the guaranteed futures that the old systems would have offered. They knew that their own futures were extremely uncertain. But most preferred the new uncertainties to the old guarantees. They believed, admittedly with varying degrees of confidence, that they would be able to build better futures for themselves in their countries than the old systems would have delivered. Far from envying their elders, the young people considered themselves to be the privileged age group. They believed that they would live to see the benefits of the reforms. Unlike in the West, which has known nothing comparable since the 1960s, young people in independent Armenia, Georgia and Ukraine believed that life would be better for them than it had been for their parents, and even better for their own children than it would be for themselves.

The young people's optimism was based more on self-confidence than trust in big institutions. All the countries had become low trust societies. People had little confidence in politicians, state officials, large enterprises, banks or strangers. The 'habitus' in which they lived had become fragile and unreliable. In the West this condition is sometimes read as a symptom of progression into a postmodern state. In the post-communist countries it was the mixture of progress in some, alongside regression to pre-modern conditions in other spheres, that was responsible. Most young people felt that their best strategy was to rely on themselves, and most had confidence in their ability to cope. Their typical aims were to complete their education, then, equipped with qualifications and skills, to find good jobs or build their own businesses and establish families. They seemed to be making thoroughly realistic appraisals of their situations. Some were demoralised and apathetic, willing to depend on their families in the short term and on fate in the longer run, but they were in the minority. A message from our research to the countries involved is that, up to 1995 at any rate, most of their young people had not been shattered by the impact of the reforms. Many of the war veterans and refugees appeared traumatised, but theirs were extreme rather than typical experiences.

MESSAGES FROM POST-COMMUNIST YOUTH

We believe that our research has further messages for Ukraine, Georgia and Armenia. Overall the messages are encouraging. In general the countries' young people were resilient and resourceful. They had not become an estranged, lost generation. Forecasts that children schooled under communism would prove unable to cope with freedom were being confounded (see Suchy, 1991). The messages are also encouraging in that some of the measures that our evidence supports would not imply huge immediate outlays that the governments could not afford.

Young people in all the countries differed in their experiences and views. In all the countries there were some who, if it had been possible, would have opted for restoring the past, but this was a minority preference. Rather than preserving old jobs, most of the young people wanted opportunities to gain the education, qualifications and work experience that would at least allow them to envisage building financially secure futures in, and deriving rising living standards from the private sector economies. Rather than a revival of the old youth organisations, the majority wanted to see commercial leisure provisions continuing to develop. Young people's political inactivity was not a sign of indifference. Most were politically aware and concerned but preferred to discuss political issues mainly within their private social networks and to confine their public participation to voting in periodic elections. In these respects they resembled most citizens in Western countries. All told, although most of the young people had undergone and were still experiencing considerable discomfort, the ways in which their countries were in fact changing were in general accord with their own preferences.

Developments which, according to our evidence, would be widely welcomed by young people in Armenia, Georgia and Ukraine, and which would impact positively on their quality of life, would not all require expensive programmes. Such developments include the strengthening of sex education and contraceptive services, the expansion of housing markets through which young people could at least envisage ways of obtaining independent accommodation, national currencies and banks in which they could have confidence, law and order enforced impartially, and a phasing out of military conscription in favour of professional volunteer armed forces. Rather than just the wishes of youth, these should probably be seen as demands of the new generation of adult citizens in all three countries.

Our evidence also carries messages, challenges indeed, for much Western social thought. First, the situations in Armenia, Georgia and Ukraine reveal how naive it is to assume that investment in education will more or less automatically lead to economic success for either individuals or their societies. Education may expand primarily to fill life space that is surplus to productive requirements. Second, our evidence shows that young people can still make recognisable transitions to adulthood even in conditions of extreme adversity. Western commentators need to pause before assuming that the levels of youth unemployment in their countries will be fatal for young people's longer-term progress and cast them into never ending limbo. Third, the biographies of young people in Ukraine, Armenia and Georgia are a reminder that in most parts of the modern world military experience for males is a normal part of growing up. In most countries this strengthens gender divisions and creates divisions between males who serve and the rest. Fourth, some supposedly world-wide trends are in fact less global that much Western social thought suggests. It is difficult to square theses on the decline of the nation state with the disintegration of the USSR. The re-appearance of housewives, and the predominance of males in business and politics in the new independent countries, challenges notions of a global trend towards sex equality.

The new independent countries may soon dethrone much Western social theory. Its recent track record has been chequered. Few Western experts predicted the collapse of communism. The expert advisers from the West did not predict the extent to which the post-communist economies would collapse once market processes began to prevail. Nor did they warn that recovery could take decades or never happen. All these unpredicted developments give new dimensions to the meaning of 'risk society'. In the former communist world the new risks have arisen not as a result of the societies developing beyond industrialism and Fordism but through the collapse of modern institutions and, in many respects, regression to pre-modern conditions. Social scientists and other citizens in the post-communist countries now want answers to the big questions posed by the twentieth century just as the classical sociological theorists interpreted nineteenth century developments in Europe. The big events of the twentieth century have included the rise and spread, then the collapse of communism. People in the relevant countries want to know why these events happened and the futures that are possible for them. Their need to know is likely to produce the next generation of important theories. These could rapidly sideline the current Western pre-occupation with an alleged postmodernity.

REFERENCES

Academpress (1994), *Youth of Ukraine: Positions, Problems and Ways of Solution*, Kiev.

A Adibekian (1985), *Socio-Professional Orientations of Armenian Graduates*, Independent Sociological Centre, Yerevan.

A Adibekian (1986), *The Religiousness of Youth*, Independent Sociological Centre, Yerevan.

A Adibekian (1987), *Perspectives of Youth Movements*, Independent Sociological Centre, Yerevan.

A Adibekian (1991), *Political Priorities in Independent Conditions*, Independent Sociological Centre, Yerevan.

A Adibekian (1992), *The New Social Stratification and Mobility*, Independent Sociological centre, Yerevan.

A Adibekian (1995), *Social Integration in the Modern Period*, Independent Sociological Centre, Yerevan.

A L D Publisher (1995), *Young Generation of New Ukraine*, Kiev.

S Ashwin (1996), 'Forms of collectivity in a non-monetary society', *Sociology*, 30, 21-39.

J Aves (1991), *Path to National Independence in Georgia*, School of Slavonic and East European Studies, London.

J Aves (1992), 'The rise and fall of the Georgian nationalist movement, 1987-91', in G A Hosking, J Aves and P J S Rucam, eds, *The Road to Post-Communism*, Pinter, London.

A Cranston (1992), *A Study of Active Employment Policy in Czechoslovakia*, Federal Ministry of Labour and Social Policy, Prague.

V V Cybul'nyk (1994), 'Youth and market', *Rakurs*, 4.

V Cybul'nyk, H Dvorec'ka, S Makeiev, S Maslich and O Yaremenko (1994), 'The material position of youth: dynamics and perspectives', in *Youth of Ukraine: Positions, Problems and Ways of Solution*, Academpress, Kiev.

M M J Fischer and S Grigorian (1993), 'Six to eight characters in search of Armenian civil society amidst the carnivalisation of history', in G E Marcus, ed, *Perilous States*, University of Chicago Press, Chicago.

A T Hatenuik and I M Hrabovs'ka (1994), 'Youth and ecological situation', in *Youth of Ukraine: Positions, Problems and Ways of Solution*, Academpress, Kiev.

International Labour Office (1995), *The Ukrainian Challenge*, Central European University Press, Budapest.

International Monetary Fund (1991), *Armenia*, Washington.

International Monetary Fund (1992), *Economic Review - Georgia*, Washington.

B Jung (1994), 'For what leisure? The role of culture and recreation in post-communist Poland', *Leisure Studies*, 13, 1-15.

N M Komarova (1994), 'Some aspects of the socio-economic position of youth', in *Youth of Ukraine: Positions, Problems and Ways of Solution*, Academpress, Kiev.

J Konings, H Lehmann and M E Schaffer (1995), *Employment Growth, Job Creation and Job Destruction in Polish Industry: 1988-91*, Working Paper 38/1995, Leuven Institute for Central and East European Studies, Catholic University of Leuven.

O A Korniyevs'kyi and V M Lytvyn (1994), 'Socio-political orientations of youth', in *Youth of Ukraine: Positions, Problems and Ways of Solution*, Academpress, Kiev.

O A Korniyevs'kyi and M D Mishchenko (1995), 'Youth in transitional society: political analysis of its socio-political orientations' in *Youth of Ukraine: Positions, Problems and Ways of Solution*, Academpress, Kiev.

L Ray (1994), 'The collapse of Soviet socialism: legitimation, regulation and the new state', in P Brown and R Crompton, eds, *Economic Restructuring and Social Exclusion*, UCL Press, London.

K Roberts and B Jung (1995), *Poland's First Post-Communist Generation*, Avebury, Aldershot.

K Roberts and A Kurzynowski (1996), *Young People and their Employers in Present-Day Poland*, Occasional Paper 6, Department of Sociology, Social Policy and Social Work Studies, University of Liverpool.

J Suchy (1991), 'The Slovak youth and international society', in L Machacek, ed, *Youth and State, CSFR 1991*, Slovak Academy of Sciences, Bratislava.

M I Tomchuk (1994), 'Psychological peculiarities of the readiness of youth for military service in the Ukrainian army', in *Youth of Ukraine: Positions, Problems and Ways of Solution*, Academpress, Kiev.

N Tregubova (1992), 'What are youth keeping silent about?' *Politolohichni Chytannia*, 1.

F Varese (1994), 'Is Sicily the future of Russia? Private protection and the rise of the Russian mafia', *Archives of European Sociology*, 35, 224-258.

M Vlachova and M Stanek (1992), 'Young men's value orientation and its relation to their attitudes towards the Czechoslovak military', *Sociologia*, 24, 47-48.

L S Volynec, H I Onishchenko and J M Yakuboba (1995), 'The problems of complex analysis of the youth family and the construction of a model of its reproductive behaviour', in *Young Generation of New Ukraine*, A D L Publisher, Kiev.

C J Walker (1991), *Armenia: the Survival of a Nation*, Routledge, London.

C Wallace (1995), 'Young people and their families in Poland: changing times, changing dependencies', *Journal of European Social Policy*, 5, 97-109.

P Watson (1993), 'Eastern Europe's silent revolution: gender', *Sociology*, 27, 471-487.

J R Wedel (1988), *The Private Poland*, Facts on File Publications, New York.

O O Yaremenko and N M Komarova (1995), 'The secondary employment of youth in the big Ukrainian cities', in *Young Generation of New Ukraine*, A L D Publisher, Kiev.

V B Yevtukh, A I Vushniak and M A Molchanov (1994), 'Socio-political orientations of Ukrainian youth', in *Youth of Ukraine: Positions, Problems and Ways of Solution*, Academpress, Kiev.

CHAPTER 6

UKRAINE: CURRENT ISSUES AND U.S. POLICY

STEVEN WOEHREL

HISTORICAL INTRODUCTION

Area: 235,443 sq. mi., larger than Poland, Hungary, the Czech Republic and Slovakia combined

Population: 51.4 million

Ethnic Composition: Ukrainians 37.4 million (73%), Russians 11.3 million (22%), Jews 486,000 (.9%), Belarussians 450,000 (.9%)

GNP: $121.1 billion in 1996 (PlanEcon estimate in 1993 US$ at a Purchasing Power Parity rate)

Ukraine's history has been shaped by its status as a border region; indeed, "border region" is the original meaning of its name. For almost all of its history, Ukraine has been divided between opposing great powers, who have tried to assimilate it. This has led to a fragile sense of national identity and to considerable differences between the regions of Ukraine. Polish culture helped orient western Ukraine to the West, although attempts to Polonize Ukraine created resentment. The dominant influence on most of the rest of Ukraine has been Russia. For centuries, Russian leaders have often pointed to a common historical heritage, similarities in language and a common Orthodox religion to assert that Ukraine belongs in the same state with Russia or that Ukrainians were merely the "Little Russian" offshoot of the "Great Russian" nation. Tsarist efforts to Russify Ukraine met with considerable, but not complete success: the elite and city-dwellers were largely Russian-speakers, but the Ukrainian language remained strong in rural areas.

The Soviet impact on Ukraine was mixed. Industrialization of Ukraine accelerated. Stalin's territorial aggrandizement incorporated ethnic Ukrainian-majority regions from Poland, Czechoslovakia and Romania into Ukraine. But faced with the resistance of Ukrainian peasants to collectivization, Stalin engineered a famine in 1932-1933 that starved to death an estimated three to eight million Ukrainians. The Stalinist and post-Stalinist leadership restricted education and cultural activities in the Ukrainian language in favor of Russian. The Soviet economic model left the Ukrainian economy in a catastrophic state. The Gorbachev era provided the opening for a revival of Ukrainian national feeling that later led to independence. The accident at the Chernobyl nuclear reactor in Ukraine and Gorbachev's economic mismanagement led even many ethnic Russians and others not particularly attracted to Ukrainian nationalism to believe that Ukraine could manage its affairs better on its own. Gorbachev's policy of glasnost and partial democratization permitted Ukrainian reformers to seize on these issues, and the national issue, to combat the arch-conservative Ukrainian Communist Party. During the March 1990 elections to the Ukrainian Supreme Soviet, Ukrainian nationalists and democrats won over a quarter of the seats in the parliament. Even though a minority, the opposition (with the support of public opinion) was able to pressure the Communist majority into approving a declaration of sovereignty for Ukraine on July 16, 1990. The declaration asserted the precedence of Ukrainian laws over the center central governments laws and asserted Ukraine's control of all economic assets on its territory.

Gorbachev's efforts to keep the union together by peaceful decentralization were shattered by the abortive coup in August 1991. On August 24, the Ukrainian Supreme Soviet declared Ukraine's independence from the Soviet Union. On December 1, 1991, voters approved a referendum on the declaration of independence, with 90% in favor. Independence was supported by overwhelming majorities (83-98%) in most regions and among all ethnic groups. One exception was the Crimea, where Russians make up two-thirds of the region's population. There, independence was approved by a relatively modest 54%. The decisive, country-wide vote in favor of independence surprised many observers, especially those in Russia who expected strong opposition to independence in the largely Russified south and east of Ukraine. The winner of the presidential election held on the same day was Leonid Kravchuk, chairman of the Ukrainian Supreme Soviet. Kravchuk's strategy as President was to try to hold on to the support of former party functionaries and the economic elite in part by refusing to embark on rapid economic reform. He also tried to garner support among the nationalist opposition by firmly defending Ukrainian sovereignty. In response to deadlock with the Supreme Soviet (many of whose members criticized Kravchuk for concentrating too much power in his own hands at the expense of the parliament and local soviets) and the threat of strikes and demonstrations from miners from eastern Ukraine angry at deteriorating economic conditions, Kravchuk and the parliament called early elections for parliament on March 27, 1994, and for President on June 26, 1994.

POLITICAL SITUATION

SUPREME RADA

Ukraine's 450-seat parliament (only 417 seats are filled), known as the Supreme Rada, is polarized along ideological and regional lines. The largest faction is the Communist Party, with 89 seats. The factions of its allies, the Socialists and the Agrarians, have 24 and 26 members respectively. The strength of the leftist parties is largely in eastern Ukraine. In June 1995, reform-minded members of the Agrarian faction (mainly from western Ukraine) broke away from the then 55-member Agrarian faction and formed the 25-member Agrarians for Reform faction.

The "Center" faction, with 29 members, is dominated by members of the pre-independence Communist nomenklatura (bureaucratic elite) who gave up

Communist Party membership but kept positions in government and the economy. They style themselves "centrists" who shun the ideological "extremes" of the reestablished Communists and the national-democrats and liberals, favoring Ukrainian independence with economic reform at a very gradual pace.

A center-left faction, Social-Market Choice, has 31 members. It is headed by former Prime Minister Yevhen Marchuk, who was fired by President Kuchma in May 1996. He has said that he will challenge Kuchma in the 1999 presidential election. Two other left/center groups are Unity (24 members) and the Interregional Group (21 deputies). These three groups favor economic reform, social protection and closer ties to Russia. Many of its members are leading Ukrainian industrialists and businessmen who have profited from the division of property in post-Soviet Ukraine, in part because of their ties with top Ukrainian officials. They have few philosophical differences. These factions differ mainly in their regional bases of support within eastern Ukraine, and their affiliation with powerful individuals, such as Marchuk, former Donetsk governor Volodymyr Shcherban (Social-Market Choice) and Prime Minister Pavlo Lazarenko (Unity).

The national-democratic group Rukh has a 29-member faction. Another national-democratic faction, "Statehood," has 29 members. Both favor economic reforms, but insist that Ukraine remain as independent as possible from Russia. Many of these deputies are from nationally-oriented western Ukraine. "Reforms", a moderate democratic group favoring economic reforms, has 30 deputies. A largely centrist Independents faction has 27 members.[1] In September 1996, the "Constitutional Center" faction was formed, taking deputies from the "Statehood" and "Reform" factions. Several extreme nationalists were elected to the parliament. An extreme nationalist/paramilitary organization, the UNA-UNSO, won 3 seats. One western Ukrainian newspaper characterizes 9 other deputies as "right radicals." Leftist forces in the new parliament helped elect Socialist Party leader Oleksandr Moroz as speaker on May 18, 1994.

PRESIDENT AND GOVERNMENT

On July 10, 1994, former Prime Minister and missile factory director Leonid Kuchma defeated incumbent President Leonid Kravchuk by a margin of 51.57% to 45.46%. Kuchma's election, and victories by non-leftist forces in parliamentary elections to fill vacant seats, shifted the balance of power away from the left and towards the center, although the left remains a powerful force.

Until June 1996, Ukraine operated under a heavily amended version of its old, Soviet-style constitution. Provisions of the constitution dealing with the separation of powers were unclear and often contradictory. As a result, the President, Cabinet of Ministers, and the parliament spent much time battling to a stalemate on constitutional issues. These problems also extended to conflict between local legislatures and executive agencies. There has also been conflict between the central government and the localities over power. Moroz and the

---

[1] FBIS Trends, March 25, 1996, 6.

leftist forces in parliament favor a weak presidency and a strong parliament. They also favor stronger state controls over the economy and a slow pace of economic reform.

After years of wrangling, the Ukrainian parliament finally approved a new Constitution for Ukraine on June 28, 1996. In order to break the deadlock by bypassing the parliament, President Kuchma had decreed two days earlier that a referendum be held in September 1996 to approve a draft constitution that had been drawn up by a constitutional commission. The move may have sparked fears among Chairman Moroz and hard-line leftists that the public would approve the constitution draft, marginalizing the parliament as a political force. In response, the parliament, in a marathon 16-hour session, produced an amended, compromise version of the commission draft. The constitution was approved by a vote of 315-36.

The new constitution preserves strong powers for the President. In a boost for economic reform, the new constitution guarantees the right to private ownership, including the right to own land. It also gives the President the authority to issue economic reform decrees. The new constitution recognizes Crimea's status as an autonomous republic, with its own constitution, which must be consistent with Ukraine's constitution and must be approved by the Ukrainian parliament. The constitution bars the deployment of foreign troops on Ukraine's territory, but, in recognition of the continuing Black Sea Fleet issue, a transitional clause permits the temporary leasing of bases for foreign troops.

After the approval of the Constitution, President Kuchma re-appointed Pavlo Lazarenko as Prime Minister and Hennady Udovenko as Foreign Minister. Valeriy Shmarov was replaced as Defense Minister by Gen. Oleksander Kuzmuk.

In July 1996, Prime Minister Lazarenko narrowly escaped assassination when a radio-controlled bomb planted under a Kiev highway exploded near his car. Lazarenko said that he believes the attack was linked to his efforts to uncover embezzlement and corruption by Donetsk coal mining officials. Two days later, President Kuchma fired Volodymyr Shcherban from his post as head of the Donetsk regional government. In November 1996, his brother, businessman and Rada deputy Yevhen Shcherban, was killed in what observers have called a "gangland-style hit" at Donetsk airport.

Many analysts view these events as evidence of an increasingly open struggle for power and property among two powerful, regionally-based, political-economic "clans." Both Shcherbans are considered to be leaders of the "clan" from the coal mining region of Donetsk in eastern Ukraine. On the other hand, Kuchma, Lazarenko and many other top central government officials are from the key industrial region of Dnipropetrovsk, also in eastern Ukraine. Members of both groups are widely believed to have links to organized crime. Some analysts believe members of the Dnipropetrovsk faction thought that Yevhen Shcherban had been behind the attempted assassination of Lazarenko and decided to retaliate. Other observers assert that Shcherban was killed because of his efforts to break into the lucrative natural gas distribution business, reportedly now monopolized by Lazarenko cronies. High-level corruption and powerful and violent organized crime groups are key hurdles to political and economic reform in Ukraine, as in other parts of the former Soviet Union.

Ukraine will hold new parliamentary elections in March 1998 and presidential elections in 1999. Political maneuvering for the elections has already begun. President Kuchma has supported the establishment of the People's Democratic Party (PDP) and the Agrarian Party of Ukraine. The PDP is viewed by some analysts as a "party of power," that is, a vehicle to consolidate members of the political and economic elite around President Kuchma and his re-election bid. These two groups are aimed at countering the strength of the leftist Agrarians and Communists in the Rada. It is uncertain whether these parties will acquire a significant public following. Kuchma is also courting Rukh, which opposed Kuchma in 1994, but has been pleasantly surprised by Kuchma's defense of Ukraine's sovereignty since his election. In addition, Kuchma appears to be concerned about a challenge in 1999 from Prime Minister Lazarenko, who is politically well-connected and reportedly wealthy through proceeds from corruption. This may be one reason why Kuchma has been reluctant to dismiss Lazarenko from his post, despite differences between the two men on economic reforms; keeping Lazarenko in the government blunts possible criticism from the Prime Minister while possibly saddling him with responsibility for continued economic stagnation or unpopular reform measures.

REGIONAL ISSUES

Ukraine's regional diversity presents a major political challenge for its leaders. In addition to the struggle between regionally-based elite "clans" in eastern Ukraine, there are also cultural, linguistic and historical differences between western Ukraine (especially the regions of Lviv, Ivano-Frankivsk and Ternopil) and the eastern and southern regions of the country. In general, western Ukrainians are more nationally conscious than those in other regions and led the drive for Ukrainian independence. They form the leadership and much of the rank-and-file of the Rukh national-democratic movement, as well as other, more radical, nationalist groups. In contrast, eastern Ukrainians, subjected to centuries of Russification, tend to look more skeptically on Ukrainian nationalism. They are more interested in the economic benefits independence provides or does not provide. Much of the Communist Party support comes from eastern and southern Ukraine, including the key Donets basin (Donbas) area.

Ethnic Russians make up 22% of Ukraine's population, and are concentrated in the east and south. In contrast to other regions of the former Soviet Union, there has been no significant ethnic tension or violence in Ukraine. Ethnic Russians by and large supported Ukrainian independence for pragmatic, economic reasons. Many ethnic Russians are disturbed by the occasionally confrontational relations between Russia and Ukraine. They strongly support efforts to restore critical economic ties with Russia, including an economic union with Russia and other CIS countries. Some, especially Communist supporters, feel nostalgia for the Soviet Union, and advocate that Ukraine join a new political union with Russia, Belarus and Kazakhstan. Others support greater autonomy for their region within Ukraine. During the March 27, 1994 legislative elections, voters in the Donetsk and Luhansk regions of Eastern Ukraine voted overwhelmingly in favor of local consultative referendums calling for a federal structure for Ukraine (over 84% in Donetsk), making Russian an official language in Ukraine alongside Ukrainian (91% in Donetsk), and calling for Ukraine to become a full member of the CIS economic union (93% in Donetsk.)

The 1994 presidential elections showed a sharp regional split. Perhaps the key issue in the race was relations with Russia, with Kuchma favoring stronger ties with Russia and Kravchuk supporting the status quo in relations with Moscow. In the second round, Kravchuk won decisively in western Ukraine (93.7% in Lviv oblast, for example, to Kuchma's 3.9%). However, this was not enough to offset Kuchma's victories in more heavily populated eastern and southern Ukraine. In Crimea, Kuchma won 89.7% of the vote to Kravchuk's 8.8%.[2] Although he ran on what many observers viewed a eastern Ukraine-based, "pro-Russia" platform, Kuchma has staunchly upheld Ukrainian sovereignty since becoming President.

Crimea. With respect to one region, Ukraine's territorial integrity is potentially fragile. Russians make up 67% of Crimea's population, Ukrainians, only 26%. In December 1991, a bare majority of Crimeans voted for Ukraine's independence. But public opinion shifted against Ukraine as economic conditions deteriorated. In May 1992, the Crimean Supreme Soviet declared Crimea's independence from Ukraine, but suspended the resolution after Kravchuk warned Crimea that bloodshed could occur if Crimea tried to implement it. Tension escalated sharply once again when the newly elected, nationalist-dominated Crimean parliament restored the pro-independence constitution in May 1994. The restored constitution said that the relations between Ukraine and Crimea would be regulated on the basis of bilateral treaties, established a separate Crimean citizenship, and permitted Crimea to have its own armed forces.

On March 17, 1995, after nearly a year of demanding that the Crimean constitution be brought in line with the Ukrainian constitution and laws, the Ukrainian parliament abolished the pro-independence Crimean Constitution and the post of President of Crimea (established during Crimea's March 1994 elections). On March 24, 1995, the parliament followed up by scheduling local elections on the peninsula for June 1995. On April 1, 1995, Kuchma issued a decree putting the Crimean government under his direct control. There was little reaction among the general public in Crimea to Kiev's actions. On April 25, the Crimean parliament voted to call a referendum to ask voters whether they support the Crimean constitution or Kiev's actions to abolish it. Another question would have asked if they favor an economic and political union

---

[2] The Economist, July 16, 1994, 42.

between Russia, Ukraine and Belarus. Facing Ukrainian leaders' threats to dissolve the Crimean parliament, the Crimean legislature backed down, voting to cancel the June 25 referendum on its banned constitution. The Crimean parliament also approved a new constitution in line with Ukrainian legislation. On June 8, the Crimean parliament canceled the second referendum question after Kuchma canceled his decree subordinating the Crimean government to his direct control. In August 1995, Kuchma issued a decree relinquishing direct control over the Crimean government, putting it back in the hands of the local authorities.

Ukraine's new Constitution, approved in June 1996, guarantees Crimea's status as an autonomous republic within Ukraine, and permits the region to have its own constitution. However, the Crimean constitution must be consistent with the Ukrainian one, and must be approved by the Ukrainian parliament. Crimean parliamentary speaker Yevhen Suprynyuk said the new Ukrainian constitution, while not ideal, was an acceptable compromise. He said the peninsula will amend its draft constitution to make it consistent with the new Ukrainian one. Many observers note that the influence of Crimean separatism appears be waning at least temporarily, and economic reform and organized crime appear to be the key political issues on the peninsula.

Another facet of the Crimea question is the issue of the Crimean Tatars. Stalin expelled the Tatars from Crimea during World War II. Since the late 1980s, Crimean Tatars have begun to return to the peninsula, often living in tents or other makeshift dwellings; over 240,000 have arrived to date (composing about 10% of Crimea's population), and roughly as many more live scattered throughout the former Soviet Union. Tatar representatives want Crimea to become an autonomous Tatar state within Ukraine. Crimea's election law set aside 14 seats of the 98 seats in the Crimean parliament for the Tatars.

Crimea has been a potentially dangerous issue in the Russo-Ukrainian relationship. Crimea was part of Russia until 1954, when Khrushchev transferred the peninsula to Ukraine to commemorate the 300th anniversary of the union of Ukraine with Russia. Many Russians feel that Crimea rightfully belongs to Russia. Russian President Boris Yeltsin has thus far ruled out a territorial claim to Crimea, but influential forces have advocated raising such a claim. In March 1995, Russian government officials ignored Crimean demands to put Russian-Ukrainian negotiations on a friendship treaty on hold because of Ukraine's abolition of Crimea's constitution. Observers believe that Ukraine timed the move against Crimea to occur when Russia was preoccupied with Chechnya. However, subsequent strong protests against Russia's acquiescence in Kiev's actions among members of the Russian parliament evidently persuaded Yeltsin to postpone a scheduled trip to Kiev. Nevertheless, Russia's lack of consistent support for Crimea in its dispute with Kiev forced the Crimean legislature to back down on the threatened referendum.

On December 5, 1996, the upper house of Russia's parliament, the Federation Council, passed a resolution laying claim to the Black Sea port city of Sevastopol. The move followed similar resolutions passed by the Communist and nationalist-dominated Duma by nearly unanimous votes on October 23 and 24. The moves disturbed Ukrainian observers, because of the overwhelming support both measures received from strong Yeltsin loyalists in both bodies. The vote was preceded by a statement from Prime Minister Chernomyrdin demanding that Kiev recognize the "illegality" of its sovereignty over Sevastopol.

In a long-awaited Russia-Ukraine friendship treaty, signed by President Yeltsin and President Kuchma on May 31, 1997, Russia formally recognized Ukraine's territorial integrity, including sovereignty over Sevastopol and the rest of Crimea. President Yeltsin's move was denounced by hardliners in the Duma and by Moscow mayor Yuri Luzhkov.

ECONOMIC ISSUES

Aside from Russia, Ukraine was the Soviet Union's most economically important republic. In 1990, it accounted for almost 17% of Soviet industrial output. Unlike many of the newly independent states, it has a significant natural resource endowment, with deposits of coal, iron ore, manganese, and sulfur. Production is heavily concentrated on heavy industry, especially coal mining and ferrous metallurgy. These two sectors alone accounted for 40% of industrial assets and 20% of output in 1990. Coal mining is concentrated in the Donets Basin (Donbas), forming an integrated complex with heavy industry, also located in the Donbas and along the Dnieper River bend, centered near the city of Dnipropetrovsk. Ukraine, often called the "breadbasket" of the Soviet Union because of its rich, black soil, provided about 20% of Soviet agricultural production in 1990. On the other hand, Ukraine's coal and iron ore are expensive to extract, are polluting, and less easily sold on world markets than oil and other natural resources. Ukraine's heavy industries pose similar environmental problems and are voracious consumers of increasingly expensive energy.

The collapse of trading links among CIS states hurt the Ukrainian economy, since the economies of the CIS countries were highly interdependent. The most critical problem is fuel; Ukraine imports about 90% of its oil needs, almost all of it from Russia. About 80% of Ukraine's natural gas is imported from Russia (about 60%) and Turkmenistan (about 20%). Both countries have cut off supplies intermittently in an effort to force Ukraine to pay mounting debts for past deliveries. However, Ukraine also has some leverage that has prevented a permanent shut-off -- gas pipelines to Western countries run through Ukrainian territory. Ukraine can divert gas from the pipeline or raise transit tariffs to pressure Russia. In January 1995, the Ukrainian parliament approved the building of a new oil terminal at the Black Sea port of Odessa. The construction of the terminal, which would enable Ukraine to lessen its dependence on Russian oil by receiving supplies from other countries via oil tanker, has been delayed by a lack of financing and other difficulties. Efforts to restructure the largely obsolete coal sector, and force greater energy conservation among wasteful enterprises have also been slow to materialize. Failing major reforms, Ukraine may continue to face energy debt crises.

On March 20, 1995, Russian and Ukrainian negotiators reached a gas debt rescheduling agreement. Ukraine will pay its $2.5 billion debt to the Russian government over 12 years, with a two-year grace period. Ukraine would pay only $68 million by March 1997. Under a separate accord on Ukraine's $1.7 billion debt to the Russian natural gas monopoly Gazprom, Kiev would issue promissory notes to pay off the debt gradually over 12 years. Gazprom would be able to use part of the notes to buy shares in privatized Ukrainian enterprises. Ukraine would also supply about $500 million dollars in goods and services (including housing for Gazprom workers) over 3 years. In December 1995, fearing that the agreement could lead to greater Russian economic domination of Ukraine, the Ukrainian parliament told the government to renegotiate the Gazprom deal. In June 1997, Russian Deputy Prime Minister Valeriy Serov said that, as part of a deal on the division of the Black Sea Fleet. Russia agreed to write off $97.75 million each year of Ukraine's debt to Russia as payment for leasing naval bases in Crimea.

ECONOMIC REFORM

Economic reform efforts in Ukraine from 1991-1994 were hampered by the country's absorption with securing its independence and by the predominant position of ex-Communist Party functionaries, who have little enthusiasm for or understanding of the free market. Power struggles between free market reformers and conservatives led to a proliferation of reform plans, with very little in fact being done. A key failure of Ukrainian economic policy was very lax fiscal and monetary policies that fuelled hyperinflation. Ukraine ran a very large budget deficit. The Ukrainian central bank gave huge low-interest loans to collective farms and enterprises. According to Deputy Prime Minister Roman Shpek, real GDP fell by 34% from 1990-1993, and an additional 23% in 1994. Inflation was 1,210% in 1992, 4,735% in 1993 and 892% in 1994. Ukraine's currency, the karbovanets, was dramatically undermined by this policy. Very little privatization occurred, with the exception of some small-scale privatization carried out by local authorities in several regions, with the help of the World Bank.

After his election in July 1994, President Kuchma vowed to move forward with radical economic reform. With the help of experts from international financial institutions, Ukraine developed a comprehensive reform program, which included tight fiscal and monetary policies, price liberalization, foreign trade liberalization and accelerated privatization. Kuchma said Ukraine would "fully complete" small-scale privatization in 1995, and would convert 8,000 larger state enterprises into "open shareholding associations." The parliament approved the plan in principle on October 19, 1994. However, parts of the plan, especially accelerated privatization and sharp price increases caused by reductions in government subsidies, have met resistance from leftists in parliament.

Kuchma signed many economic reform decrees, including ones on liberalizing prices, exchange rates, and foreign trade. He also signed decrees on accelerating privatization of state-owned firms, privatization of land, and liberalization of agricultural trade. In January 1995, regional privatization centers began to open throughout Ukraine. The centers provided information and conducting auctions for citizens converting their privatization vouchers into shares in enterprises. By October 1996, about 36,576 small enterprises had been privatized, and the government has declared that small privatization has been completed. In addition, 3,506 medium-sized and large firms had been privatized (i.e. 70% or more of their stock was privately owned) by October 1996. A second stage of privatization is planned, involving the sale of shares for cash, including to foreign investors. A list of 208 strategic firms was drawn up for cash privatization. Parliament passed laws in late 1996 in an effort to stop the privatization of strategic firms, just as it had done during earlier stages of privatization. Strong opposition in parliament from Moroz and collective farm chairmen has also stymied land reform; in November 1996, the parliament rejected a government-sponsored Land Code that would encourage private ownership of land and a land market.

Kuchma's efforts to create macroeconomic stability have been a success. The National Bank has pursued a tough monetary policy. The Ukrainian parliament passed more austere budgets for 1995 and 1996 than in previous years, in order to qualify for IMF financing. Inflation dropped from 376.7% in 1995 to 80.2% in 1996 and is continuing to fall.[3] In September 1996, seeking to take advantage of its success in fighting inflation, Ukraine introduced a new currency, the hryvna. The launch of the new currency was a success, and the new currency stabilized quickly.

Ukraine's economic performance in other areas is less impressive. Gross Domestic Product continues to plunge. It fell 11.8% in 1995 and plunged another 10.6% in 1996. Although experts point out that perhaps as much as one-third to one-half of Ukraine's economy is underground, these figures show Ukraine is still far from economic recovery. Analysts underline that Ukraine must accelerate privatization and other structural reforms. It must revise its tax code and free the economy from oppressive state regulation. Some analysts believe that the Lazarenko government has moved to re-regulate the economy in order to maximize chances for corruption, another critical problem Ukraine must resolve. These problems are driving foreign investment away from Ukraine, at a moment when it is desperately needed to modernize Ukraine's dilapidated industry. Current per capital foreign direct investment in Ukraine is less than $30. Government policies and corruption have driven Motorola and other high profile Western investors away from Ukraine in recent months.

An economic reform package introduced by Deputy Prime Minister Pynzenyk in October 1996 included provisions to lighten the tax burden by eliminating unjustified tax privileges for some interest groups and reducing tax rates; and proposals to make it easier to open new businesses, including reducing the number of government licenses required, which have been an important source of government corruption. However, the plan remains stalled

---

[3] Plan Econ Review and Outlook for the Former Soviet Republics, March 1997.

in parliament because of resistance from the affected interest groups. The parliament has also refused to approve a 1997 in line with IMF requirements, delaying needed IMF loans to Ukraine. Frustrated, Pynzenyk resigned from the government in April 1997. He was replaced by Valeriy Tyhypko, a Dnipropetrovsk banker who has vowed to push the reform program through.

FOREIGN POLICY AND DEFENSE

Since independence, Ukraine has tried to develop ties with the West. On February 8, 1994, Ukraine joined NATO's Partnership for Peace program. Under the program, countries of central and eastern Europe and the former Soviet Union cooperate with NATO in such issues as peacekeeping and joint exercises but do not receive the formal security guarantees that full NATO membership would entail. On September 12, 1994, Ukrainian soldiers participated in a peacekeeping training exercise, the first under the aegis of the Partnership for Peace program. During a May 1995 summit meeting with President Clinton, President Kuchma shifted away from his earlier opposition to NATO enlargement, saying he favored the "evolutionary" expansion of the alliance. He later said that Ukraine's current doctrine of non-alignment was "obsolete" in the face of NATO's inevitable expansion. However, Ukrainian officials have expressed opposition to the stationing of nuclear weapons on the territory of new NATO members and have proposed a nuclear-free zone for central Europe.

On September 14, 1995, Ukraine and NATO agreed on an Individual Partnership Program that laid out concrete areas of cooperation between NATO and Ukraine within the Partnership for Peace Program. NATO and Ukraine agreed to open consultations on key European security issues. In November 1996, Ukrainian officials submitted proposals to NATO for a special partnership between Ukraine and the alliance, that would go beyond cooperation in the North Atlantic Cooperation Council and Partnership for Peace. On May 29, NATO and Ukraine initialled a "Charter on a Distinctive Partnership." The partnership document will be signed at the NATO summit in July 1997. The agreement will not provide Ukraine with a NATO security guarantee, but will give Ukraine a right to consult with NATO if it feels its security is threatened. The document also reiterates security assurances provided to Ukraine as part of the Trilateral Statement of 1994 on the removal of nuclear weapons from Ukraine. Ukraine will send a military liaison mission to NATO Headquarters. A NATO-Ukraine Commission will meet at least twice a year to review NATO-Ukraine relations. Ukrainian officials say that Ukraine does not seek to join NATO at present, but wants to keep open at least the possibility of NATO membership at some unspecified point in the future.

Ukraine wants to increase ties with the European Union, with the long-range objective of membership. On June 14, 1994, the European Union signed a partnership agreement with Ukraine that will give Ukraine most-favored-nation status and other trade advantages, and opens the possibility of a free trade agreement after 1998, if Ukraine makes significant progress toward a free market economy. Ukraine is also seeking associate status in the Western European Union defense grouping.

Ukraine played an important role in U.N. peacekeeping efforts in Bosnia-Hercegovina, where it had 1200 peacekeepers. While these troops were withdrawn after the signing of the Bosnian peace accords in November 1995 and the transfer of authority from the U.N. peacekeeping force to the NATO implementation force (IFOR), Ukraine still participates in the U.N. peacekeeping force in Croatia's eastern Slavonia region.

While Kiev is building closer ties with the West, Ukraine's most important (if less than friendly) relationships for the foreseeable future will continue to be with the Commonwealth of Independent States countries, and above all, with Russia. Ukrainian leaders have seen the CIS as a forum for discussion of and cooperation on a wide variety of important political, economic and military issues. However, Ukraine has resisted Russian efforts to use the CIS to reintegrate the former Soviet republics under its leadership, insisting that Ukraine will not surrender its sovereignty to a supranational body. In 1993, Ukraine become an associate member of the CIS economic union, but declined full membership. President Kuchma has rejected Russia's efforts to give real powers to CIS economic union bodies. Kuchma has also rejected Russian pressure to sign a treaty providing for joint Russian-Ukrainian patrolling of Ukraine's borders. In August 1996, Russia announced that it would levy a 20% value added tax on Ukrainian imports. The move aroused strong objections from Kiev, since Russia is Ukraine's largest trading partner.

After years of wrangling, President Yeltsin and President Kuchma signed a Russia-Ukraine friendship treaty on May 30, 1997, pledging wide-ranging cooperation in many fields. In the treaty, Russian formally recognized the sovereignty and territorial integrity of Ukraine, including over Sevastopol and the rest of Crimea. The two sides will start to formally demarcate the Russian-Ukrainian border. A key stumbling block to the treaty, the status of the Black Sea Fleet, also appeared to be settled at the Kuchma-Yeltsin summit.

Ukraine scored another diplomatic success on June 2, 1997, when Kiev signed a treaty with Romania. In the treaty, Romania recognized Ukraine's current border. Each side pledged to abide by international and European standards for ethnic minorities in each country. Until now, Romania had refused to formally recognize Ukraine's sovereignty over regions of Romania seized by Stalin in 1940 as part of the Molotov-Ribbentrop pact and incorporated into Soviet Ukraine. Many ethnic Romanians live in these regions. With the signature of this treaty, Ukraine now has signed treaties resolving outstanding problems with all of its neighbors. Romania needed the treaty to bolster its prospects for NATO membership.

DEFENSE ISSUES

On January 3, 1992, Ukraine started to form its own armed forces from former Soviet forces stationed in Ukraine. Ukraine required soldiers on its soil to declare a loyalty oath to Ukraine. While some made the pledge out of support for Ukraine, many others (especially Russians) did so in order to keep their jobs and housing benefits in Ukraine. At the July 1992 CSCE summit, Ukraine received a ceiling of 450,000 soldiers in an intergovernmental agreement among CSCE states on limiting each country's manpower level. Under the Conventional Forces in Europe (CFE) treaty, Ukraine was obligated to destroy large stocks of tanks, armored combat vehicles (ACVs) and combat aircraft, by November 1995. After the CFE cuts, Ukraine still retained a formidable arsenal of 4,063 tanks, 4,847 armored combat vehicles, 294 attack helicopters, 940 combat aircraft, and 3,121 artillery pieces. [4] There were about 396,000 men in Ukraine's armed forces in December 1996. However, these impressive numbers do not mean Ukraine's armed forces are highly capable; as is the case in Russia and other former Soviet states, years of meager defense budgets have sharply diminished readiness and morale in Ukraine's military.

Black Sea Fleet. A key area of friction between Russia and Ukraine has been the Black Sea Fleet. At the breakup of the USSR, the Black Sea Fleet possessed over 350 ships, including 55 major surface combat vessels (about 26% of the Soviet total) and 20 attack submarines (roughly 7% of the Soviet total). The fleet's major base is at Sevastopol on the Crimean peninsula, although there are other bases elsewhere in Crimea, as well as mainland Ukraine and Russia. Russian and Ukrainian officials and military leaders have engaged in a war of words over who should control the Fleet. Tension has been heightened by sporadic incidents between pro-Ukraine and pro-Russian elements of the Fleet. On June 9, 1995, President Kuchma and President Yeltsin signed another in a series of Russo-Ukrainian agreement on the principles for dividing the Black Sea Fleet. Half of the Fleet will be allocated to Ukraine and half to Russia, but Russia will buy out most of Ukraine's share, leaving Kiev with 18.3% of the total fleet.

In November 1995, Russian Defense Minister Pavel Grachev and Ukrainian Defense Minister Valery Shmarov agreed on the details of dividing up the Fleet. The division of the fleet then proceeded more rapidly than in the past. However, contentious issues remain that continued to block a final resolution of the Black Sea Fleet dispute. The most important one is that Russia wants full control of the main naval base at Sevastopol in Crimea, while Ukraine (perhaps fearing a future Russian bid to seize the city and the entire Crimean peninsula) insists on keeping at least some ships there. In addition, the terms of the Russian Fleet's lease of bases and facilities on the peninsula are still uncertain. The new Ukrainian constitution, approved in June 1996, bans foreign bases on Ukraine's soil, but transitional provisions allow for temporary leasing of bases.

At a meeting in Kiev on May 28, 1997, Russian Prime Minister Viktor Chernomyrdin and Ukrainian Prime Minister Pavlo Lazarenko signed agreements aimed at finally settling the Black Sea Fleet dispute. Both the Russian and Ukrainian Black Sea Fleet will be based in Sevastopol, albeit in

---

[4] Arms Control and Disarmament Agency, "Treaty on Conventional Armed Forces in Europe (CFE): Implementation, Adaptation, Implications," February 12, 1997.

separate areas. Russia will lease the facilities (which Moscow has recognized as Ukrainian territory) for 20 years. Russia will write off $97.75 million each year of Ukraine's debt to Russia as rent for the bases.

Nuclear Weapons. In December 1991, Ukraine announced that it would agree to have all tactical nuclear weapons removed from Ukraine to Russia, where they were to be destroyed. On May 6, 1992, a CIS military spokesman said that all tactical nuclear weapons had been removed from Ukraine. Ukraine had 176 ICBMs (130 SS-19s and 46 SS-24s) as well as 42 nuclear-equipped strategic bombers. U.S. officials estimated the total number of warheads left in Ukraine after the withdrawal of tactical nuclear weapons at about 1,900 warheads. On May 23, 1992, the United States, Ukraine, Russia, Belarus and Kazakhstan signed the Lisbon protocol to the START Treaty that made the new states parties to the treaty. The non-Russian CIS states also agreed to eliminate all nuclear weapons on their territory within the 7-year reduction period envisioned by START and pledged to sign the Nuclear Non-Proliferation Treaty (NPT) as non-nuclear states.

Despite pleas from Kravchuk, the Ukrainian parliament repeatedly put off ratification of the START treaty until November 1993, when it ratified the treaty but attached many stringent, and for the United States largely unacceptable, conditions. On January 14, 1994, the United States, Russia, and Ukraine signed an agreement designed to meet some of the Ukrainian parliament's objections and clear the way for the elimination of nuclear weapons on Ukrainian soil. The Trilateral Statement committed Ukraine to transfer nuclear weapons on its territory to Russia "in the shortest possible time," within the 7-year implementation period for the START Treaty. In exchange for sending nuclear warheads on its soil to Russia, Ukraine was to receive low enriched uranium for its nuclear power plants "within the same time period."

The accord specified that the first 200 warheads (from both SS-19 and the more modern SS-24 missiles) were to be sent to Russia within 10 months in exchange for 100 tons of low-enriched uranium for Ukraine. It committed Ukraine to remove the warheads from all of the SS-24 missiles on its territory within the same 10-month period. The accord provided for Ukrainian monitoring of the warhead dismantling process. The United States was to buy some of the uranium from Russia and resell it on the world market. The agreement said that once Ukraine ratifies START and joins the NPT as a non-nuclear state, Russia and the United States will "confirm" their obligations under the CSCE Final Act to respect Ukraine's "independence and sovereignty and existing borders;" will refrain from using force or the threat of force against Ukraine; will refrain from using "economic pressure" against Ukraine to secure political advantage at the expense of Ukraine's sovereignty; and will confirm its obligations under the NPT to demand immediate action by the U.N. Security Council if Ukraine (as a non-nuclear NPT signatory) is attacked with nuclear weapons or threatened with nuclear attack. On February 3, the parliament approved a resolution that retracted the earlier conditions it had placed on the exchange of the instruments of ratification for START, which must occur before a treaty formally enters into force. Kravchuk hailed a U.S. announcement that by the end of May 1994, U.S. nuclear weapons would no longer be targeted on Ukraine.

At the urging of President Kuchma, the Ukrainian parliament voted by an overwhelming 301-8 margin, on November 16, 1994, for Ukraine's accession to the NPT. Ukraine's accession to the Nuclear Non-Proliferation Treaty (NPT) formally came into effect after the U.S., Russia, and Britain signed a document providing security assurances for Ukraine at the CSCE summit in December 1994. Ukrainian accession to NPT also cleared the way for the formal entry into force of the START I Treaty.

The implementation of the Trilateral Statement proceeded largely on schedule. Russia made the initial shipments of nuclear fuel rods to Ukrainian nuclear power plants, although Ukrainian officials complained that Russia fell behind schedule in fuel deliveries. Russian officials have said that Russia will make its last fuel delivery required under the agreement later this year. On June 1, 1996, President Kuchma announced that all nuclear weapons had been removed from Ukrainian territory.

ISSUES FOR U.S. POLICY

Before the August 1991 failed coup, the Bush Administration strongly supported Gorbachev's desire for a renewed federation, mainly because the Administration did not want to undermine the Soviet leader, whom it saw as responsible for the transformation in East-West relations and as the most realistic hope for domestic reform in the Soviet Union. But after overwhelming support for Ukraine's independence during the December 1991 referendum, the United States recognized Ukrainian independence (and the independence of all the other ex-Soviet states grouped in the new Commonwealth of Independent States) on December 25.

After Ukraine's independence, the United States was faced with the question of how to balance its relations between Russia and Ukraine. Some advocated emphasizing relations with Russia, noting that it is by far the largest of the ex-Soviet republics and the one with the largest military (including nuclear) capability. They asserted that leaning toward Ukraine could aggravate Russian national feeling. Some even held out the specter of a "Weimar Russia" scenario, in which, as in Germany in the 1930s, democracy could be crushed by extreme nationalists playing on Russian chauvinism and economic chaos. Finally, they believed that without successful economic reform by Russia, none of the other post-Soviet states can succeed economically. In contrast, others argued the United States should support Kiev more. They believed that Russia's acceptance of true Ukrainian independence is weak, but that such acceptance is critical if Russia is to leave behind its heritage as an imperial state and enter the Western community. In any case, they believed, a strong Ukraine would rule out a Russian imperial resurgence, by its very strength and geographical position.

In recent years, a consensus appears to have emerged, echoed in statements by top U.S. policymakers, that good relations with a stable, democratic and independent Ukraine are a critical part of U.S. policy toward the region. The 1994 Trilateral Statement on nuclear weapons, and the final removal of those weapons in June 1996 removed an important stumbling block in U.S.-Ukrainian relations. The main focus of U.S. policy now is to bolster Ukraine's political and economic reform efforts. The importance of Ukraine to U.S. policy can be seen in the fact that in 1996 Ukraine became the third largest recipient of U.S. foreign assistance, behind Israel and Egypt, and well in front of Russia, which had previously been in the third position. Despite this U.S. assistance, however, Ukraine's economic reform efforts have been only partially successful thus far.

CURRENT ISSUES

U.S. Aid for Ukraine. From FY1992 through FY1996, the U.S. budgeted a total of $1.304 billion in aid for Ukraine. Of this total, $1.086 billion has been obligated. Included in this amount is $608.23 million in Freedom Support Act aid, mainly technical assistance. Of the total amount of aid, $886.05 million has been expended, $442.72 million in Freedom Support Act assistance. AID projects in Ukraine touch on a wide range of areas including agriculture, energy, environment, health care, stimulating private sector development, improving the food distribution system, housing sector reform, economic and financial restructuring and encouraging democratic pluralism.

In addition to aid to support economic reform and democracy in Ukraine, the United States has budgeted $395.29 million in Nunn-Lugar Cooperative Threat Reduction funds to help Ukraine dispose of nuclear weapons on its territory. Of this amount, $302.48 million of this amount had been obligated by the end of FY1996 and $254.06 million had been spent.[5] The money is being used to help Ukraine meet its destruction obligations under START, including the elimination of SS-19 and SS-24 missiles and silos. In addition, money is being spent to assist in the establishment of a materials control, accounting, and physical protection system for civilian nuclear material; to provide emergency response equipment; and to establish a government-to-government communications link to transmit notifications under the START and INF Treaties. The money is also being spent on helping Ukraine dismantle equipment and bases associated with nuclear weapons; and helping U.S.-Ukrainian joint ventures to convert former military production facilities to civilian products. Responding to Ukrainian concerns about the welfare of officers who will lose their jobs when the missiles are pulled out, the United States is spending $20 million in Nunn-Lugar money to convert a defense plant to build prefabricated housing for former officers at one missile site. At Kmelnitsky, another missile base, $16 million in Nunn-Lugar funds are being provided to build housing directly for former officers.

---

[5] "U.S. Government Assistance to and Cooperative Activities with the New Independent States of the Former Soviet Union, FY 1996 Annual Report," U.S. State Department, January 1997.

The United States is also providing other security assistance to Ukraine. In its FY1998 Congressional Presentation on Foreign Operations, the State Department estimated that the U.S. would provide $5.25 million in FY1997 to help Ukraine participate in Partnership for Peace activities, as well as peacekeeping and other operations with NATO forces. The United States spent just over $1 million in FY1996 in IMET funds to train Ukrainian officers, and plans to spend another $1 million in FY1997 and $1.2 million in FY1998 for the same purpose.[6]

Ukraine gained Most Favored Nation (MFN) status on June 22, 1992. In May 1992, the two sides also signed an agreement extending Overseas Private Investment Company (OPIC) investment guarantees to U.S. firms who want to invest in Ukraine. Since January 1994, OPIC has approved investment insurance totaling more than $23 million for Ukraine. In March 1995, the United States announced the creation of a $250 million trade credit insurance facility to help Ukraine pay for critical imports for its agricultural sector.

During the May 1995 Clinton-Kuchma summit, President Clinton stressed the need for increased trade and investment to improve Ukraine's economy. He pledged that the United States would support Ukraine's desire to join the World Trade Organization. He noted Ukraine would remain eligible for reduced tariffs on its exports to the United States under the General System of Preferences. He said the bilateral Joint Commission on Trade and Investment would help enhance bilateral commercial cooperation. The United States announced that the Export-Import Bank would make financing available to Ukraine. Export-Import Bank financing had been suspended due to Ukraine's lack of creditworthiness.

During a February 1996 meeting with President Kuchma in Washington, President Clinton reaffirmed the strong support of the United States for economic reform in Ukraine. Vice President Gore, in a meeting with Kuchma, outlined a package of $330 million in grants and $860 million in trade and investment programs. Key areas of support will include privatization, bolstering private investment in agriculture and strengthening Ukraine's energy security.[7] A State Department spokesman noted that in 1996 Ukraine will be the third largest recipient of U.S. economic aid, ahead of Russia. The Administration estimates that Ukraine will receive $330 million in U.S. grants and $675 million in bilateral credits. On March 1, 1996, the Import-Export Bank announced it would provide $187 million in financing to allow Ukraine to buy U.S. agricultural equipment. The deal was the first since Ukraine became eligible for Export-Import Bank financing in May 1995.

In September 1996, the Administration announced the establishment of a joint U.S.-Ukrainian commission headed by President Kuchma and Vice

---

[6] State Department Congressional Presentation on Foreign Operations, FY 1998.

[7] White House Press Release on President Clinton's Meeting with Ukraine President Kuchma, February 21, 1996.

President Al Gore. The body, modelled on the successful U.S.-Russian Gore-Chernomyrdin commission, will work to improve U.S.-Ukraine cooperation on a wide variety of issues. Four committees will deal with foreign policy, security, trade and investment, and economic cooperation.

The first meeting of the joint U.S.-Ukrainian commission was held during Kuchma's May 1997 visit to Washington. Vice President Gore stressed the need for Ukraine to "reinvigorate" the reform process in Ukraine, including the need to fight corruption and protect foreign investors. Discussions focused on the key sectors of promoting Ukraine's energy independence and increasing productivity in Ukraine's agricultural sector through market reforms. Gore announced that the two countries would begin talks on an agreement on nuclear cooperation, which would permit the U.S. to sell fuel and reactors to Ukraine. The two leaders signed an agreement to develop an "action plan" by the end of 1997 to create a "market-oriented, competitive, transparent and efficient gas sector in Ukraine."

In the past several years, Members of Congress expressed concern that Ukraine was not getting its "fair share" of aid money for the former Soviet Union. The foreign aid appropriations legislation for FY1994 (P.L. 103-87) said that of the $2.5 billion appropriated for the former Soviet Union "not less than $300 million should be made available for Ukraine." A Senate amendment to the FY1995 foreign aid appropriations measure earmarked $150 million in aid for Ukraine for FY1995. However, the conference committee on the bill softened the earmark to read that the United States "should" provide $150 million in aid to Ukraine. The FY1996 foreign aid appropriations measure (P.L. 104-107), approved by the President on February 12, 1996, retained a Senate earmark of $225 million for Ukraine, provided that Ukraine continues to take steps toward reform. Of this amount, the measure requires $20 million be spent for developing small and medium-sized private enterprises that (including broadcast and print media), $50 million for nuclear energy safety and energy self-sufficiency, and $5 million for victims of the Chernobyl disaster. The measure earmarks $2 million to conduct a study on Ukraine's energy distribution grid. P.L. 104-107 also earmarks $50 million for the Western NIS Enterprise Fund (including Ukraine) and the Central Asia Enterprise Fund.

The FY1997 foreign aid law (P.L. 104-208) earmarks $225 million for Ukraine out of the $625 million allocated for the countries of the former Soviet Union as a whole. Of the $225 million, $25 million is earmarked for decommissioning the Chernobyl nuclear plant; $5 million for screening and treatment of Chernobyl-related illnesses among children and $5 million for a land and resource management institute to identify nuclear contamination at Chernobyl. Further sub-earmarks include $35 million for agricultural projects; $5 million for a small business incubator project; and $15 million for reform of Ukraine's legal system. The legislation earmarks $50 million from the FY1996 and FY1997 foreign aid laws for improving safety at nuclear reactors. The measure prohibits aid to Ukraine if the President finds that Ukraine is engaged in military cooperation with Libya. However, the President may waive this provision if he determines that it is in the national security interest to do so.

In May 1997, some Members of Congress expressed concern at reports that U.S. businesses in Ukraine have been victims of corruption and arbitrary government policy. Section 4001 of the 1997 Emergency Supplemental Appropriations Act (H.R. 1871) permits the President to waive the earmark on aid to Ukraine in the FY1997 foreign aid appropriation act (P.L. 104-208) if he determines Ukraine has not made progress toward economic reform, is not taking steps to ensure that U.S. businesses in Ukraine are "able to operate according to generally accepted business principles;" or is not taking steps to cease the "illegal dumping of steel plate." Other Members strongly support maintaining current levels of aid to Ukraine.

Multilateral Assistance to Ukraine. In addition to its own bilateral assistance, the United States has urged other countries and institutions to aid Ukraine. The Group of 7 countries, meeting in Italy on July 9-10, 1994 urged Ukraine to embark on economic reforms, including price liberalization and privatization. The summit communique said that Ukraine could receive as much as $4 billion over two years from the international community if it embarked on a serious reform program. The June 15, 1995 G-7 summit in Halifax, Canada decided that an additional $2 billion beyond that already provided could be allocated for Ukraine by the end of 1996 if it continued economic reforms.

On December 17, 1996, the United States and other international aid donors agreed to provide Ukraine with $3.5 billion in financial support for 1997. About $1.1 billion will be provided by the IMF, $1 billion by the World Bank and the rest by other multinational organizations and donor nations. The aid is conditioned on continued progress toward economic reform in Ukraine, including passing an austere 1997 budget, reforming the tax system by widening the tax base and lowering tax rates; reforming the pension system and improving support for the most vulnerable groups of the population; strengthening the banking system and monetary policy; deepening the process of privatization; further liberalizing the trade system; and undertaking further deregulation to foster private sector development.[8]

On October 27, 1994, the IMF announced it had approved a loan of $371 million to Ukraine as the first tranche of a more than $700 million loan package (under the Systemic Transformation Facility, or STF), in response to Kiev's approval of a comprehensive economic reform program. In response to the parliament's passage of an austere budget with a deficit of 3.3% of GDP, the IMF released the first tranche of a $1.5 billion stand-by loan on April 12, 1995. Ukraine received several tranches of the loan in 1995, but Ukrainian non-compliance with IMF-imposed spending targets for the last quarter of 1995 and the first quarter of 1996 caused the IMF to suspend disbursement of the remaining $700 million. After Ukraine pledged to restore fiscal discipline and accelerate privatization, the IMF agreed in May 1996 to a new $867 million "stand-by" loan for the rest of the year. Ukraine's 1996 budget as passed by parliament called for a deficit equivalent to 4% of GDP, but the government

[8] IMF News Brief, December 17, 1996.

agreed with the IMF to hold the deficit to 3.5% of GDP.[9] Inflation was to be reduced to between 40 and 60% for 1996. Ukraine opened talks with the IMF for a $1.5 billion stabilization fund to support Ukraine's new currency, the hryvna. However, Ukraine's success in fighting inflation encouraged it to introduce the hryvna successfully in September 1996, without a new IMF loan. Ukraine is seeking a $2.5-3 billion, three-year Extended Fund Facility loan for the period after February 1997. The parliament's failure to pass a 1997 budget and a government-proposed tax reform bill continues to delay much needed IMF loans to Ukraine.

Since 1992, World Bank commitments to Ukraine have totalled about $1.6 billion for ten projects. World Bank officials said in early 1997 that the bank could provide up to $1 billion in loans to Ukraine in 1997, if Ukraine passes a budget and tax reform law quickly. Deputy Prime Minister Viktor Pynzenyk said that Ukraine expects to receive $900 million in World Bank loans in 1997 for energy and agriculture development projects. World Bank projects include funds for enterprise development, agricultural reform, restructuring the coal sector, and export promotion.[10]

In July 1996, the Ukrainian parliament ratified an agreement with the EU under which the EU will provide a 10-year balance of payments loan for Ukraine worth $260 million. An EU-Ukraine agreement signed in September 1996 will provide Ukraine with $675 million in technical assistance over the next three years. The EU will also provide Ukraine with $35 million to reform its energy sector, including $26.4 million to close the Chernobyl nuclear plant. Since 1990, the EU has provided Ukraine with over $1.4 billion in assistance, of which $480 million has been in the form of grants.[11]

Chernobyl. On April 13, 1995, Ukraine agreed in principle to close Chernobyl by the year 2000. However, Ukrainian officials later said the closure would be contingent on receiving over $4 billion in order to close the plant and build a gas-fired plant to replace Chernobyl. In December 1995, Ukraine signed a memorandum with the G-7 countries on closing the Chernobyl by 2000. According to the memorandum, Ukraine is slated to receive $500 million in grants and $1.8 billion in loans from the G-7 for Chernobyl's closure. The grants will be applied toward rebuilding the sarcophagus covering the fourth reactor and relocating plant employees. The loans will finance profit-making projects, including the construction of new reactors at other Ukrainian nuclear plants and modernization of non-nuclear plants. The key details of the financing were left to be worked out in bilateral talks between Ukraine and each

---

[9] Reuters news agency dispatch, May 10, 1996.

[10] Transition (a World Bank newsletter), September-October 1996.

[11] Reuters news agency dispatch, September 11, 1996.

of the G-7 countries.[12] In June 1996, the head of a G-7 delegation to Ukraine said that the G-7 countries have agreed to provide $1.4 billion over 10 years to close Chernobyl. However, Ukrainian Environment Minister Yuri Kostenko complained that the G-7 countries were slow to provide funding to complete two other nuclear stations to replace Chernobyl. He said Ukraine could reconsider its decision to close Chernobyl if funding was not forthcoming soon. In September 1996, Ukraine and the European Bank for Reconstruction and Development (EBRD) held talks on how to pay for the closure of Chernobyl and the building of two new nuclear power plants. The G-7 has tasked the EBRD to work out the details of the funding issue. Ukraine closed down one of the two working reactors at Chernobyl on November 30, 1996.

Weapons Technology Proliferation and Arms Sales. Unlike Russia, Ukraine has no nuclear weapons design or production facilities. However, some nuclear weapons components were made in Ukraine and some nuclear scientists live in Ukraine. Another proliferation threat is missile technology. Ukraine is home to two ICBM production facilities that made SS-18 and SS-24 missiles. Ukraine has pledged not to sell advanced weaponry to Iraq or other "outlaw" states, but its leaders have freely admitted (like their Russian counterparts) that arms sales will be an important source of revenue for military conversion and providing for the social needs of the military. In December 1993, the State Department said that the United States had told Ukraine that it was "very concerned" about reports about "transfers of arms to Iran." The statement said that "Ukraine assured us they would exercise restraint in arms transfers to areas of concern."

A June 1996 press report in the Washington Times said that a U.S. intelligence report revealed that Ukraine has set up a high-level intergovernmental committee to engage in "strategic cooperation," including technology transfer with Libya. Ukrainian officials denied the report. The FY1997 foreign aid law prohibits U.S. aid to Ukraine if the President determines Ukraine is engaged in "strategic cooperation" with Libya. In December 1996 the Washington Times reported that a top secret CIA report said that Ukraine had agreed to sell SS-21 Scud B short-range ballistic missile to Libya and to service its nuclear submarines for $510 million. The report also claimed that Ukraine had sold Iran large quantities of Ukrainian arms with the intent of shipping them to Libya. Ukrainian officials have strongly denied these charges.

On May 13, 1994, Vice President Gore and Deputy Prime Minister Shmarov signed a memorandum of understanding on Ukraine's accession to the Missile Technology Control Regime (MTCR), which is aimed at limiting the spread of ballistic missile technology. During the Clinton-Kuchma summit in November 1994, an agreement on space cooperation was signed, but a proposal to give Ukraine the right to launch commercial satellites was postponed, reportedly due to opposition from U.S. rocket manufacturers. During the February 1996 Clinton-Kuchma summit, an agreement was signed that will allow Ukraine up

[12] "Chernobyl Closure to be Decided by Bilateral Talks," IntelNews Weekly Digest, December 25, 1995.

to 5 launches to geosynchronous orbit for commercial customers through the year 2001, at prices that do not undercut those of U.S. competitors. The agreement allows Ukraine to win contracts for 11 more launches, provided that these are for a U.S.-Ukrainian joint venture. If the commercial launch market expands, Ukraine will be able to make four additional launches. In late May 1996, Secretary Perry warned Russia and Ukraine that it would be a "serious mistake" if either country supplied SS-18 missile technology to China, even for space launches.

A September 23, 1996 *Washington Times* article claimed that disagreement existed within the Administration over whether Ukraine should be permitted to formally join the MTCR. Ukraine wants to be able to acquire several types of missiles, including cruise missiles and ICBMs, while being part of the MTCR, which until now would ban such an effort. The report says the Administration may support Ukraine's request, in hopes of better controlling Ukraine's missile development programs within the MTCR rather than outside it. Critics of the alleged proposal have said it could destroy the MTCR's effectiveness. On May 19, 1997, National Security and Defense Council Secretary Volodymyr Horbulin said that Ukraine would continue to produce short and medium-range missiles for its own defense needs, and would not abandon the idea of producing strategic missiles. Horbulin said Ukraine would not sell missile to "pariah" states.

On October 26, 1993, the United States signed an agreement with Ukraine to set up an international science center in Kiev, similar to one already planned for Russia, to provide work for unemployed weapons scientists. The United States will contribute $10 million. Canada and Sweden, which also signed the accord, will contribute $2 million and $1.5 million respectively. The center was opened in Kiev in July 1994. During the May 1995 Clinton-Kuchma summit, the United States announced an additional $5 million in aid to the international science center. In December 1995, the center funded its first 13 projects worth $1.7 million and employing over 200 Ukrainian weapons scientists and engineers.

The Administration has asked Ukraine to commit to establishing a stringent export control regime. Ukraine has little experience in this area, since military technology controls in the old Soviet Union were the domain of the State Planning Agency in Moscow. The United States has offered $13.26 million in Nunn-Lugar assistance for this purpose to Ukraine. As of March 1997, over $9.43 million has been obligated and $6.48 million has been spent. A May 1996 study released by the Monterey Institute of International Relations says that while Ukraine had made progress in export controls, particularly in nuclear and missile technology controls, Ukraine lacked a comprehensive export control law.[13]

Adherence to Democratic Values and Human Rights. As a member of the OSCE, Ukraine has pledged itself to adhere to the principles of the Helsinki Final Act and the Charter of Paris, which include respect for

[13] Nuclear Successor States of the Soviet Union, 57, 71.

democratic values and human rights (including minority rights). International observers generally viewed the 1994 legislative and presidential elections as largely free and fair, but criticized the election law under which the voting was carried out and pointed out several troubling cases of potential fraud. The 1996 State Department human rights report said that Ukraine generally has a good human rights record. Print media are not censored, and express a wide variety of views. However, government-controlled newspapers receive subsidies, while others must fend for themselves. The report says both government-controlled and private newspaper engage in self-censorship on matters sensitive to the government. Many believe state-controlled television also avoids viewpoints critical of or embarrassing to the government. Programs on state-controlled government that have discussed such issues have had to fend off government efforts to push them off the air. Ukraine's judicial and prison systems are largely unreformed and underfunded. In the area of minority rights, Ukraine's citizenship law that does not impose language or residency restrictions. Ukrainian leaders also stress the importance of reconciliation with Jews in Ukraine because of anti-Semitism in Ukraine's past, a problem common to many countries in the region.

©1992 Magellan Geographix[SM] Santa Barbara, CA (800) 929-4627 Nov. '93

Prepared by the Geography and Map Division for the Congressional Research Service

CHAPTER 7

RUSSIAN-CHINESE COOPERATION: PROSPECTS AND IMPLICATIONS

STUART D. GOLDMAN AND ROBERT G. SUTTER

INTRODUCTION

In the past few years, Russia and China have increased their cooperation significantly on a broad range of political, economic, and military issues. As both countries face the prospect of continued and perhaps increased tension in their relations with the West, particularly the United States, some observers warn of the possible emergence of a Sino-Russian strategic alliance.[1]

Others argue that there are serious limits to Russian-Chinese cooperation and major obstacles to a strategic alliance between them.[2] The condition that would be most conducive to the emergence of a Sino-Russian strategic alliance would be a crisis or rupture in Russia's or China's relations with one of the other major powers, such as the United States or Japan.[3] Absent such a development, or a mounting strategic confrontation, the limits to Russian-Chinese cooperation seem substantial and the obstacles to a strategic alliance formidable. (See below, Limits on Cooperation, p. 10-13.)

Both China and Russia face the prospect of potentially destabilizing political succession struggles. In neither country, however, does the issue of

---

[1] For example, Peter Rodman (a Reagan and Bush Administration senior National Security Council staffer and former Director of Policy Planning at the State Department), warned that, "... another strategic problem is looming in East Asia .... a rapprochement between Russia and China that has disturbing geopolitical implications...." "A New Russia-China Alliance?," *Los Angeles Times*, March 25, 1996. A *Wall Street Journal* headline warned, "Russia and China Getting Together Again; Anti-Western Mood Shifts Moscow's Focus Eastward." December 30, 1995. For a fuller discussion of the threat of a Sino-Russian alliance, see, Hung P. Nguyen, "Russia and China: The Genesis of an Eastern Rapallo," *Asian Survey*, March 1993.

[2] See, for example, Peggy Falkenheim Meyer, "From Cold War to Cold Peace? U.S.-Russian Security Relations in the Far East," *Russian Security Policy in the Asia-Pacific Region: Two Views*, Stephen Blank, ed., U.S. Army War College, Strategic Studies Institute, May 1996.

[3] The hypothesis here is that if Russia or China -- and particularly if both of them -- were to become locked in protracted geostrategic confrontation and hostility with the United States and/or a resurgent Japan, that could push Moscow and Beijing to forge a strategic alliance to counter their powerful common enemy. One such scenario might be if China and Russia, for whatever reasons, simultaneously became embroiled in conflicts with Taiwan and with some of the Soviet successor states, provoking confrontation or conflict with the United States and its allies, that could lead to a Moscow-Beijing alliance.

their bilateral relations appear to be an important factor in the domestic political competition.

BACKGROUND

China and Russia have had a long and often troubled history. Tsarist Russia's expansion into the Far East came largely at the expense of the declining Chinese empire. Nineteenth century treaties saw vast stretches of territory formerly under Beijing's rule become part of the Russian Empire. China's internal weakness and political dislocation during the first half of the 20th Century provided opportunities for Lenin and Stalin to seek allies and foster revolutionary movements favorable to the U.S.S.R. Soviet involvement was often ham-handed and, on occasion, worked against the immediate interests of the communist guerilla movement in China led by Mao Zedong.[4]

Seeking economic support and strategic backing in the face of an indifferent or hostile West, Mao Zedong's newly formed People's Republic of China sought an alliance with Stalin's U.S.S.R. in 1949. After many weeks of hard bargaining, the alliance was signed on February 14, 1950. The alliance relationship was essential to China's security and its military, economic and social development in the 1950s. Soviet aid, advisers and guidelines were key features fostering the changes underway in China. But steadily escalating differences arose over strategy toward the United States and international affairs, the proper ideological path to development, and the appropriate leadership roles of Mao and Khrushchev in the world communist movement. Soviet aid was cut off in 1960. Polemics over strategy and ideology led to more substantive disputes over competing claims to border territories. Armed border clashes reached a point in 1969 where the Soviet Union threatened to attack Chinese nuclear installations and Chinese leaders countered with a nation-wide war preparations campaign against the "war maniacs" in the Kremlin. Party relations were broken, trade fell to minimal levels, and each side depicted the other in official media as a dangerous international predator.

The start of Sino-Soviet talks on border issues in October 1969 eased the war crisis, but each side continued preparations for a long-term struggle against its neighboring adversary. As the weaker party in the dispute, China attempted to break out of its international isolation and gain diplomatic leverage against perceived Soviet efforts at intimidation and threat. Beijing's opening to the Nixon Administration was an important element in this policy. The Soviet Union continued past efforts to build up military force along the Sino-Soviet and Sino-Mongolian borders in order to offset any perceived threat from China. They also pursued this course to provide a counterweight useful against any Chinese effort to exert pressure on countries around China's periphery that were interested in developing closer relations with the U.S.S.R. (e.g., India, Vietnam).

---

[4] For background, see among others *Chinese Foreign Policy in Asia and the Sino-Soviet Summit*. CRS Report 89-298 F, May 15, 1989.

The death of Mao Zedong in 1976 and the gradual emergence of a more pragmatic leadership in China reduced the importance of ideological and leadership issues in the Sino-Soviet dispute; but the competition in Asia again reached a crisis in 1979. China countered Soviet-backed Vietnam's invasion of Cambodia by launching a limited military incursion into Vietnam. The Soviet Union responded with warnings and large-scale military exercises along China's northern border. China also denounced the Soviet invasion of Afghanistan in 1979 and sided with the U.S.-backed anti-communist guerillas in Afghanistan.

Subsequently, both countries attempted to moderate tensions. Soviet leader Brezhnev made several public gestures calling for improved economic, government and party relations with China before he died in 1982. This prompted the start of a series of political, economic, technical, and cultural contacts and exchanges.

By 1982, the Soviet leadership concluded that their post-1969 strategy toward China (including the massing of forces along the eastern sector of the border and a media campaign of denunciation) had backfired. The post-1972 normalization in China's relations with the United States and Japan and the signing of the 1978 China-Japan friendship treaty showed a strategic convergence among the United States, China and Japan, which added to the Soviet defense burden, and worsened the security environment on its long, remote, thinly-populated eastern flank. To undo this problem, Brezhnev and later leaders held out the olive branch to the Chinese leadership. Political contacts and trade increased and polemics subsided, but real progress came only after Mikhail Gorbachev consolidated power and made rapprochement with China an urgent priority. In particular, Gorbachev was prepared to make major changes in what China referred to as the "three obstacles" to improved Sino-Soviet relations: Soviet troops in Afghanistan, the buildup of Soviet forces along the border (including the deployment in Mongolia), and the Soviet-backed Vietnamese military occupation of Cambodia.[5]

Motivated by a desire to repair relations with China, to ease the defense burden on the Soviet economy, and to reciprocate China's reduction of its 4 million troops to 2.95 million from 1982 to 1986, the Soviet government announced in 1987 that a phased reduction of its troops (roughly 65,000 in number) from Mongolia would be initiated with the aim of eliminating the deployment by 1992.[6] The Soviet formations in Mongolia had been kept at a higher level of readiness than others along the border, and the Chinese had long viewed them as a first-echelon strike force aimed at Beijing. In December 1988, Gorbachev announced at the United Nations that Soviet conventional forces

---

[5] Professor Rajan Menon of Lehigh and Columbia Universities has written extensively on recent Russian-Chinese relations. This section draws heavily on his analysis, especially "The Transformation of Russian-Chinese Security Relations," conference paper July 3, 1996.

[6] For a review of the military situation, see among others, James Clay Moltz, "Regional Tensions in the Russo-Chinese Rapprochement," *Asian Survey*, June 1995.

would unilaterally be reduced by 500,000. Soviet spokesmen later clarified that, of the total, 120,000 would come from the troops arrayed against China, and that remaining Far Eastern units would progressively be reconfigured in a defensive mode. In late 1989, following Gorbachev's visit to Beijing in May, Chinese and Soviet officials began negotiations on reducing forces along the border, and during Chinese Prime Minister Li Peng's visit to Moscow in April 1990, an agreement was reached on governing principles regarding force reductions. By the time the Soviet Union collapsed in 1991, five rounds of talks on force reductions had been conducted.

The reduction of the conventional threat to China was complemented by the 1987 U.S.-Soviet INF treaty under which Moscow, accepting the concept of a "global zero," dismantled all its medium- and intermediate-range nuclear missiles, including 180 mobile SS-20s that were based in Asian regions of the U.S.S.R.

Meanwhile, the U.S.S.R. agreed under the April 1988 Geneva Accords to withdraw its combat forces from Afghanistan by May 1989 and encouraged Vietnam to evacuate its troops from Cambodia by the end of 1989.

High level political contacts helped to alter the adversarial character of Sino-Soviet relations, the most important being the visits of Eduard Shevardnadze and Gorbachev to Beijing in 1989 and of Li Peng and Chinese Communist Party General Secretary Jiang Zemin to Moscow in 1990 and 1991 respectively. Talks on resolving the border dispute, which had been derailed by the Soviet invasion of Afghanistan, resumed in 1987. A treaty delimiting the eastern sector of the border was signed in May 1991. These military and political transformations in Sino-Soviet relations were supplemented by a significant growth in trade --especially along the border -- and agreements providing for thousands of Chinese workers to be employed in construction projects in Siberia and the Soviet Far East.[7]

Chinese leaders welcomed Gorbachev's military withdrawals from around China's periphery, and the collapse of the U.S.S.R. in 1991 removed the Soviet military threat that had been the centerpiece of Beijing's strategic planning since the 1960s. The changes came at a time when Chinese leaders were beleaguered in the face of national and international resentment over their handling of the Tiananmen Square demonstrations of 1989. Representing one of the few surviving communist regimes in the post-Cold War world, Chinese officials were especially suspicious of Boris Yeltsin and his avowed democratic reforms that were anathema to Chinese leaders determined to maintain the communist party's monopoly of political power. Nevertheless, more pragmatic consideration of the national interests of China and Russia have seen Yeltsin and Chinese leaders continue the process of gradually improving relations begun in the 1980s.

---

[7] See among others Stephen Uhalley, "Sino-Soviet Relations: Continued Improvement Amidst Tumultuous Change," *Journal of East Asian Affairs*, Winter-Spring, 1992.

POLITICAL RELATIONS

The ideological grounds for polemics between Moscow and Beijing were basically removed in the Gorbachev years -- party-to-party ties were re-established during the 1989 Deng-Gorbachev summit. The end of Communist Party rule in Russia and the reforms that China has embarked upon since 1978 render the old schismatic disputes about "revisionism," "social imperialism" and "hegemonism" irrelevant. China's poor human rights record and Beijing's use of force to suppress Tiananmen demonstrations are criticized by Russians but have not become major problems in government-to-government relations. Also, unlike the United States, Russia has not allowed its expanded economic ties with Taiwan to offend Beijing. Meanwhile, progress on resolving Russo-Chinese border disputes continued. The May 1991 eastern sector border agreement was followed by the signing of an agreement in September 1994 on the western sector of the border. As a result, except for some small sectors, the entire Russo-Chinese border is settled.[8]

Both countries have maintained the momentum of political contacts at the highest levels. Yeltsin visited Beijing in 1992 and 1996 and Prime Minister Viktor Chernomyrdin in 1994. Chinese President Jiang Zemin visited Moscow in 1994 and 1995 and Prime Minister Li Peng in 1994 and 1996. In addition, there have been numerous meetings between the foreign ministers, defense ministers, and economic officials of both countries.

MILITARY ISSUES[9]

In 1992, Yeltsin's government completed the withdrawal of troops from Mongolia initiated by Gorbachev in 1987. By May 1996, Russia reportedly had cut 150,00 troops from its Far Eastern deployment and the Pacific Fleet had been reduced by 50 percent from its 1985 level. At the eighth round of negotiations on force reductions along the border in December 1992, both sides agreed that their formations would be pulled back 100 kilometers from the border. Offensive weapons (tanks, strike aircraft, artillery, and tactical nuclear weapons) are to be reduced in the 200-kilometer zone that results.

Efforts to reduce forces and institute confidence building measures (CBMs) along the border became multilateral with the addition of the Soviet successor states Kazakhstan, Kyrgyzstan, and Tajikistan -- all of whom share borders with China -- to a joint Commonwealth of Independent States (CIS) delegation. Guidelines, including force reductions, warnings preceding military exercises, and the attendance at exercises of observers from the signatories, were incorporated in an agreement signed by the leaders of the four CIS states and China in Shanghai during Yeltsin's April 1996 visit.

---

[8] See Moltz, "Regional Tensions."

[9] See discussion in Menon, "Transformation," p 7-14.

A Joint Declaration signed at the end of Yeltsin's visit to China in December 1992 called for reducing troops along the border to "a minimal level" and for increased contact between Chinese and Russian military personnel. Each party also pledged to eschew the use of force against the other, including in the domain of third countries, and not to enter any "military and political alliances directed against the other Party, or sign with third countries any treaties or agreements detrimental to the state sovereignty and security interests of the other Party."[10]

In July 1994, Russian and Chinese defense ministers agreed on measures (such as preventing accidental missile launches, ending the electronic jamming of communications, and establishing signals to warn aircraft and ships in danger of violating the other side's border) to reduce the danger of inadvertent military escalation. In September 1994, the two sides agreed to the principle of no-first-use for nuclear weapons and to re-target nuclear missiles away from each other's territory. In May 1994, Chinese warships from the North China Fleet visited Vladivostok. Units of the Russian Pacific Fleet called at Qingtao that August. Local Chinese commanders have also visited Russian military districts.[11]

RUSSIAN ARMS SALES[12]

China has become the largest customer for Russian arms, having purchased $2 billion worth in 1994 alone. Figures are not available for 1995 and 1996, but it seems clear they exceed the 1994 level.[13] Major purchases in recent years include 72 Su-27 fighter-ground attack aircraft, 50 T-72 tanks, 100 S-300 surface-to-air missiles, 10 Il-76 transport aircraft, several Kilo-class (diesel-electric) submarines, and most recently, two Sovremenny-class destroyers.[14]

---

[10] Moltz, "Regional Tensions," p. 518.

[11] Reviewed in Menon, "Transformation," p 9.

[12] See *China's Rising Military Power*, CRS Report 96-66 F, January 16, 1996, p. 18-19. See also IISS, *Military Balance 1995-1996*, London, 1995 p. 171.

[13] *Conventional Arms Transfers to Developing Nations, 1988-1995*. CRS Report 96-677 F, August 15, 1996, p. 55, ff.

[14] The destroyer deal reportedly was completed during Li Peng's December 1996 visit to Moscow. The Sovremenny-class destroyers are highly capable, modern vessels. They would be China's largest and most formidable surface warships. They reportedly will be equipped with the SS-N-22, a very fast anti-ship cruise missile designed to counter U.S.-built Aegis cruisers and destroyers and which could also threaten aircraft carriers. U.S. military officials said this purchase was China's direct response to the deployment in March 1996 of two U.S. aircraft carriers to waters near Taiwan during the tension surrounding Taiwanese elections and Chinese military exercises and missile firings. (See note 22, below.) Bill Gertz, "Pentagon Says Russians Sell Destroyers to China," *Washington Times*, January 10, 1997, p. A1, 10.

Two submarines had been delivered by the end of 1995, but at least four, and most likely more, are expected to be sold. Moscow is also providing China with technology to improve the accuracy of surface-to-surface and air-to-air missiles, and training in Russia for personnel who will operate the weapons purchased. Several of the sales have been difficult. The Su-27 transaction has been in the works since 1992, and the first 24 aircraft were delivered that year. Additional deliveries were held up by a dispute over China's desire to pay for two-thirds of the cost through barter. Although precise details of how the dispute was settled are unavailable, after the visit to Russia in December 1995 by Chinese military leader Liu Huaqing, the way was finally cleared for the delivery of the remaining 48 Su-27s, and an agreement was reached (reportedly worth $2 billion) allowing China to manufacture this highly capable aircraft under license.

At bottom, these sales reflect a pragmatic marriage of important bilateral needs. For Russia, arms sales to China supply much-needed hard currency and consumer goods from China, provide orders for severely distressed Russian defense industries,[15] and reduce the tendency of the United States, Japan and others to take Russia for granted in the post-Cold War Far East. Russia's political disarray also facilitates these arms sales, as reduced central control from Moscow gives defense industries more independence to make such deals. For China, the Russian equipment is relatively cheap, compatible with the existing Chinese inventory, and comes without political or other preconditions. Both Russian and Chinese leaders are sensitive to concerns in the United States, Japan, and among Asian governments along China's periphery that the Russian transfers could substantially add to China's power projection and alter the prevailing military balance in East Asia. In general, Russian and Chinese officials say that China has a long way to go before it can use the recently acquired Russian weapons effectively or project its augmented power in ways that would seriously upset the military balance in the region.[16] There is debate in the West over when and if such weapons will alter the regional balance.

ECONOMIC AND SOCIETAL CHANGES

Trade between the two countries has grown substantially from a low base. In 1985, Sino-Soviet trade was $300 million. Russian-Chinese trade peaked in 1994 at $7 billion, and cross-border trade, which resumed in 1982 and is conducted largely in barter,[17] accounted for a third of the volume, although its

---

[15] The defense industries, however, do not directly receive the hard currency payments. These payments go to the Russian treasury.

[16] Consultations with Chinese and Russian officials, Washington, D.C., Beijing, 1996.

[17] Chinese food, textiles, and consumer goods and Russian raw materials predominate.

proportion is falling in accordance with the desire of both governments. China has become Russia's second largest trade partner after Germany.[18]

Along the economically more important eastern section of the Russo-Chinese border, roads and rail connections now link 19 working border checkpoints between the two sides, with two more planned. In addition, direct postal and telephonic links have been created between northeastern China and the Russian Far East. Russia also has signed contracts to build nuclear and hydroelectric power plants in China.

Problems caused by an influx of Chinese into the Russian Far East, particularly those who remain in violation of visa regulations, led Russia and China to work out a more stringent visa regime in 1994. But the problem of Chinese migration into the Russian Far East is likely to persist. Both countries face the unprecedented challenge of managing the movement of what could be millions of people across a long border. Russia, in particular, cannot afford to pump large sums of money into securing that border more effectively. There is a structural supply and demand dynamic at work: the high population density and unemployment that obtains on the Chinese side stimulates people to cross into the Russian Far East, which has traditionally suffered from severe labor shortages. The entire eastern third of Russia (east of Lake Baikal, a territory almost the size of the continental United States) has fewer than 20 million inhabitants -- and its population is shrinking as people re-migrate back toward Russia's European heartland. This is exacerbated by economic distress in the Russian Far East that is worse than in most other regions, including severe food and energy shortages and wage arrearages.

FUTURE PROSPECTS

The sorts of political, economic, and military cooperation between Russia and China described above are likely to continue for quite some time and perhaps to increase somewhat. Political and economic conditions faced by both countries favor such continued cooperation.

Continued Cooperation Likely. China and Russia both find that their relations with the advanced industrial democracies, particularly the United States, have become more difficult in recent years. China faces problems over human rights abuses, trade and weapons proliferation questions, the status of Tibet, and especially the Taiwan question. With Russia it is problems concerning its relations with other Soviet successor states, tension over NATO enlargement, and nuclear proliferation. Internationally, Russia supports China's position on Taiwan and China backs Russia's opposition to NATO enlargement. Each opposes international interference in what the other views as its internal affairs. Some Chinese and Russians perceive U.S. policy as aimed at "containing" or encircling them. Both countries view themselves as outsiders vis-a-vis the G-7, which they see as the "rich countries' club". As still-developing

---

[18] Reviewed in Menon, "Transformation," p. 14-17.

economies, they tend to resist certain G-7-supported economic and trade policies in areas such as protectionism, dumping, intellectual property rights, transparency, and government regulation.

Russia badly needs the China market to export arms and industrial products for which, for various reasons, it has relatively few other buyers who can afford to pay.[19] Food and inexpensive consumer goods from China play a vital role in helping sustain the Russian Far East. These factors helped propel China into the position of Russia's second largest trade partner. Economically, China is far less dependent on Russia. But Russia can provide advanced weapons, nuclear reactor technology, and other industrial products relatively cheaply to China that might otherwise be much more costly for Beijing or unavailable for political reasons.

Both Russia and China find it helpful, to some extent, to use their improving bilateral relations for leverage vis-a-vis the West, particularly the United States. This strikes some as reminiscent of Nixon/Kissinger's famous playing of the "China card" against the Soviet Union. Moscow tends to be more explicit about this than Beijing. Many Russian officials, for example, have warned that NATO enlargement could drive Russia into much closer cooperation, even a strategic alliance, with China.

Moscow has been emphasizing this linkage with increasing frequency. For example, on January 20, 1997, while NATO Secretary-General Javier Solana was holding difficult talks with Foreign Minister Primakov in Moscow about NATO enlargement, Russian Deputy Foreign Minister Grigori Karasin announced a summit meeting between the Russian and Chinese presidents in April. Karasin said the two sides were drafting a document that would outline a common Russian-Chinese view on international realities in a multi-polar world.[20] Put more generally, as a Russian Foreign Ministry official explained while Yeltsin was in Beijing in 1996, "when Russia speaks with the West, if it has at its back a reliable China, it can speak with more ease."[21] China can, and sometimes does, play the same game. In connection with the increased tension in U.S.-

---

[19] Most Russian non-military manufactured goods are qualitatively uncompetitive on the international market. Many of Moscow's traditional customers are unable to pay in hard currency. Some traditional customers who can pay, such as Iraq, Libya, and Serbia, are inaccessible to Russia because of U.N. trade sanctions. Russian officials argue that Moscow would be less eager to sell arms to customers that make the United States nervous, such as China and Iran, if Washington cooperated in giving Russia a share in the arms trade with "more civilized" countries.

[20] Jamestown Monitor, January 21, 1997.

[21] Joseph Kahn and Claudia Rosett, "China and Russia Rekindle Their Romance." *Wall Street Journal*, April 24, 1996, p. A11, quoted in a forthcoming Cato Institute policy analysis by Stanley Kober, *Why Spy? The Uses and Misuses of Intelligence.*

Chinese relations in the spring of 1996[22], a Chinese specialist on Russian affairs in the Chinese Academy of Sciences told American journalists, "We want to give the Americans a warning. Our relations with Russia can become closer and closer."[23]

China and Russia share some other common interests that strengthen the basis of their cooperation. For example, both see the possible spread of radical Islam in Central Asia as a threat to their own domestic stability and national security.[24] Both countries desire regional stability in Asia, want to avoid any crisis on the Korean Peninsula, and wish to forestall the reemergence of Japan as a major military power.

Limits to Cooperation. Despite the broad basis for Russian-Chinese cooperation discussed above, there are serious limits to that cooperation -- and even more to the creation of a strategic alliance between them.

In the aftermath of the collapse of the Soviet Union and loss of its peripheral territory and population, Russia's relative economic weakness and political instability vis-a-vis China make many Russians nervous. Russia's population (roughly 147 million) is about half that of the of the former Soviet Union -- and the sparsely populated Russian Far East is losing people. Russia's economy has contracted significantly during the still far from complete transition to a market economy. Industrial production may be as low as 50 percent of the 1991 level.[25]

Even if President Yeltsin makes a full recovery from his heart surgery, the political situation is still unstable. One aspect of that instability is the difficulty Moscow has controlling distant regions, such as Eastern Siberia and the Far East. Leaders in those resource-rich regions seek greater autonomy from Moscow and some flirt with the idea of separatism.[26] Finally, many Russians

---

[22] China conducted military exercises and missile firings near Taiwan in an apparent effort to intimidate Taiwanese voters prior to their national elections. The United States dispatched two aircraft carriers to the vicinity as a show of support for Taiwan. This show of strength in the Taiwan Straits irked Beijing.

[23] Kahn and Rosett, "China and Russia Rekindle Their Romance."

[24] During the period of the Sino-Soviet split, Moscow and Beijing vied for influence in Central Asia. That competition is now greatly reduced and in some respects ended.

[25] PlanEcon, *Review and Outlook for the Former Soviet Republics*, August 1996, p. 31. Others who say that this estimate is too bleak because it does not adequately take unreported production into account, estimate that the decline in industrial production since 1991 is roughly one-quarter to one-third.

[26] Russian "great-power" nationalists view these centrifugal tendencies with alarm, fearing that they weaken Russia and, some believe, increase its vulnerability to a dynamic and potentially expansionist China. For a history of the Russian Far East and an assessment of the possibility of separatism in that region see, John J. Stephan, *The*

are keenly aware of the deterioration of their country's military strength. The Russian Army's remarkably poor performance in Chechnya is one indication of this. Russia's Armed Forces presently number about 1.5 million troops, compared to 4.5 million Soviet troops in the early 1980s. Weapons procurement, readiness, and morale are all, even by Russian standards, alarmingly low. Outer Mongolia was a de facto Soviet protectorate until 1991 and the staging area for powerful Soviet armored forces that threatened North China. All Russian military forces and most Russian political influence are gone now, and Mongolian leaders express concern that because of Russian weakness and western indifference, their country may fall under Chinese domination again, as in centuries past.

In contrast, from Moscow's perspective, China -- with its dynamic economy, huge and growing population, apparent national self-confidence and assertiveness, stable, authoritarian political system, and large and modernizing army -- seems strikingly robust. Some among the Russian policy elite find Beijing's example admirable and see in China both a model to emulate and a natural ally. Others -- mindful of Russia's declining power vis-a-vis China and of the history of Russia's seizure of vast territories in Eastern Siberia and the Russian Far East from China in "unequal treaties" in the later part of the 19th century -- see China's renaissance and burgeoning power as a challenge and potential threat. Russians' nightmare scenario from this perspective is that a resurgent China might try to retake vast, thinly populated territories from a weakened Russia.

There is a policy debate in Moscow about the proper orientation of Russian foreign policy in general, and also with regard to China. It does not split neatly along ideological lines. Andrei Kozyrev, Yeltsin's Foreign Minister from 1991 to January 1996, was a democrat and a westernizer who championed a western orientation for Russia. His successor in the Foreign Ministry, Yevgenii Primakov, advocates a more eastern orientation, including, "as a very high priority," building closer relations with China as a strategic partner to counterbalance American "unilateralism."[27] Gennady Zyuganov, head of the Communist Party and of the newly formed Popular Patriotic Front which combines communist and nationalist parties, proposes alliance with China. But Vladimir Zhirinovsky, head of the ultranationalist Liberal Democratic Party, warns of the danger of Chinese revanchism. Pavel Grachev, Defense Minister from 1992 until June 1996, used to hint broadly about Russia's need to "find allies in the East" to counter NATO enlargement. The new Defense Minister, Igor Rodionov, while asserting Russia's intent to build a "strategic partnership with China in the 21st century," criticized some Russian officers for "questioning the correctness of Russia's official military-political course with regard to China."[28] Sergei Rogov, head of the prestigious Institute for the Study of the

---

Russian Far East : A History, Stanford, Calif, Stanford University Press, 1994.

[27] Open Media Research Institute, OMRI Daily Digest, June 26, 1996.

[28] Interfax, January 14, 1997.

U.S.A. and Canada, also says that NATO enlargement might drive Russia into alliance with China, but warns that such an alliance would be "suicidal" for Russia in the long run.[29] Vladimir Lukin, Chairman of the Duma's International Affairs Committee,[30] calls for a balance in Russia's relations with China and the West: "The level of our relations with the PRC in the field of security must not be inferior to our corresponding relations with the West but must not appreciably exceed them either."[31]

Although Russia's sale of advanced weaponry to China is widely believed to be motivated in large part by economic necessity on Russia's part, and is strongly supported by the defense industrial sector, there are serious reservations in the Russian security community. Some Russian commentators question the wisdom of helping to modernize the military of a country that might well become a threat to Russian security in the future. These reservations reportedly extend to the Russian General Staff. While acquiescing in the sale of Su-27 jets and T-72 tanks to China, the General Staff is said to have vetoed proposed deals for top-of-the-line Su-35s and T-80s.[32] Some regional leaders in Eastern Siberia and the Russian Far East criticize Moscow's cession of some disputed territory to China in the border demarcation agreements and seek to block implementation of the agreements.[33]

There is no consensus in the Russian policy community about relations with China. Objectively it seems reasonable to say, as some Russians do, that in the short-run China represents an opportunity for Russia, but in the long-run, if China's power continues to grow, it may become more of a threat.

On the Chinese side too, there are significant limitations and constraints on cooperation with Russia. The radical swings in Soviet and Russian domestic politics and foreign policy since the mid-1980s inevitably make Russia appear somewhat unreliable in Chinese eyes. Russia's economic, political, and military weakness has been duly noted by Chinese strategic planners, who nonetheless remain vigilant for signs of revival of Russian strength that could complicate Chinese interests in Asia.

---

[29] Martin Sieff, "Russians Feel Isolated as NATO Grows, Policy Could Push Ties to Iran, China" *Washington Times*, September 23, 1996.

[30] Lukin, a leader of the democratic opposition Party, Yabloko, was Ambassador to Washington, 1992-1995 and a long-time critic of Kozyrev's pro-western policies.

[31] Foreign Broadcast Information Service, *Central Eurasian Daily Report*, FBIS-SOV, June 2, 1994, p. 60-62.

[32] CRS interview with a senior Russian Foreign Ministry official, September 1994.

[33] Yevgenii Nazdratenko, Governor of Primorsky Krai (Russia's Pacific Ocean Maritime Province) and officials from Chita Oblast have taken this position. Peggy Falkenheim Meyer, "From Cold War to Cold Peace?," p. 16.

Also, Russia is much less important economically to China than vice-versa. Their bilateral trade peaked at $7 billion in 1994. It slipped to about $5 billion in 1995 and is expected to be about $5.5 billion in 1996. Although this makes China Russia's second largest trade partner, Russia accounts for less than 2 percent of China's $300 billion in foreign trade. China's trade with and credits and investments from the G-7 countries weigh far more heavily in Beijing than Russo-Chinese trade. In a policy crunch, China would be loathe to jeopardize its vital economic relations with the advanced industrial democracies on Russia's behalf.

In short, the markets, financing and technology of the West and the developed countries of East Asia represent a key link in China's ongoing program of economic modernization. And economic modernization and the concrete benefits it gives to the broad masses of Chinese people are the key sources of political legitimacy for post-Mao leaders. Those leaders do not have the charisma or power of Mao and his revolutionary cohorts. They and the Chinese Communist Party are able to justify their continued monopoly of political power largely on the basis of the solid economic achievements China has achieved under their rule. It is difficult to imagine circumstances where they would allow closer military, political or other ties with an economically anemic Russia to jeopardize China's vital links with the world's most important economies -- unless China faced a major crisis or geostrategic confrontation with the United States or Japan.[34]

IMPLICATIONS FOR THE UNITED STATES

Russian-Chinese-American relations do not a constitute a zero-sum game. Instead, Russian-Chinese cooperation is a mixed bag for the United States, with positive as well as negative implications.

The calming of the intense Sino-Soviet hostility of the Brezhnev period serves U.S. interests. This goes beyond the obvious benefit of removing the threat of war between those two military giants. Dampening down their previous level of hostility and the militarization that accompanied it enhances stability throughout much of Asia. It also improves the prospects for further progress on nuclear and conventional arms control in many venues.

The improvement in Russian-Chinese relations enhances stability on the Korean Peninsula, the most dangerous flash-point in Asia. Both Beijing and

[34] A recent example of China's unwillingness to jeopardize these economic ties for the sake of other important priorities relates to Chinese relations with Japan -- a major market for China, the largest source of bilateral aid to China, and a major source of technology and foreign investment. Despite growing popular sentiment and nationalistic feelings directed against Japan's control of disputed islands in the East China Sea, Chinese officials took steps to dampen anti-Japanese rhetoric and demonstrations in China and to handle the dispute with Japan quietly, mainly through diplomatic means. See CRS Report 96-864 F, *Japan-China Relations*, October 30, 1996.

Moscow want to avoid nuclear confrontation in Korea -- a development that could be calamitous for both countries that border on North Korea. They also both want to expand trade relations with economically dynamic South Korea. The rapprochement between China and Russia tends to reduce North Korea's room for maneuver. It was the Sino-Soviet split that gave Pyongyang the leverage to play Moscow and Beijing off against one another, causing them to compete for influence in Pyongyang by supporting some of Kim Il-sung's dangerous policies and providing economic support and arms transfers. Now both Russia and China have distanced themselves from North Korea, leaving Pyongyang without a big power patron or protector.

On the other hand, some aspects of Russian-Chinese cooperation clearly have negative implications for the United States. Russia accelerates China's military build up, providing Beijing with advanced weaponry, military technology, and training that might otherwise not be available to it. Opinions vary among U.S. specialists about the extent of the danger to U.S. security and interests of China's military build up, and of the importance of Russia's contribution to that build up. But virtually all western observers view it as a negative development.

In addition, deepening cooperation between China and Russia in the United Nations Security Council, the World Trade Organization (if and when they join), and other international fora could further complicate U.S. diplomacy on such matters as economic and trade issues, the imposition of economic sanctions, and the protection of human rights. Moscow and Beijing are often uncomfortable with U.S. initiatives in these areas, but sometimes go along anyway. Greater cooperation between them might well stiffen their resistance.

And finally, there is the specter of a strategic alliance between Russia and China, driven in part by their hostile responses to such U.S. policies as NATO enlargement, perceived "containment," and support of Taiwan. Some observers dismiss this prospect as, at most, a "marriage of convenience." Others warn that even on that basis, a Russian-Chinese alliance could be dangerous, pointing out, for example, that the Hitler-Stalin Pact of August 1939, one of the most cynical "marriages of convenience" in history, triggered the outbreak of World War II in Europe.

On balance, however, as stated above,[35] the emergence of a Sino-Russian strategic alliance seems highly unlikely -- unless there is a major crisis or rupture in Russia's or China's relations with one of the other major powers, such as the United States or Japan.

---

[35] See Introduction and explanation in footnote 3.

CHAPTER 8

RUSSIA'S NUCLEAR FORCES: DOCTRINE AND FORCE STRUCTURE ISSUES

AMY F. WOOLF AND KARA WILSON

INTRODUCTION

When the Soviet Union dissolved at the end of 1991, the Russian Federation inherited most of the nuclear weapons and much of the nuclear command and control system that had been a part of the Soviet arsenal. Russia also inherited key elements of Soviet nuclear doctrine and employment strategy, along with the Soviet status as the only nation capable of destroying the United States with nuclear weapons if a global conflict were to occur.

Nevertheless, there are numerous differences between Russia's nuclear posture and that of the Soviet Union. First, the threats that Russia believes it faces are different from those of the Soviet era; Russia focuses less on the prospects for a global conflict with the United States and more on the prospects for smaller conflicts with and among nations along its periphery. In addition, changes in Russia's political stature abroad and its economic distress at home have combined with the decline in its conventional military capabilities to alter the role that Russia sees for its nuclear arsenal. According to Russia's military strategy and statements from Russian officials, nuclear weapons may play a political role in enhancing Russia's stature and deterring challenges from regional adversaries, along with a military role if Russia's conventional forces prove unequal to the task in a regional conflict.

Russia's nuclear force structure resembles that of the Soviet Union and remains capable of inflicting massive damage on any adversary. But arms control and economic pressures have altered its current shape and future prospects. All the nuclear warheads have been removed from the other former Soviet republics, leaving Russia as the sole nuclear power to emerge from the collapse of the Soviet Union. In addition, sharp constraints on funding for nuclear weapons and the command and control network have raised questions about the near- and long-term reliability and viability of those forces. And, although Russia continues to produce some new missiles and submarines to replace aging systems, the rate of modernization has declined sharply since the end of the Soviet era, raising questions about whether Russia has the economic or political resources to maintain force levels that are equal to those of the United States.

These two contrasting trends -- Russia's growing reliance on nuclear weapons as a political and military tool and increasing financial pressures on the size and reliability of its nuclear force -- raise numerous questions about the future of Russia's nuclear arsenal. Most experts believe that Russia's forces will continue to decline in quality and quantity. Others, however, argue that Russia will devote whatever resources are necessary to maintain a robust nuclear arsenal because these forces are the only remaining basis of Russia's superpower status and only source of political stature needed to counter the power and influence of the United States and U.S. allies.

Most agree that Russia will seek to maintain a nuclear balance with the United States in spite of its economic difficulties. As a result, some argue that now is an ideal time for the United States and Russia to negotiate further reductions in nuclear weapons through formal arms control agreements. This would not only relieve the economic pressures on Russia, it would also reduce the threat to the United States from the Russian arsenal. Others, however, believe that Russia might not be willing to accept further limits on its forces now because it would want to maintain its nuclear options in an era of conventional weakness and growing regional and international insecurity. Still others argue that the presence or absence of arms control agreements is irrelevant to Russia's nuclear future because economic constraints will force Russia to reduce its forces regardless of the arms control environment.

This report provides information and analysis on the future of Russia's nuclear forces. It also seeks to address the question of how changes in Russia's nuclear strategy and nuclear force posture might affect U.S. national security. The answer to this query might be clear if all agreed that Russia would continue to maintain a robust, modern nuclear arsenal with a solid and comprehensive command and control structure or if all agreed that Russia would pursue a coherent, orderly plan to reduce its nuclear arsenal. In either case, the United States might be able to predict the outcome, measure the threat, and devise an appropriate response to Russia's remaining nuclear arsenal.

But the answer to this query may be less obvious if Russia's nuclear forces and command and control structure continued to age with little modernization, particularly if this occurred without the predictability offered by arms control constraints or coherent policy. Some would argue that this outcome serves the U.S. interests because it would undermine the effectiveness and threatening nature of Russia's forces. Still others would see new threats in this circumstance because, as long as Russia continues to rely on nuclear weapons for its status and its security, it might seek ways to remain confident in its declining force posture. And some of Russia's solutions to the weaknesses in its nuclear posture could create new problems for U.S. security.

This report is divided into three sections. The first two describe Russia's nuclear strategy and its nuclear force structure. They highlight areas where Russia's nuclear posture differs from the posture it inherited from the Soviet Union and areas where the two remain similar. Both sections also identify ways in which Russia's economic and political positions have affected Russia's nuclear posture and ways in which these factors could affect Russia's nuclear forces in the future. The third section of this report reviews how Russia might structure its forces under alternative arms control scenarios. The analysis reflects the current limits in the START I and START II treaties and proposed limits for a START III agreement. In each case, the report identifies ways in which the United States might be affected by Russia's force structure choices.

RUSSIA'S NUCLEAR STRATEGY

The end of the Cold War and collapse of the Soviet Union ushered in a dramatically altered strategic reality for Russia. Russia has been unable to retain an international posture as commanding as that of the Soviet Union and is concerned about any decline in its influence in international affairs. This external situation has been exacerbated by fragile economic and military conditions throughout the country. In response to these events, Russia has adopted a nuclear doctrine and strategy that differ in several respects from those of the Soviet Union.

CHANGES IN NUCLEAR DOCTRINE

Soviet Nuclear Doctrine

Throughout much of the Cold War era, the Soviet Union valued nuclear weapons for both their political and military attributes. From a political perspective, nuclear weapons provided the Soviet Union with stature and influence in the international arena. They were not the only measure of Soviet status -- the Soviet Union's massive army and alliance structure also enhanced the Soviet Union's position as a leader in international affairs -- but nuclear parity with, or superiority over, the United States also offered the Soviet Union prestige and influence in international affairs. From the military perspective, the Soviet Union considered nuclear weapons to be instrumental to its warfighting plans. Soviet leaders apparently believed that it could prevail in a conflict against the United States and NATO if it both stationed superior numbers of conventional forces in Central Europe and also threatened to use nuclear weapons offensively and on a large scale if a conflict did occur.

Although the Soviet Union integrated nuclear weapons into its warfighting strategy and doctrine, it also espoused a policy of "no-first use" for nuclear weapons. This policy can be traced back to the Brezhnev era of the 1970s, when the Soviet Union and United States began an effort at detente and the Soviet Union sought to expand its influence among developing nations. Most U.S. analysts doubted that the Soviet Union's "no-first use" pledge would influence its actual warfighting plans, but the policy did place the Soviet Union on the moral high ground with non-aligned nations when the United States and its NATO allies refused to adopt a similar pledge or policy. The United States and NATO, in fact, explicitly relied on the option of first use of nuclear weapons to counterbalance the Soviet-Warsaw Pact advantages in conventional forces along the Central European front.

The Soviet Union reiterated its no-first-use policy during the Gorbachev era from 1985 to 1991. During this time, actual Soviet military doctrine may have become more consistent with this declaratory doctrine as the Soviet Union began to reduce its emphasis on nuclear warfighting strategies. This noteworthy change was primarily a result of Gorbachev's belief that the willingness of the Soviet Union to escalate to the nuclear level against the United States or NATO in a conflict would lead to catastrophic consequences. As such, he believed the Soviet Union should avoid the use of nuclear weapons if at all possible. Nevertheless, nuclear weapons remained a key tool in the Soviet arsenal for deterring and, if necessary, fighting a large-scale conflict with the United States and NATO.

Russia's Nuclear Doctrine

Russia maintains the Soviet belief that nuclear weapons can serve both political and military objectives.[1] Nevertheless, a comparison of Russia's policy with Soviet doctrine provides some interesting contrasts. For example, where nuclear weapons were but one measure of the Soviet Union's superpower status, many believe they remain as the sole indicator of Russia's stature in international affairs.[2] In addition, the Soviet Union declared that it *would not be the first to use nuclear weapons*, but it actually planned for their offensive use by stressing their utility for surprise attack and preemptive strike options. Russia, in contrast, *explicitly rejected a no-first-use policy* in its 1993 Doctrine, but it seems to view nuclear weapons more as a tool for defensive, war-prevention and termination goals than for offensive operations and surprise attack.[3]

In their statements explaining their nuclear policy, Russian officials have sought to emphasize the deterrent nature of Russia's nuclear weapons and to play down the implicit threat to use these weapons first in a conflict. For example, the 1993 military doctrine stated:

> The aim of the Russian Federation in the sphere of nuclear weapons is to eliminate the danger of a nuclear war by deterrence against the unleashing of aggression against the Russian Federation and allies. Russia, does not see nuclear weapons as a means of conducting military acts, rather as a means of deterrence against such aggression.[4]

Former Foreign Minister Andrei Kozyrev further elaborated:

---

[1] Russia first outlined its nuclear policy in its 1993 Basic Provisions of the Military Doctrine of the Russian Federation. See *Jane's Intelligence Review*, Basic Provisions of the Military Doctrine of the Russian Federation, January 1994, pp. 6-12.

[2] General Igor Sergeyev, Commander of the Strategic Missile Forces, recently told the media that Russia's strategic missile forces can "evolve into a real measure of Russia's military might which will ensure strategic stability in the world [and] maintenance of Russia's status as a great power." Interfax, April 23, 1997.

[3] Spencer D. Bakich, Toward a New Quality: The Russian Military Doctrine and Eurasian Security, *Journal of Social, Political, and Economic Studies 21*, Spring 1996, p. 10.

[4] Spencer. Toward a New Quality: The Russian Military Doctrine and Eurasian Security, p. 10.

> It would be a mistake to make out that our new approach to nuclear weapons [the abandoning of the no-first-use pledge] increases the risk of nuclear war. The fact that we do not intend to be the first to use any weapons, and see nuclear weapons as a last resort, is of fundamental importance.[5]

Nevertheless, Russian officials have underscored that Russia believes the threat to use nuclear weapons in a conflict is an essential part of Russia's military strategy. Former Defense Minister Pavel Grachev stated that a purely defensive posture is unrealistic; Russia must have the option of employing those types of weapons that are most effective against an aggressive action.[6] This point of view has remained evident in further iterations of Russia's military doctrine.[7] And, in early 1997, when Russian officials were voicing strenuous objections to NATO's plans to enlarge by adding nations in Central Europe, Ivan Rybkin, head of Russia's Security Council, stated that Russia reserved the right to use nuclear weapons first in a conflict. He told a Russian newspaper that "we are not talking of a preventive nuclear strike but if an aggressor starts a war against us using conventional weapons, we may respond with nuclear ones." He highlighted the deterrent nature of this threat by stating that the threat to use nuclear weapons first could "discourage miliary adventurers bent on exploiting Russia's difficulties," but he made it clear that Russia was prepared to respond to a direct military challenge with nuclear weapons.[8] Although many officials in the Yeltsin government sought to play down these comments, Rybkin's statement is consistent with Russia's military strategy.

THE CONTEXT FOR RUSSIA'S NUCLEAR POLICY

In recent years, Russia's leaders have grown concerned about regional threats from an expanded NATO or other nations along Russia's periphery. But Russia may not be able to rely on its conventional forces alone as a credible deterrent to these local and regional threats. The poor handling of the Chechen rebellion and careful analysis of the U.S. success in the Persian Gulf War

---

[5] Spencer. Toward a New Quality: The Russian Military Doctrine and Eurasian Security. p. 16.

[6] Grachev, Pavel S. Drafting a New Russian Military Doctrine: Guidelines for the Establishment of the Russian Armed Forces, *Military Technology*, February 1993, p. 1.

[7] In late 1996, reports in the Russian press indicated that the Ministry of Defense and the Defense Council had produced a new document that outlined a new military doctrine and plans for military reform. This document reportedly stated that "in the event of aggression moving from the phase of a regional armed conflict into a wide-scale war, Russia may be the first to employ nuclear weapons to deliver a disarming strike against military targets." See, Military Reform in Russia, Army Soon to Ax About 500 Generals. *Nezavisimaya Gazeta*, Moscow, December 16, 1996. Translated in FBIS-SOV-96-242.

[8] Khalip, Andrei. Russia may use nukes first in self-defense. Reuters. February 11, 1997.

demonstrated that Russia's conventional forces have declined in quality and are not up to international standards. The emphasis on the possible use of nuclear weapons in these conflicts does not indicate that Russia believes any conflict, even one with a break-away republic, could become nuclear. In contrast, many in Russia believe that it might actually deter challenges to its security by reminding potential adversaries that Russia has nuclear weapons at its disposal.

Potential Threats to Russian Security

As the possibility of a global nuclear conflict has decreased, Russia has shifted its attention toward threats in its immediate vicinity. Of primary concern are local wars and armed conflicts in the near abroad (meaning the other former Soviet republics) and in other nations around its periphery. Russia has also shown a concern with possible challenges from states who possess or may acquire weapons of mass destruction. For example, General Yuri Yashin, Chairman of Russia's State Technical Commission, expressed concern in December 1994 that Britain, France, and China were modernizing their nuclear arsenals as Russia embarked on major reductions in its strategic offensive weapons systems under START I and II.[9] In addition, several nations that may have nuclear, chemical, or biological weapons -- such as Iran, Iraq, India, and Pakistan -- ring Russia's southern flanks. With its weakened conventional forces, Russia may believe it needs to demonstrate to these countries that it retains the ability and intent, with its nuclear forces, to counter their possible use of weapons of mass destruction.

NATO's plans to add new members from Central Europe also worries many in Russia. Not only have these plans renewed some Russia's historic fear of encirclement, they also have raised concerns about a change in the balance of power -- to Russia's disadvantage. Many fear that NATO will move advanced weapons and technology to the borders of Russian territory, and that NATO's new members will offer basing rights to the United States. Some in Russia also believe that NATO's enlargement will isolate Russia. In December 1995, Dr. Alexander Konovalov, Director of Moscow's Center for Military Policy and Systems Analysis, stated, "The West is taking advantage of Russia's current weakness to gain the most favorable strategic position for further confrontation."[10] Such sentiment goes a long way in casting NATO's conventional strength in a threatening light and pushing Russia toward adopting a flexible response policy similar to NATO in the 1950s. Namely, because Russia cannot match NATO's conventional forces with its own, it may view nuclear weapons as a more likely means of deterrence and response.

Russia also sees U.S. development of theater missile defenses as a provocation because it believes these systems could undermine strategic stability.

---

[9] Mathers, Jennifer G. Deja Vu: Familiar Trends in Russian Strategic Thought, *Contemporary Security Policy*, v. 16, December 1995, p. 390.

[10] Ulbrich, Jeffrey. NATO Expansion Threatens to Isolate Russia: East Bloc Nations Want In, *Washington Times*, September 19, 1995, p. A12.

Many are convinced that an advanced theater missile defense system, like the Theater High Altitude Area Defense (THAAD), could protect large areas of the United States. This would undermine Russia's confidence in its ability to launch a devastating attack after absorbing a first strike.[11] Perhaps more disturbing to Russia is the chance that the United States might be more prone to initiating an attack if it believed its troops or territory could be shielded from a retaliatory strike.

Russia may also view Chinese military modernization efforts as a potential growing threat.[12] The pace and direction of Chinese modernization efforts, particularly in aircraft and missiles, could threaten Russia should relations between the two countries sour.[13] As a result, Russia may eventually have to decide if the benefits of arms trade with China to generate cash outweigh the growing military power of a neighbor.

Russia's Conventional Forces

The weakened state of Russian conventional forces may also influence Russia's nuclear strategy. Russia's Army faces severe problems that have already greatly diminished its combat-readiness and overall capability to function. Plagued by severe personnel and housing shortages, discipline problems, and rampant corruption, morale is unsurprisingly low.[14] But Russia cannot now afford the high defense expenditures needed to correct the problems. Current levels of defense spending, which equal approximately 3.4% of Russia's GDP, have produced frequent and chronic underfunding of the defense establishment.[15] Projections for future defense spending mark 5.4% of GDP

---

[11] Mendelsohn, Jack. START II & Beyond, *Arms Control Today*, October 1996, p. 4.

[12] Steady increases in Chinese military expenditures since 1986 have resulted in an official military budget reaching $7.5 billion in 1995-96 or 9.9% of China's total state expenditures. See Shambaugh, David. China's Military: Real or Paper Tiger? *Washington Quarterly*, v. 19, Spring 1996, p. 21.

[13] Some believe Russia may be causing its own problems by selling military hardware to China. For example, in 1991, China purchased 48 Su-27 fighters from Russia (with a follow-on order placed in April 1996) and more recently ordered 4 Kilo class submarines (with future expectations of acquiring an additional twelve). See, Bluth, Christopher. Beijing's Attitude to Arms Control, *Jane's Intelligence Review*, July 1996, p. 330. See, also, U.S. Library of Congress. Congressional Research Service. *Russia-Chinese Cooperation: Prospects and Implications*. CRS Report 97-185 F. by Stuart D. Goldman and Robert G. Sutter. January 27, 1997.

[14] Slagle, New Russian Military Doctrine, p. 89.

[15] FBIS Daily Report, "Russia: Economic Side of Defense Industry, Military Reforms," FBIS-UMA-96-216-S, October 17, 1996.

as a realistic goal, but Russia will not reach this level at least until the year 2000.[16]

Many in Russia recognize the need to restructure and reform the military to maintain its combat capabilities. Officials have announced a plan for reform, but there are no assurances that they will follow through. This plan contains two stages. Stage I, which would occur from 1997-2000, envisions a 30% reduction of the armed forces, to 1.2 million troops, and the development of a unified command and control system. During Stage II, between 2000 and 2005, Russia would shift toward a professional army of contract serviceman (rather than conscripts) and trained reserve units.[17]

Russia hopes these structural changes will create a highly capable and mobile army. Until then, however, nuclear weapons will assume an enhanced deterrent role for Russia. Although these forces also suffer from funding shortfalls, they remain more coherent and cohesive than Russia's conventional forces. The commander of Russia's Strategic Rocket Forces, Army General Igor Sergeyev, stated in December 1996 that the rocket forces have maintained their combat readiness and continue to perfect their skills at launching intercontinental ballistic missiles.[18]

RUSSIA'S NUCLEAR FORCE STRUCTURE

INITIATIVES INHERITED FROM THE SOVIET UNION

Withdrawals and Reductions of Nonstrategic Nuclear Weapons

During the Cold War, the Soviet Union deployed thousands of tactical nuclear weapons in the Warsaw Pact nations of Eastern Europe and in republics outside Russia.[19] The Soviet Union had moved most of these weapons to facilities on Russian territory prior to the end of 1991. Hence, by the latter half

---

[16] "Russia: Economic Side of Defense Industry, Military Reforms," Translated in FBIS, October 17, 1996.

[17] FBIS Daily Report, "Russia: Paper Sketches Main Provisions of New Defense Doctrine," FBIS-SOV-96-242, December 16, 1996.

[18] FBIS Daily Report, "Russia: Commander on Combat Readiness, Future Prospects," FBIS-SOV-96-243, December 16, 1996.

[19] NRDC Nuclear Notebook. Estimated Russian Stockpile, End of 1996. *The Bulletin of the Atomic Scientists*, March/April 1996. v. 53, p. 63.

of 1991, Belarus, Ukraine, and Kazakhstan were the only non-Russian former Soviet republics with nuclear weapons on their territories.[20]

Responding to a U.S. initiative,[21] President Gorbachev announced in October 1991 that the Soviet Union would withdraw all land-based and sea-based non-strategic weapons (those with ranges of less than 360 miles) from deployment and place them in storage areas in Russia.[22] Although official estimates remain classified, many U.S. experts calculated that these initiatives could affect several thousand nuclear warheads in the Soviet Union. After the Soviet Union collapsed, the other former Soviet republics continued to transfer non-strategic nuclear weapons to Russia. According to officials in Russia and the other former republics, all of the warheads for land-based systems had been returned to Russia by July 1992 and all sea-based tactical nuclear weapons had been removed from operation by mid-1993.[23]

Russian officials contend that they have begun to dismantle warheads removed from these nonstrategic nuclear weapons and that they can do so at a rate of 2,000 warheads each year. The United States has little direct evidence to support Russia's claims because U.S. officials have not observed the dismantlement process. Nevertheless, some have stated that Russia's force of nonstrategic nuclear weapons may have declined by more than 25% from its peak of around 25,000 warheads in the late 1980s.[24] In addition, Russia has consolidated its storage facilities for the remaining warheads for land-based

---

[20] U.S. Library of Congress. Congressional Research Service. *Nuclear Weapons in the Former Soviet Union: Location, Command and Control*, CRS Issue Brief 91144, by Amy F. Woolf, Updated Regularly.

[21] On September 21, 1991, President Bush announced that the United States would withdraw all its land-based and sea-based tactical nuclear weapons (those with ranges of less than 360 miles) from bases outside the United States. He noted that these withdrawals were not dependent on Soviet reciprocity. But he suggested that Soviet President Gorbachev take similar steps, in part to remove nuclear weapons from regions where independence movements or political unrest raised questions about the safety and security of Soviet nuclear weapons. See "The Peace Dividend I Seek Is Not Measured in Dollars," Text of Presidential Address, *Washington Post*, September 28, 1991. p. A23 and The White House, Office of the Press Secretary. Presidential Initiative on Nuclear Arms; Fact Sheet. September 27, 1991.

[22] Gorbachev Announces Wide Arms Reductions in Response to Bush. *Washington Post*. October 6, 1991. p. A1.

[23] Congressional Research Service. *Nuclear Weapons in the Former Soviet Union: Location, Command and Control*, IB91144, updated regularly.

[24] Russian Defense Budget Continues Downward Spiral, Says CIA, DIA. *Arms Control Today*, v. 24, September 1994. p. 27.

nonstrategic nuclear weapons, reducing these facilities from more than 600 to perhaps less than 100 locations.[25]

Many in the United States remain concerned about the safety and security of Russia's warheads from nonstrategic nuclear weapons, so U.S. officials have urged Russia to further consolidate its storage infrastructure. In addition, some storage facilities for these weapons remain close enough to operational bases for Russia to return some of these weapons to deployment if it believed they would be needed in a conflict. Such an option would be consistent with Russia's growing emphasis on nuclear deterrence in regional contingencies.

Reductions in Strategic Nuclear Weapons

Russia has reduced the Soviet Union's strategic nuclear forces while implementing the 1991 Strategic Arms Reduction Treaty (START I).[26] The table below summarizes the changes that have occurred in those weapons that count under the START I treaty. By mid-1996, Russia had destroyed more than 430 ICBM launchers, 275 SLBM launchers, and 40 bombers to comply with START I. And it had removed from service hundreds more warheads by deactivating weapons in Ukraine and Russia. These weapons still count under START I, and, therefore, appear on the table below, because the launchers have not been destroyed according to treaty procedures. Subtracting them out of the totals in the table would leave Russia with fewer than 6,000 warheads deployed on its operational strategic offensive forces. This compares with the more than 11,000 warheads on Soviet forces before START I entered into force.

Table 1: START I Reductions in Soviet Strategic Nuclear Weapons

	September 1990		January 1997	
	Launchers	Warheads	Launchers	Warheads
ICBMs	1,398	6,612	877	4,574
SLBMs	940	2,804	664	2,496
Bombers	162	1,776	123	914
Total	2,500	11,192	1,664	7,984

Source: U.S. Arms Control and Disarmament Agency, Arms Control Association

In addition, Belarus, Kazakhstan, and Ukraine have all returned to Russia the nuclear warheads that were on their territories after the collapse of the

---

[25] Estimated Russian Stockpile, End of 1996. *The Bulletin of the Atomic Scientists, March/April 1996*. v. 53, p. 64.

[26] For details on the provisions in this treaty see, U.S. Library of Congress, Congressional Research Service, *The START I and START II Arms Control Treaties: Background and Issues*, by Amy F. Woolf. June 30, 1993.

Soviet Union. Belarus returned 81 SS-25 ICBMs and their warheads to Russia by late November 1996. Kazakhstan had returned all 370 bomber weapons and 1,040 warheads from the SS-18 ICBMs on its territory by May 1995, and had destroyed all the silos on its territory by September 1996. Ukraine completed the removal of all the nuclear warheads from its territory by June 1, 1996; it has begun to destroy the silos on its territory. Russia also plans to buy back 19 Blackjack bombers and 25 Bear H bombers currently based in Ukraine.[27]

NUCLEAR MODERNIZATION PROGRAMS

Modernization During the Soviet Era

During the 1970s and 1980s, the Soviet Union consistently added to the quantity and quality of its strategic offensive nuclear weapons. It simultaneously produced several different ICBMs, SLBMs, and ballistic missile submarines and introduced improved versions of its missiles every few years. The United States, in contrast, produced only one or two new missile types at a time and would then deploy each system for at least 20 years before introducing a new system to replace aging weapons.

There are several possible explanations for the vigorous weapons modernization programs in the Soviet Union. First, there are the "arms race" explanations. The Soviet emphasis on weapons modernization may have reflected Soviet efforts to achieve first, parity, then superiority, over the United States in terms of the numbers of warheads deployed on its strategic offensive forces. Second, some Soviet modernization may have been driven by "bureaucratic" factors. The Soviet Union may have produced several types of missiles simultaneously because it had several missile design bureaus working on new missiles at the same time. It did not require any competition or selection among the design bureaus. The United States, in contrast, customarily requests that several defense contractors offer designs for new missiles, but then "down selects" to one contractor who produces a single system for the U.S. force.

In addition, the Soviet Union may have introduced new missiles into the force before they carried the most advanced technologies, then modified the missiles to accommodate new technologies when they became available. The United States, in contrast, designs its missiles to take advantage of the most advanced technologies available, and therefore, has less need for later modifications. Finally, some have noted that the Soviet Union never expected its missiles to last for 20-30 years, as the United States does, but, instead,

---

[27] Negotiations on this sale have not reached a conclusion. As a result, the aircraft remain at bases in Ukraine. According to press reports, they have not received enough maintenance to remain fully operational. See Colonel General Volodymyr Antonets Believes That the Question of the Transfer of Strategic Bombers to Moscow Must Be Decided Not by the Military but by Politicians. Nezavisimoye Voyennoye Obozreniye, Moscow, February 15, 1997. Translated in FBIS-SOV-97-035.

designed them knowing that they would be replaced by a modified or new missile within 10 years of their initial deployment.

Recent Changes in Modernization Programs

By the time the Soviet Union collapsed in 1991, economic pressures and the improving relationship with the United States had combined to slow the Soviet Union's nuclear modernization efforts. In October 1991, Soviet President Gorbachev announced that he planned to curtail or cancel several nuclear weapons programs.[28] He announced that the Soviet Union would forgo the deployment of additional rail-mobile ICBM launchers and that it would not modernize the SS-24 ICBMs that were already deployed on 46 of these systems. He also announced that the Soviet Union would cancel the modernization program for its SS-25 road-mobile ICBM. However, as is discussed below, the Soviet Union and Russia have proceeded with the production of a new single warhead silo-based ICBM that may also replace existing mobile SS-25 ICBMs.

Russian President Yeltsin also canceled some programs in 1992. He stated that Russia would cease production of new Bear H and Blackjack bombers. He also announced that Russia would cancel production of a new long-range sea-launched cruise missile and long-range air-launched cruise missile.[29] Russia has not, however, completely ceased to modernize its nuclear forces. It continues to produce a new single-warhead ICBM and to design a new SLBM, a new class of ballistic missile submarines, and some new bomber weapons. According to recent press reports, it has also continued to construct underground subways and command posts that its leadership could try to use to survive attack and to command its forces in the event of a nuclear war.[30]

Russia's Ongoing Nuclear Modernization Programs

ICBM Modernization

Russia is currently producing a new, single warhead ICBM. This missile, known as the Topol-M in Russia and the SS-27 in the United States, is a follow-on to the SS-25 road-mobile ICBM (known as the Topol in Russia). The new missile will resemble the older version with its three-stage, solid fuel design. It

---

28 As with the withdrawal of nonstrategic nuclear forces, this announcement responded to a similar initiative by U.S. President Bush. In September, President Bush announced that the United States would cancel its mobile launcher programs for two new ICBMs and that it would cancel plans to modernize its air-launched short-range attack missile.

29 Duncan, Andrew. Russian forces in decline - Part 5. *Jane's Intelligence Review, v. 9*, January 1997. p. 14.

30 Gertz, Bill. Moscow Builds Bunkers Against Nuclear Attack. *Washington Times*, April 1, 1997. p. 1. See also, Expert Says Report on Secret Bunkers in Moscow Partially True. Interfax. April 3, 1997.

will have a throwweight of 1,200 kilograms and a range of more than 10,000 kilometers when equipped with a single nuclear warhead.[31] With its size and reported throwweight, the missile probably could be equipped to carry 3 or 4 warheads without losing the ability to strike at intercontinental range. The new missile may also be more robust than its predecessor, with major overhauls needed after 15, rather than 10 years.[32] Russia is designing the missile for deployment in fixed ICBM silos, such as those that currently hold SS-18 and SS-19 ICBMs, but it might also produce a road-mobile version in the future.[33]

Russia conducted its first successful flight test of the new Topol-M ICBM in December 1994, its second in September 1995, and its third in July 1996. According to Russian officials, each of these tests demonstrated the capabilities of the new missile system.[34] However, financial pressures may have altered the plans for the Topol-M. In recent years, the program may have received only one-third of the funds needed for development and flight testing. Some sources indicate that Russia had initially planned to conduct around 20 flight tests in 1995 and 1996, but had only completed one each year. Although Russian officials seem pleased with the results of these tests, they may be insufficient to offer high levels of confidence in the system. In addition, Russia had initially announced that the Topol-M would begin deployment in late 1996, and that 10 missiles would be operational by the end of 1997. But the chief of the Strategic Rocket Forces, General Sergeyev, has stated that the missile may experience problems "with its development rates due to insufficient and uneven financing."[35] As a result, the initial deployment has now slipped until later in 1997, in part because construction at missile deployment sites was behind schedule.[36] And, with production rates as low as 12 missiles per year, Russia may take several years to deploy a significant number of these ICBMs.[37]

---

[31] Litovkin, Viktor. Nonetheless We are Making Missiles! Details of New "Topol-M" Missile System. Moscow, *Izvestia*. January 20, 1995.

[32] Handler, Joshua. The Future of Russian Strategic Forces. *Jane's Intelligence Review*, v. 7, April 1995. p. 163.

[33] Litovkin, Viktor. Nonetheless We are Making Missiles! Details of New "Topol-M" Missile System. Moscow, *Izvestia*. January 20, 1995.

[34] Yurkin, Anatoliy. Russia: Officials Comment on Test of Intercontinental Missile. Moscow, ITAR-TASS. July 25, 1996. Translated in FBIS-TAC-96-009.

[35] Dzhibuti, Vitaliy. A Superpower's Final Attribute: New-Generation Missiles Will Go on Alert Status Before Year's End. Interfax. March 17, 1997. Translated in FBIS-SOV-97-076.

[36] Yudin, Pyotr. Moscow Budget Squeeze May Stall New Nuke Missile. *Defense News*, v. 11, August 19-25, 1996. p. 1.

[37] Estimated Russian Stockpile, End of 1996. *The Bulletin of the Atomic Scientists*, March/April 1996. v. 53, p. 62.

SLBM and SSBN Modernization

Russia reportedly has several programs in place to modernize the sea-based leg of its strategic triad. First, it is developing a new ballistic missile for deployment on its existing Typhoon submarines. At least two of the six Typhoons in the fleet are currently in shipyards where they will be fitted with the new missile, and all six may have been scheduled for this modification.[38] Russia has apparently made little progress with this program, however and some reports indicate that it may have cut off all funding for overhauls and upgrades so that it can focus its resources on submarine operations and new construction.[39] As a result, several reports cite rumors that the overhaul program for the Typhoon submarines may stall and at least two of these submarines may be retired during the next ten years.[40]

Second, in late October 1996, Russia laid the keel for the first boat in a new class of ballistic missile submarines. This is the first new ballistic missile submarine to begin construction in Russia (or the Soviet Union) in over ten years and, when completed, it will be the first new submarine to enter the fleet since 1990. Russia is also reportedly developing a new ballistic missile for this new class of submarines.[41]

Russian sources report that the new submarines will be larger than current 16-missile Delta IV submarines but smaller than the 20-missile Typhoon submarines. Russia plans to complete construction of this first boat by 2002-2003 and some reports indicate it may construct 10 or 12 submarines in this class by the year 2010.[42] Others, however, doubt that this program is feasible. In late 1996, workers at the shipyard went on strike to protest unpaid wages

---

[38] Handler, Joshua. The Future of Russian Strategic Forces. *Jane's Intelligence Review*, v. 7, April 1995. p. 163.

[39] Pengelley, Rupert. Grappling for Submarine Supremacy. *Jane's International Defense Review*, v. 7, September, 1996. p. 49.

[40] Estimated Russian Stockpile, September 1996. *The Bulletin of the Atomic Scientists*. September/October 1996, p. 62. See also, Sutyagin, Igor. Sharks of Strategic Designation. *Submarine Review*, October 1995, p. 78; and Handler, The Future of Russian Strategic Forces. p. 165.

[41] Russian Stockpile, End of 1996. *The Bulletin of the Atomic Scientists*, March/April 1996. v. 53, p. 62.

[42] Litovkin, Viktor. The Nuclear Submarine that Luzhkov and Chubays Are Going To Board Will Surface in the 21st Century. Russia Prepares for Construction of New Class of Submarines. Moscow, *Izvestia*. October 25, 1996. Translated in FBIS-TAC-96-010.

and, according to some in Russia, it could take 50 years to finish even the first submarine if funding levels do not improve.[43]

Bombers and Bomber Weapons

Russia may also need to modernize its bomber fleet if it wants to retain a bomber component for its strategic forces. At the present time, most of the Soviet Union's Blackjack bombers and many Bear H bombers remain at bases in Ukraine. Russia and Ukraine have been negotiating a sale of these aircraft back to Russia, but they have been unable to agree on the terms of a deal.[44] If Russia eventually recovers these aircraft, it may lack the spare parts and maintenance funds needed to return them to service.[45] Blackjack bombers have long been plagued by maintenance and operational problems, and only six aircraft are currently operational in Russia.[46] As a result, according to press reports, Russia is developing a new long-range bomber to bolster its force in the 2005-2010 timeframe. In the meantime, it may upgrade the Bear and Blackjack bombers by deploying a new non-nuclear cruise missile.[47] This program might enhance the conventional capabilities of Russia's aircraft, and could be a response to Russia's new emphasis on regional conflict and to the lessons learned by watching U.S. bombers in the Persian Gulf War.

Reports indicate that Russia is also developing a new medium-range bomber to replace the Air Force version of the medium-range Backfire bomber. The Navy has already retired its older Backfires, but the Air Force may upgrade those in its fleet while it awaits delivery of the new aircraft.[48] If funding is tight, Russia may place a higher priority on this aircraft than on the long-range

---

[43] Defense Workers Protest at Russian Wage Delays. Reuters, September 19, 1996. See also, Gavrilenko, Andrey. Yuriy Dolgorukiy Would Not Have Approved. At No Other Time in the 20th Century Has Russia Been Building So Few Ships. February 12, 1997. Translated in FBIS-SOV-97-031.

[44] Colonel General Volodymyr Antonets Believes That the Question of the Transfer of Strategic Bombers to Moscow Must Be Decided Not by the Military but by Politicians. Nezavisimoye Voyennoye Obozreniye, Moscow, February 15, 1997. Translated in FBIS-SOV-97-035.

[45] NRDC Nuclear Notebook. Russian (C.I.S.) Strategic Nuclear Forces, End of 1995. *Bulletin of the Atomic Scientists*, March/April 1996. p. 63.

[46] Comments attributed to Petr Deynekin, Commander-in-Chief of the Russian Air Force. Feature examines role of strategic aviation. Vesti newscast, Moscow Russian Television Network, April 5, 1997. Translated in FBIS-UMA-97-095

[47] Butowski, Piotr. Russia's Air Force Looks Beyond 2000. *Jane's Defense Weekly*, January 17, 1996. p. 29. See, also, NRDC Nuclear Notebook. Estimated Russian Stockpile, September 1996. *The Bulletin of the Atomic Scientists*. September/October 1996, p. 62.

[48] Butowski. Russia's Air Force Looks Beyond 2000. p. 29-30.

bomber because bombers have never played a significant role in Russian or Soviet nuclear forces. As a result, Russia may believe that the medium-range bomber would be better suited to the regional threats highlighted in Russia's recent military plans.

Deep Underground Command and Control Facilities

Russia continues to construct deep underground facilities that could protect its leadership during a nuclear conflict. The Soviet Union initiated many of these projects in the 1970s and 1980s, and Russia has proceeded with them in spite of their high costs and financial constraints in Russia's economy. One project, a huge underground military complex, is reportedly located at Yamanatau in the Ural Mountains. Neither Russian nor U.S. officials have specified that this facility is a command and control center, but it could serve that purpose because it would be able to withstand a nuclear attack.[49] Recent reports indicate that Russia has also continued to construct "a nuclear-survivable, strategic command post" at Kosvinsky Mountain; this may be the site where Russian officials would gather to implement Russia's nuclear employment plans. Russia may also be upgrading and expanding a dedicated subway system in Moscow that would evacuate leaders from the city to two bunkers, at Voronovo and Sharpovo, that are about 35-45 miles outside Moscow.[50]

Officials in the Clinton Administration do not believe these programs threaten the United States.[51] They note that money spent on these projects is not spent on offensive forces, which would pose a direct threat. They also point out that the United States has pursued its own programs to ensure "continuity of government" during a nuclear crisis. Additionally, the Administration has stated that these programs are not new and have not accelerated in the past few years. Russia may simply be completing efforts begun in the past, even if the need for the projects has diminished.

Some analysts, however, believe that Russia's continuing efforts to build defensive bunkers for leadership and command and control do pose a threat to the United States because they indicate that Russia continues to believe it might need to fight and win a nuclear war with the United States.[52] They also

---

[49] Gordon, Michael R. Despite Cold War's End, Russia Keeps Building a Secret Complex. *New York Times*, April 16, 1996. p. 1.

[50] Gertz, Moscow Builds Bunkers Against Nuclear Attack. *Washington Times*, April 1, 1997; and Expert Says Report on Secret Bunkers in Moscow Partially True. Interfax. April 3, 1997.

[51] See, for example, the comments of Kenneth H. Bacon, Assistant Secretary of Defense for Public Affairs. DOD News Briefing, April 1, 1997.

[52] See the comments of Peter Pry in Gertz, Bill. Moscow Builds Bunkers Against Nuclear Attack. See also, Expert Says Report on Secret Bunkers in Moscow Partially True. Interfax. April 3, 1997.

believe that these projects show a misuse of scarce resources, given Russia's current economic condition, and argue that these resources would be better used to dismantle nuclear weapons and improve security at nuclear storage facilities.

Future Prospects For Russia's Modernization Programs

Although Russia continues to design and produce new strategic offensive nuclear weapons, most experts agree that these efforts differ sharply from those of the Soviet Union. It is pursuing a much smaller number of simultaneous programs than did the Soviet Union and each program is proceeding at a much slower pace than did Soviet modernization efforts.[53] For example, in 1991, the Soviet Union reportedly produced 175 strategic ballistic missiles. Between 1992 and 1993, the production rate for strategic ballistic missiles dropped by 50 percent, from around 70 to 35 total missiles. Some estimates indicate that Russia may now be producing fewer than a dozen new ICBMs each year.[54]

Although the improving relationship between the United States and Russia may have contributed to some of the slowdown in modernization, Russia's lack of economic resources is probably also a significant factor. Insufficient funding has already slowed the Topol-M ICBM modernization program and could impede Russia's efforts to construct new ballistic missile submarines. Russia may, however, continue to modernize its strategic offensive weapons, in spite of its economic difficulties. As was noted above, until Russia has the means to reform and modernize its conventional forces, it has placed a greater emphasis on nuclear deterrence in its military strategy. Hence, Russia may view these programs as essential to its efforts to maintain its superpower status and protect its national security.

NUCLEAR WEAPONS MAINTENANCE AND OPERATIONS

To remain confident in the reliability of its nuclear forces, Russia must maintain, test and train with the weapons in its arsenal. But reports in both the Russian and U.S. press paint contradictory pictures of the quality of Russia's nuclear forces. On the one hand, Russia has continued to test its

---

[53] For example, General Eugene Habinger, Commander in Chief of the U.S. Strategic Command, stated "Ten years ago, if I were to list all the emerging strategic systems that the Russians were developing, there would be column after column after column. Today there are four systems. One of the four is doing well. The other three are not." See Aging weapons alone will prompt Duma's okay of START II: General. *Aerospace Daily*. v. 181, August 30 1996. p. 324. See also, the testimony of Walter B. Slocombe, Undersecretary of Defense for Policy, before the International Security, Proliferation and Federal Services Subcommittee of the Senate Governmental Affairs Committee. Hearing on the Future of Nuclear Deterrence. The Federal Document Clearing House, Transcript, February 12, 1997.

[54] Handler, Joshua. Working Paper on The Future of Russian Strategic Forces. Greenpeace. February 16, 1995. p. 2. See, also, Russian Defense Budget Continues Downward Spiral, Says CIA, DIA. *Arms Control Today*, v. 24, September 1994, p. 27.

nuclear weapons systems and to train the forces that operate these systems. On the other hand, many officials in Russia have complained that insufficient financing has led to low morale among the troops and lower than necessary levels of training and maintenance for the forces. Over time, these factors could undermine the effectiveness of Russia's nuclear forces.

Ongoing Tests and Training

In 1996 and early 1997, Russia conducted several tests of older weapons in its force structure. On June 6, 1996, Russia conducted a flight test of its 6-warhead SS-19 ICBM. Around 100 of these missiles may remain in Russia's force under the START II Treaty. Even so, it is important to note these missiles entered the Soviet force structure in the 1970s and may be reaching the end of their expected service lives. As a result, Russia used the flight test to evaluate the tactical and technical characteristics of this type of missile and to determine if its life could be extended past the year 2003. Russian officials announced that the test proved the missile remained reliable.[55] In late November 1996, Russia test-fired a 10-warhead SS-24 ICBM from a rail-mobile launcher.[56] This was the first test of this type of missile in more than 6 years. And, although all SS-24 missiles would be eliminated under the START II Treaty, the test demonstrated that the missiles remain reliable and could remain in the force if the United States and Russia never implement START II. In April 1997, Russia conducted a similar flight test with a 20-year old SS-18 ICBM. This test also was designed to confirm the operational performance of an older missile and to provide information about the possibility of extending the system's life. Officials in Russia declared the test a complete success.[57] Although these missiles would be banned under the START II Treaty, some may remain in service if START II does not enter into force.

In late June 1996, Russia conducted a nuclear staff exercise that included test launches of three SLBMs from three different ballistic missile submarines. Russian officials stated that this was the first time that Russia had launched missiles simultaneously from separate submarines and that the exercise was a successful check of the submarine fleet's combat readiness.[58] The officials also noted that the exercise had tested "new methods of combat management in coordination with other kinds of strategic forces and with Russia's ballistic missile early warning system." They further stated that missiles fired in the test

---

[55] Russia Launches "Unique" Intercontinental Ballistic Missile. Interfax. June 6, 1996.

[56] Kemp, Ian. Russia: NATO expansion may prompt retargeting. *Jane's Defense Weekly*, December 4, 1996. p. 5.

[57] 20-year-old SS-18 test-fired from Baikonur. *Aerospace Daily*, v. 182, April 23, 1997. p. 134.

[58] Pacific Fleet Fires Ballistic Missiles in Nuclear Staff Exercise. Interfax. July 1, 1996.

had been in storage for a number of years, so the exercise demonstrated the continued readiness of Russia's older missile systems.[59]

Russia conducted a similar exercise in early October 1996, when its forces simultaneously launched an SS-25 ICBM, an SLBM, and two bomber-carried cruise missiles. These tests coincided with an exercise of Russia's central command and control authority; press reports stated that a signal was transmitted by satellite from Moscow to initiate the launch of all three nuclear systems. General Sergeyev, chief of the Strategic Rocket Forces, stated that the missile tests demonstrated reliability and technical readiness of his troops.[60]

In November 1996, the Strategic Missile Forces Military Council stated that its forces were capable of fulfilling their tasks. It concluded that the training and operational launches during the year had confirmed the high reliability of the missiles and command and control system and the high skills of the troops. The Council noted that all the missile flight tests were rated as excellent, 76% of units were assessed as good and the remainder were satisfactory.[61]

Russia has continued to test its strategic offensive forces during the first few months of 1997. For example, in January and February 1997, Russia conducted two separate tests of missiles launched from Delta III submarines; one of the submarines launched 2 missiles in a short time span. Officials stated that these tests were designed to verify the combat readiness of the missiles and to demonstrate that the crews retained their high level of combat training.[62] And, in March 1997, Russia launched 19 SS-N-20 SLBMs from Typhoon submarines (it had launched one missile in a similar fashion in late 1996). These tests were used to destroy the missiles, rather than to test their operational capabilities, but Russian officials also noted that these launches tested the capabilities of the Navy's forces and demonstrated the continuing reliability of the missiles.[63] This information may be useful if Russia retains Typhoon submarines under START II, but lacks the funds to backfit them with new SLBMs.

---

[59] Two SLBMs fired in Russian Fleet Exercises. *Aerospace Daily*, v. 182, July 18, 1996. p. 91.

[60] These tests were a part of on ongoing military staff exercise -- known as Redoubt-96 -- that was designed to practice Russia's management of all of its armed forces and to check on the readiness of all kinds of troops. See Russia test fires cruise missiles -- agencies. Reuters. October 3, 1996.

[61] Baychurin, Ilshat. Strategic Missile Forces Remain Russia's "Nuclear Shield". Moscow, Krasnaya Zvezda. November 16, 1996. Translated in FBIS-Sov-96-224.

[62] Russian Arctic Sub Successfully Tests Ballistic Missile, Interfax. January 15, 1997; and Russian Nuclear Sub Makes Two Successful Missile Launches, Interfax. February 5, 1997.

[63] Russian Navy destroys SS-N-20s by low-level launches. *Aerospace Daily*, v. 182, April 7, 1997. p. 40.

Concerns about Manpower and Maintenance

General Sergeyev has stated that the Strategic Rocket Troops are as ready for combat as they were 10 years ago, and that they are capable of performing all their required missions.[64] Nevertheless, he and other Russian officials have highlighted some concerns about the effects that budget constraints are having on maintenance, manpower and morale in the land-based Strategic Rocket Forces. For example, General Sergeyev and Defense Minister Rodionov have both noted that ICBM units are undermanned, so the troops must stay on their posts in launch facilities for 13-15 days per month.[65] This has allowed the troops to maintain their combat readiness, but it has increased stress and fatigue, while reducing morale within the ranks. The troops have also faced a shortage of housing and lack of pay. In addition, they have had trouble procuring spare parts and fuel needed to operate mobile systems. This has created problems with routine servicing and maintenance of weapons systems.[66] Funding shortfalls have also reduced the number of tactical drills and exercises for the forces. In addition, more than half of Russia's ICBMs have exceeded their "warrantied" service lives, and, therefore, would have been retired if new missiles were available to replace them. But many remain in the force because low funding has slowed the production of the new Topol-M ICBM that will eventually replace them.[67]

Problems with aging and inadequate financing have also affected Russia's ballistic missile submarine force. As was noted above, Russia may lack the funds to modernize and maintain its older Delta and Typhoon submarines. As a result, only one or two Typhoon submarines may be operational at the present time. In addition, in late 1996, U.S. sources reported that Russia appeared to have stopped all major maintenance work on its existing classes of submarines and that it was reducing the number of deployed submarines so that it could devote additional resources to the construction of its new class of submarines.[68] According to some sources, Russia has already withdrawn more than 35 ballistic missile submarines from its fleet.[69] These funding restrictions have also

---

[64] Commander: Strategic Missile Forces Guarantee Russian Security. Interfax. April 23, 1997.

[65] RUSSIA: Commander Says Missile Troops Guarantee of Russian Security, Interfax, December 14, 1996. Translated in FBIS-SOV-96-242.

[66] Commander: Any Conflict May Evolve into Nuclear War Today. Interfax. March 9, 1997. Translated in FBIS-TAC-97-068.

[67] Commander: Any Conflict May Evolve into Nuclear War Today. Interfax. March 9, 1997.

[68] Holzer, Robert. *Defense News*. September 9-15, 1996. p. 14.

[69] Ovcharenko, A.M. Russia's Strategic Naval Forces. *Problems and Prospects*. Moscow Vooruzheniye, Politika, Konversiya. December 26, 1996. Translated in FBIS-UMA-96-245-S.

sharply reduced the combat patrol rates for Russia's ballistic missile submarines. Most spend much of their time moored in their ports, although they can maintain their alert status and launch missiles from their bases.

Russia currently has perhaps 26 operational ballistic missile submarines.[70] Because most of these have a 25 year "warrantied" service life, only the newest Typhoon and Delta IV submarines (there are currently 6 Typhoon and 7 Delta IV submarines) may remain in service into the next decade if they receive the required maintenance.[71] Nevertheless, even if Russia constructs one new submarine each year between 2003 and 2010 -- a pace that some believe it cannot sustain -- its fleet may decline to 10-12 submarines, with only 800-1200 warheads on SLBMs, as new boats replace aging Typhoons.[72]

Finally, reports indicate that some of Russia's military bases, including those that house nuclear weapons, have been unable to pay their utility bills. In September 1995, electricity was cut at submarine bases, the Plesetsk ICBM test site, and Moscow's central command and control center for the Strategic Rocket Forces. In late September 1995, the Yeltsin government banned any more power cutoffs to military facilities, but the bills remain unpaid and energy disruptions continue to occur.[73]

COMMAND AND CONTROL OF NUCLEAR WEAPONS

Russia's Nuclear Command and Control System

Early Warning

Timely and accurate warning of emerging threats is the foundation of a robust, secure command and control system. Russia uses both orbiting satellites and radars and sensors located throughout its territory to monitor the possible launch of missiles towards Russian territory. This is the information that the leadership in Russia (or in the United States) would use to determine whether an attack might be underway.

---

[70] NRDC Nuclear Notebook. Estimated Russian Stockpile, End of 1996. *The Bulletin of the Atomic Scientists*, v. 53, May/June 1997. p. 62.

[71] Ovcharenko. Russia's Strategic Naval Forces. *Problems and Prospects*. December 26, 1996.

[72] Maslyukov, Yuriy Dmitriyevich. Chairman of the Duma Committee on Economic Policy. Degradation of Russia's Nuclear Forces: This alarming Process Must be Kept in Mind Constantly in Discussing the Fate of the START II Treaty. Moscow, Nezavisimoye Voyennoye Obozreniye. February 5, 1997. Translated in FBIS-UMA-97-025-S.

[73] Emergency at Russian Nuclear Submarine Base Tass. Reuters, September 21, 1995. Russian Strategic Missile Troops Stationed at Plesetsk Denied Electricity Supply, Reuters, September 15, 1995. Russian Premier Bans Power Cutoffs to Military, Reuters, September 24, 1995.

High-Level Decisions

If the officers who man the early warning system detect evidence of a missile launch in the direction of Russian territory, they would notify key political and military leaders who would then decide whether Russia should prepare to launch its own nuclear weapons in response to the attack. These steps require both reliable communications channels and a clear identification of political and military leaders who will participate in the high-level decisions. Although the lines of communication include numerous transmitters, receivers, and channels -- a system known as "Kazbek" in Russia -- most analysts focus on the "nuclear suitcase" as the pinnacle of this communications structure. This is the briefcase that holds the communications set through which leaders at the highest levels would receive notice that an attack were underway, consult about the appropriate response, and transmit the codes needed to authorize the use of nuclear weapons.

According to most reports, three individuals -- the President, Boris Yeltsin; the Minister of Defense, and the Chief of the General Staff -- hold versions of the nuclear suitcase and all three would participate in the decision on whether to launch Russia's nuclear weapons.[74] Most descriptions of this process assume that the President must approve a decision to authorize the use of nuclear weapons and that the military leadership cannot initiate a strike without his concurrence. Nevertheless, some analysts believe that the military's central command post for the General Staff, at least during the Soviet era, may have had the ability to override or replace orders received from the political leadership.

The political process and participants who would authorize a nuclear response may have changed in recent years. For example, the Chief of the General Staff may have lost his access to a nuclear suitcase in the latter days of the Soviet Union, when the Chief's role in the abortive coup raised questions about the loyalty of many senior military leaders. And frequent changes in this position since 1991 may have left Russia's Chief of the General Staff out of this decision-making loop. Former Defense Minister Rodionov may also have lost his suitcase when he retired from the military and retained his government position

---

[74] Several U.S. and Russian analysts have offered descriptions of the decision-making process for nuclear authorization. They differ in their assessments of whether the President, Minister of Defense, and Chief of the General Staff would have to concur in such a decision. See, for example, Blair, Bruce. The Logic of Accidental Nuclear War. Washington, D.C., The Brookings Institution, 1993. p. 72. For a more detailed description, see also, Blair, Bruce. Global Zero Alert for Nuclear Forces. Washington, D.C., The Brookings Institution, 1995. pp 46-51. See, also, Volkov, Oleg and Vladimir Umnov. In Whose Hands is the Button?: The President Has Authorized the Premier to Carry the Nuclear Suitcase For a While. Moscow, Ogonek. September 1, 1996. Translated in FBIS-SOV-96-212-S.

as a civilian.[75] If these changes remained in place, then the Russian president would have the sole responsibility for authorizing a nuclear attack. Although such a circumstance could relieve some concerns about rogue military commanders overruling the political leadership, it could also raise concerns about nuclear control in the event of a coup or illness that removed President Yeltsin from his position of authority.

Authorizing and Enabling a Nuclear Launch

Once they decide that a nuclear response is warranted, the key political and military leaders would transmit their decision to the commanders-in-chief of the nuclear forces, who would pass that decision along to the launch officers in the field and on board submarines. According to Alexei Arbatov, the Deputy Chairman of the Duma Defense Committee and an expert on Russia's nuclear force posture, "The nuclear button transmits presidential sanction for the use of nuclear weapons to command centers where general staff officers are on duty around the clock. On receiving the coded signal, officers, using appropriate codes, determine that it was the President who sent it, rather than someone else. When the authenticity is confirmed, duty officers open safes with their own codes and send them to missile launch pads and SSBNs."[76]

The procedures and technologies employed in this process are designed to minimize the risk of a nuclear launch without the proper authorization. For example, the military commanders would only open the communications channel used to transmit the authorization for a nuclear launch *after* they had received confirmation that Russia was under attack and considering a nuclear response.[77] In essence, then, they could not communicate launch orders to officers in the field unless the President and other key officials had decided a nuclear response might be needed. Troops in the field reportedly could not launch their missiles without proper authorization because Russian systems carry permissive action links (PALs) and other technical blocking devices that preclude the launch of missiles and arming of nuclear weapons without the proper codes. In their communications to the launch crews, the commanders-in-chief of the nuclear forces would transmit the *enabling* codes needed to unlock the PALs and to arm the missiles.[78]

---

[75] Golotyuk, Yuriy. Russia's Nuclear Forces Control System Will Probably Change. Together with it, the Alignment of Forces is Changing in Top Military Leadership. Moscow, Segodnya. December 17, 1996. Translated in FBIS-SOV-96-244.

[76] Shchedrov, Oleg. Russian Nuclear Button Signals Presidential Power. Reuters, November 5, 1996.

[77] Blair, Bruce. Global Zero Alert for Nuclear Forces. p. 48.

[78] For a description of the specific launch procedures for Soviet/Russian strategic forces, see, U.S. Library of Congress, Congressional Research Service. *Nuclear Weapons in the Former Soviet Union: Location, Command and Control*. CRS Issue Brief 91144, by Amy F. Woolf, Updated Regularly. p. 10-11. See, also, De Andreis, Marco and Francesco Calogero. *The Soviet Nuclear Weapon Legacy*. Stockholm International Peace

Concerns about Russia's Command and Control System

Concerns about Russia's nuclear command and control system first surfaced during the 1991 coup and the subsequent collapse of the Soviet Union. At the time, many in the United States wondered who in the Soviet political and military leadership had the ability to authorize the use of nuclear weapons and whether a launch might occur, either by accident or at the bidding of a rogue commander, without authorization from the central command authorities in Moscow. Assurances from Moscow, in spite of the lack of hard knowledge in the West about the political and military participants in Russia's command and control system, have eased many of the early fears of accidental or unauthorized launch.

But concerns remain about the possibility that continuing financial and political pressures could eventually undermine Russia's command and control system. These were exacerbated in early 1997 when Russia's Defense Minister Rodionov noted that he was worried by "deteriorating reliability and stability in the command system of the strategic nuclear forces."[79] He said that Russia could soon pass a point when its missiles and nuclear systems would become unmanageable. In response to these concerns and at the request of President Yeltsin, Prime Minister Chernomyrdin inspected the command posts and concluded that Russia's nuclear weapons were under firm and effective command and control. But he did note that there could be long-term problems if continued shortfalls in funding stalled modernization.[80]

For some in the United States, Rodionov's statements recalled concerns about Russia's ability to maintain control over the *non-use* of its nuclear weapons; they speculated that the risk of accidental or unauthorized launch might increase.[81] Others understood Rodionov's statements as a warning that Russia might not be able to control the *use* of its nuclear weapons, i.e. that it might not have the ability to launch weapons when the central command structure authorized their use. Many saw the warning as a plea for added funds; if Rodionov raised concerns about Russia's ability to control its nuclear

---

Research Institute. 1995. pp. 32-35.

[79] Rodionov Said "Powerless" over Disintegration of Army. Moscow, Interfax, February 7, 1997. Translated in FBIS-SOV-97-026.

[80] Dolinin, Aleksandr and Aleksandr Pelts. Nuclear Shield as Firm and Reliable as Ever. Russia's Government Head Viktor Chernomyrdin Has Visited the Strategic Missile Forces Central Command Post. Krasnaya Zvezda, Moscow. February 22, 1997. Translated in FBIS-SOV-97-038.

[81] Bykov, Robert. A Nuclear Launch May Happen Accidentally. *Komsomolskaya Pravda*. March 15, 1997. See also, Threat? What Threat? *Washington Times*. October 29, 1996. p. 16.

weapons, then the military might receive a larger budget for the modernization and maintenance of its command and control system.[82]

Russia's command and control system has come under increasing financial stress in recent years. For example, Defense Minister Rodionov noted in his statements in February 1997 that many of Russia's weapons and command and control systems would need to be modernized and replaced to remain effective in the future. Other Russian observers have voiced similar concerns about aging problems in Russia's command and control system. One analyst has noted that the "Kazbek" system -- the communications network used to transmit authorization codes from the political leadership to military commanders -- has been on active duty since 1983. It originally was intended to last only 10 years, but Russia's leadership has not provided the money needed for repairs or modernization. In addition, this analyst noted that many of the scientists and engineers who designed the system have left their research institutes due to a lack of funding and salaries, so there are few people left with the knowledge needed to repair the system.[83]

Another Russian military expert has said that "Russia's strategic missile system is currently in a state of full battle readiness and is functioning effectively. However, the failure to strengthen and modernize the system could mean that early in the next century a series of components, including the information infrastructure, will be in a critical state."[84] According to one observer, this stage has already been reached in some areas. He stated that "the missile troops' biggest headache is communications, the quality of which is often only a little better than the average telephone network in Russia." Instead of investing in repairs and improvements, the troops are devoting all their resources to security and weapons maintenance.[85]

Some have also focussed on weaknesses in Russia's early warning network. For example, Defense Minister Rodionov noted that the early warning system had deteriorated due to a shortage of new satellites needed to track an adversary's nuclear force. He stated that this had led to gaps in coverage that lasted several hours each day.[86] Others have also highlighted holes in Russia's

---

[82] Gertz, Bill. Rodionov's Armageddon talk chalked up to angling for funds. *Washington Times*. February 8, 1997. p. 2. See also, Diamond, John. U.S. unable to assess status of Russia's nuclear weapons. Associated Press. April 29, 1997.

[83] Umnov, Vladimir. Who Will Repair the "Nuclear Suitcase"? Moscow, Ogonek. March 1, 1997. Translated in FBIS-SOV-97-060.

[84] Russian PM to Visit Strategic Rocketry Central Command Post. Interfax. February 19, 1997.

[85] Security at Ivanovo Nuclear Missile Base Examined. Vremya. February 15, 1997. Translated in FBIS-SOV-97-032.

[86] Rodionov Said "Powerless" over Disintegration of Army. Interfax, February 7, 1997.

ground-based early warning radars and space-based satellites, both because many had exceeded their "warrantied service life" without receiving the funds needed for modernization and because funds did not exist to produce and deploy new systems.[87] In addition, after the breakup of the Soviet Union, some radar stations, such as the Skrunda radar in Latvia, ended up outside Russia's territory in other former Soviet republics. This reduces Russia's control over their operations, maintenance, and modernization.[88]

Finally, political instability could undermine confidence in the security and reliability of Russia's nuclear command and control structure. This issue received a significant amount of attention in late 1996, when President Yeltsin prepared to undergo heart bypass surgery. At the time, it was not clear who would assume responsibility for the President's nuclear suitcase while he was under anesthesia. In the United States, such a responsibility would fall on the Vice President, first, then on other officials outlined in the line of succession to the President. But Russia does not have a similar line of succession. The Russian constitution states that the Prime Minister would become acting President if the President died or were incapacitated, but he would have to call a new presidential election within 90 days. It is not clear whether he would gain authority over the nuclear suitcase as acting President. As a result, shortly before his surgery, President Yeltsin signed a decree that passed authority for the nuclear suitcase to Prime Minister Chernomyrdin for the time when the President was under anesthesia. Russia still lacks a formal transfer protocol for nuclear authority if the President dies or becomes incapacitated.

IMPLICATIONS

At first glance, it may appear that the declining quantity and quality of Russia's nuclear forces and the weaknesses in its command and control network could contribute to a further reduction in the threat of nuclear war. If Russia cannot rely on its ability to detect a nuclear attack on its territory, identify the appropriate leaders who will assess that attack and develop a response, communicate a decision to respond with nuclear weapons to its forces in the field, and, finally execute those orders by launching its nuclear forces, then it might reduce its reliance on nuclear weapons as a guarantor of national security. Or, knowing about these weaknesses in Russia's nuclear forces, an adversary may alter its assessment of the likelihood that Russia could or would respond with nuclear weapons if attacked.

---

[87] See, for example, Maslyukov, Yuriy Dmitriyevich. Chairman of the Duma Committee on Economic Policy. Degradation of Russia's Nuclear Forces: This alarming Process Must be Kept in Mind Constantly in Discussing the Fate of the START II Treaty. Moscow, Nezavisimoye Voyennoye Obozreniye. February 5, 1997. Translated in FBIS-UMA-97-025-S.

[88] Security at Ivanovo Nuclear Missile Base Examined. February 15, 1997.

But this scenario presumes that Russia will accept the decline in its nuclear deterrent without taking any steps to compensate for its weakness, a prospect that is by no means assured. While it is unlikely that Russia would be able to allocate sufficient sums of money in the near term to reverse this decline, it could seek other solutions to counteract the effects described above. Some of these solutions could weaken central control over Russia's nuclear weapons, increase the possibility of an unintended or unauthorized use of nuclear weapons, and increase the threat to U.S. national security.

For example, weaknesses in Russia's early warning network, such as the gaps in radar and satellite coverage, could reduce Russia's ability to identify and characterize potentially threatening events. In the current environment, with the improved relationship between the United States and Russia, it is extremely unlikely that Russia would face a coordinated nuclear attack. But it is possible that Russia might think that nuclear missiles were heading its way if it were unable to identify the source of an object in space or to accurately track the trajectory of a missile.[89] Under such a circumstance, Russia could choose not to respond to warnings unless it was certain the incident was a nuclear attack, or it could choose to respond to all warnings where the threat might be a nuclear attack. In the second case, Russia might raise its nuclear alert on the basis of incomplete information about a benign event. This type of response could result in an unintended escalation of alert rates between the United States and Russia and, possibly, an increased risk of nuclear launch.

Similarly, the age and technical limits of Russia's communications system could lead Russia to take steps that might weaken central control over nuclear weapons. As communications links age and wear out, Russian leaders might not be certain that troops in the field could receive the messages that would authorize the use of nuclear weapons and provide the enabling codes needed to launch those systems. Consequently, the central command authority could choose to disperse some of the needed codes during peacetime to relieve the pressure on the communications system during a crisis. This type of response would remove some of the safeguards against an unauthorized launch because the commanders in the field would need less information from the central authorities to employ their weapons. Hence, although these steps might increase the likelihood that a launch would occur when intended, it might also make it easier for commanders in the field to employ nuclear weapons without receiving proper or complete authorization from central authorities.[90]

---

[89] This may have happened in 1995, after the launch of the Norwegian scientific rocket triggered a false alarm in Russia's early warning system. See, Blair, Bruce G. *Global Zero Alert for Nuclear Forces*. p. 47.

[90] In 1996, press reports indicated that the U.S. Central Intelligence Agency expressed concerns in 1991 about the possibility that some of these changes might have already occurred and that the commanders of the Strategic Rocket Forces and commanders on Russia's submarines may have acquired the ability to launch their missiles without receiving authorization from central political authorities. See Threat? What Threat? *Washington Times*, October 29, 1996. p. 16

The lack of clarity in Russia's political line of succession could also undermine confidence in central control over nuclear weapons. Because the nuclear suitcase serves as a symbol of political power and authority, the death or incapacitation of the President could generate an ad hoc scramble for power and control. Alternatively, without a clear civilian successor, control of Russia's nuclear weapons could fall to the military, without direction from the nation's political leadership. In either case, the risk of the an unintended nuclear attack might increase if the resulting struggle for power produced significant levels of instability and uncertainty.

Possible U.S. Responses

These scenarios raise the question of whether and how the United States should react to the declining quality of Russia's nuclear forces and its command and control structure. For example, the United States could stand by and do nothing, hoping that Russia responded to these weaknesses by reducing its reliance on nuclear weapons. Alternatively, the United States could encourage the Russians to take steps that would strengthen central control over nuclear weapons. For example, some have suggested that the United States and Russia share early warning data from U.S. satellites and sensors to enhance Russia's ability to detect threats and to reduce the likelihood that Russia would feel compelled to respond to false or incomplete data from its own early warning network.[91]

As another alternative, some analysts have offered suggestions for steps that both sides might take to step away from the nuclear "hair-trigger" and, therefore, reduce the threat that either side would launch an intentional or unintended nuclear strike.[92] Two of these proposals include removing nuclear weapons from a high state of alert and removing and placing in storage the nuclear warheads carried by deployed missile systems.

According to those who favor this idea, the United States and Russia could relieve the pressure on the Russian command and control system if the two nations agreed to remove their deployed nuclear forces from alert status.[93] At the present time, with a significant portion of their forces on a high state of alert (i.e. the forces are postured so that they can be launched in just a few minutes), both nations place a high premium on receiving, understanding, and responding to early warning information quickly. Both sides might believe that their weapons would be destroyed before they could use them if they tried to "ride-out" an attack by the other side. Advocates of this option believe that, if

---

[91] The United State and Russia have, in the past, held preliminary discussions about this type of cooperation.

[92] See, for example, von Hippel, Frank. Paring Down the Arsenal. *The Bulletin of the Atomic Scientists*, v. 53, May/June 1997. p. 33-40. See also, Blair, Bruce G. *Global Zero Alert for Nuclear Forces*.

[93] Blair, Bruce G. *Global Zero Alert for Nuclear Forces*.

both sides removed their weapons from high alert, so that neither could launch on a moment's notice, then neither would have to fear that the other had just launched a surprise attack. And, if a surprise attack were not likely, then neither side would have to make a quick decision about how to respond. This would help the Russians address the weaknesses in their early warning satellites, because, with the reduced likelihood of a surprise attack, Russian leaders would have time to collect added data on a perceived threat before they authorized a, perhaps unnecessary, nuclear response. And it would help address weaknesses in the communications systems because the longer time available to assess and respond to threats would reduce the pressure on Russia to get messages to troops in the field quickly.

Some believe that the United States and Russia might also reduce the risks of inadvertent (and intentional) nuclear attacks if they not only removed their weapons from alert but also removed the warheads from the deployed weapons. The theory here is that it would take each side weeks or longer to put the warheads back on missiles, and, if each allowed the other to monitor activities around the warhead storage facilities, then both would have a significant amount of warning if the other sought to restore an operational missile force. While the warheads remained in storage, neither side would have to rely on early warning systems to detect missile launches from the other, because missiles would have no warheads on them, and neither would have to decide on a response or communicate with troops in the field quickly because the likelihood of a missile launch would be so low. On the other hand, many who oppose this idea have noted that it could make both the United States and Russia vulnerable to attack by terrorists or other nations with nuclear weapons. They contend that it would be far easier to destroy a nation's nuclear retaliatory force if all the warheads were concentrated in a small number of storage areas then if they were spread out on hundreds of missiles and aircraft. In addition, this type of deployment could be very destabilizing if it fueled a "rearmament race" when one or the other side detected evidence that the other had begun to restore warheads to missiles.

Hence, there is little agreement on what steps, if any, the United States should take to help Russia address the evident weaknesses in its nuclear force posture and command and control systems. Nevertheless, most experts agree that Russia will continue to experience severe economic pressures that could undermine its own confidence in the reliability of its nuclear arsenal and U.S. confidence in Russian control over those forces. For many, arms control offers a promising response. If the United States and Russia agree to reduce further the numbers of warheads on their deployed weapons systems, they might not only reduce the economic costs of maintaining and modernizing those weapons, but they might also eventually reduce their reliance on, and therefore, the threat from the remaining nuclear forces.

ARMS CONTROL AND THE FUTURE OF RUSSIA'S NUCLEAR FORCE STRUCTURE

STATUS OF ARMS CONTROL EFFORTS

The United States, Russia, Ukraine, Belarus, and Kazakhstan are all implementing the 1991 START I Treaty. This treaty requires each side to reduce its strategic offensive forces to no more than 6,000 accountable warheads on 1,600 strategic offensive delivery vehicles. Ukraine, Belarus, and Kazakhstan must eliminate all the launchers for strategic offensive delivery vehicles on their territories and return the nuclear warheads from those launchers to Russia. All the parties are required to complete the reductions mandated by this treaty by the end of the year 2001.[94]

The United States and Russia signed a second strategic arms reduction treaty, START II, in 1993. This agreement has not yet entered into force because the Russian parliament has not approved its ratification.[95] Under START II, the United States and Russia would each reduce their strategic offensive forces to between 3,000 and 3,500 deployed warheads, while eliminating completely their multiple warhead ICBMs and limiting their forces to no more than 1,750 warheads on SLBMs.[96]

The United States and Russia had initially agreed that they would reduce their forces to START II levels by the beginning of the year 2003. However, that date presumed that the treaty would enter into force shortly after it was signed in 1993. After the ratification process stalled, many in Russia argued that Russia did not have the time or money needed to eliminate hundreds of missiles and dozens of submarines in the remaining years before the treaty's deadline. As a result, during their summit meeting in Helsinki in March 1997, Presidents Clinton and Yeltsin agreed that both sides could take until the year 2007 to dismantle the ICBM launchers, submarines, and bombers eliminated by START II, as long as those systems were deactivated by the end of 2003. This change presumed that the two sides would also negotiate a third treaty, START III, that would reduce their forces to between 2,000 and 2,500 warheads on deployed strategic offensive weapons. Reductions to that level would also be completed by the end of 2007.

---

[94] For a detailed description of the provisions in this Treaty see, *The START I and START II Arms Control Treaties: Background and Issues*. CRS Report 93-617F, June 30, 1993.

[95] For a description of the Duma's concerns with START II and other issues affecting its ratification, see U.S. Library of Congress. Congressional Research Service. *START II in the Russian Duma: Issues and Prospects*. CRS Report 97-359F, by Amy F. Woolf, March 14, 1997. Washington.

[96] *The START I and START II Arms Control Treaties: Background and Issues*. CRS Report 93-617F, June 30, 1993.

ALTERNATIVE ARMS CONTROL FUTURES

The prospects for the ratification of START II and the negotiation of START III remain uncertain. The United States has long insisted, and President Yeltsin agreed in Helsinki, that negotiations on START III would not begin until START II entered into force. This position generally reflects the strong support in the United States for the START II ban on multiple warhead ICBMs. If the nations move to START III without START II in place, this ban might fall aside. But many in Russia believe that START II is a bad deal for Russia and, therefore, they support a START III treaty that would replace, not supplement, START II. This position is, in part, a reflection of dissatisfaction with the START II ban on MIRVed ICBMs and other treaty provisions that some in Russia believe favor the United States.

If this impasse remains, START I would be the only treaty limiting U.S. and Russian strategic offensive forces. In this instance, both sides could seek to keep their forces close to the levels permitted by that treaty. Alternatively, the United States and Russia could agree to reduce their forces to START II levels, even if that treaty did not enter into force, so that they could gain some of the economic benefits of smaller force structures. In this instance, they might reduce to the START II level of 3,000-3,500 warhead without abiding by the treaty provision that bans MIRVed ICBMs. On the other hand, if the impasse is broken, the two sides could complete a START III treaty that would reduce their forces to between 2,000 and 2,500 warheads by 2007. In this instance, it is likely that the ban on MIRVed ICBMs would remain in place. The remainder of this report describes each of these three alternatives in more detail.[97] In each case, the report identifies an illustrative Russian force structure and reviews the possible implications of that force for U.S. security.

START I Implementation Without Further Reductions

Under START I, the United States and Russia must reduce their strategic offensive forces to no more than 6,000 accountable warheads on 1,600 strategic offensive delivery vehicles, with no more than 4,900 warheads on their ICBMs and SLBMs. As was described above, both sides have already eliminated hundreds of ICBM and SLBM launchers and heavy bombers as they implement this treaty. Neither side has ever specified what mix of weapons it would retain in a "START I" force, in part because both expected to continue on to START II levels without stopping at a START I force. Nevertheless, Table 2, below, presents an illustrative force for each nation that would be consistent with the limits in START I.

---

97 Although it is possible that START III would enter into force without a ban on MIRVed ICBMs, this report does not assess such an outcome as likely. First, Presidents Clinton and Yeltsin linked these two treaties together during their discussions in Helsinki, so, at this time, START II remains a prerequisite to START III. Second, even if START III negotiations began without START II in place, the United States could insist that the new treaty retain the ban on MIRVed ICBMs from START II.

The first force structure in this table assumes that Russia would retain many of its older weapons systems, including 154 SS-18 ICBMs and 105 SS-19 ICBMs. It also assumes that Russia would retain 8 of its older Delta III submarines and all of the Typhoon submarines that are in need of modernization at this time. The table also assumes that Russia succeeds in buying back the bombers that are currently based in Ukraine and in providing these aircraft with the spare parts and maintenance needed to return these aircraft to service. Each of these assumptions is inconsistent with information about the age and condition of some of Russia's forces; as was discussed above, Russian officials have stated that many of the ballistic missiles have passed the end of their service lives and the bombers are not even close to operational. However, as some of Russia's recent missile tests demonstrated, Russia could possibly extend the lives of some missiles with modest investments or an acceptance of lesser reliability.

Table 2: Illustrative Russian Forces Under START I

	Retain Older Weapons		Retire Older Weapons	
ICBMs	Launchers	Warheads	Launchers	Warheads
SS-18	154	1,540 (10 RVs on each)	0	0
SS-19	105	630 (6 RVs on each)	0	0
SS-24	46	460 (10 RVs on each)	46	460 (10 RVs on each)
SS-25 SS-27	400	400 (1 RV on each)	400	1,200 (3 RVs on each)
SLBMs				
Delta III	128 (8 subs)	384 (3 RVs on each)	0	0
Delta IV	128 (8 subs)	512 (4 RVs on each)	128 (8 subs)	512 (4 RVs on each
Typhoons	120 (6 subs)	1,200 (10 RVs on each)	120 (6 subs)	1,200 (10 RVs on each
Bombers				
Bear H	85	680 (8 wpns on each)	57	456 (8 wpns on each)
Blackjack	24	192 (8 wpns on each)	6	48 (8 wpns on each)
Total	1,190	5,998	757	3,876

On the other hand, Russia may not be able to maintain this force structure for any length of time. The second force shown on Table 2 assumes that Russia eventually retires older weapons -- such as the SS-18 ICBMs, SS-19 ICBMs and Delta III SSBNs -- and abandons the bombers in Ukraine. In this case, Russia's forces would slip well below START I levels by the middle of the next decade. To offset these losses, Russia could seek to produce a new MIRVed ICBM and to accelerate production of its new class of ballistic missile submarines to replace those that it had retired. But this may not be feasible without a significant increase in resources. As was noted above, accelerating the SSBN program may not be feasible with current levels of expenditures. And Russia may need to construct a new production facility to manufacture new MIRVed ICBMs; both its SS-18 and SS-24 ICBMs were produced at a facility that is now in Ukraine. But the costs of a new production facility could be prohibitive.

Alternatively, Russia could put 3 warheads on the only ICBM currently under production, the single-warhead Topol-M (SS-27). However, because Russia has already tested this missile with one warhead, it would violate the START I treaty if it followed this approach. In addition, even if it deployed several hundred 3-warhead missiles, Russia would still be left with fewer than 4,000 warheads on its strategic offensive forces.

Implications for the United States

Although the first force structure in Table 2 assumes that Russia would continue to deploy MIRVed ICBMs, it may not create any unanticipated threats for the United States. Without START II in place, the United States could also retain 6,000 warheads on a START I force, with 500 Minuteman III ICBMs, 50 MX ICBMs, 18 Trident submarines, and around 200 B-52, B-1, and B-2 bombers. The weapons systems in this force would not be as near the end of their service lives as many of the weapons in the Russian force. In addition, the United States would probably find it possible, although not preferable, to allocate the resources needed to maintain this force for several more years than Russia could. Hence, it appears likely that the United States is in a far better position than Russia to maintain its forces at START I levels.

START II Force Levels Without Treaty Ratification

As is evident in the discussion above, age and economics may move Russia's forces towards START II levels with or without a formal treaty in place. Consequently, the two nations could agree to reduce their forces to between 3,000 and 3,500 warheads even if the Russian Duma does not approve ratification of START II. This would constitute an informal arrangement that might not include all the provisions contained in the treaty. Table 3, below, displays two possible forces that Russia might deploy under these circumstances.

The first force on Table 3 assumes that the United States and Russia would observe all the provisions of START II, including the ban on MIRVed ICBMs. Russia would have to deploy 700 single warhead Topol or Topol-M ICBMs (it currently has around 360 in its force) and retain all 6 of its aging Typhoon submarines to keep its forces near 3,500 warheads. It if could not afford these two programs, its forces would drop to less than 2,000 warheads. As an alternative, Russia could seek to retain perhaps 2 of its Typhoon submarines and it could deploy 400 Topol or Topol M missiles with 3 warheads on each missile. As Table 3 indicates, this force would put Russia at nearly 3,200 warheads, which is within the range permitted by START II. However, it includes a new MIRVed ICBM, which is not only inconsistent with START II, but, as was noted above, could also constitute a violation of START I.

Table 3: Illustrative Russian Forces at START II Levels

	With Ban on MIRVed ICBMs		Without Ban on MIRVed ICBMs	
ICBMs	Launchers	Warheads	Launchers	Warheads
SS-19	105	105 (1 RV on each)	105	105 (1 RV on each)
SS-25 SS-27	700	700 (1 RV on each)	400	1,200 (3 RVs on each)
SLBMs				
Delta IV	128 (8 subs)	512 (4 RVs on each)	128 (8 subs)	512 (4 RVs on each
Typhoons	120 (6 subs)	1,200 (10 RVs on each)	40 (2 subs)	400 (10 RVs on each
Bombers				
Bear H	55	880 (16 wpns on each)	55	880 (16 wpns on each)
Blackjack	6	96 (16 wpns on each)	6	96 (16 wpns on each)
Total	1,114	3,493	734	3,193

Implications for the United States

If the United States and Russia agreed to reduce their forces to START II levels without having the treaty enter into force, the United States could choose to deploy the same force that it planned for under START II. This force includes 500 single-warhead Minuteman III missiles, 14 Trident submarines with 5 warheads on each of their 24 D-5 (Trident II) missiles, 71 B-52 H bombers with between 8 and 20 cruise missiles on each bomber, and 21 B-2 bombers. Alternatively, the United States could retain some of its MIRVed ICBMs -- either by keeping 3 warheads on some Minuteman III missiles or by keeping some of its 10-warhead MX missiles, but these choices would put U.S. forces over the 3,500 warhead limit in START II.

Neither of the Russian forces displayed on Table 3 is likely to cause serious concerns for U.S. security; both assume that Russia would eliminate the heavily MIRVed SS-18 ICBMs that the United States has found most threatening to its deterrent forces. But the second force, where Russia deploys a 3-warhead version of its SS-25 and SS-27 ICBMs, could cause concerns because it is inconsistent with the START I Treaty. As a result, if the United States and Russia agree to reduce their forces to START II levels without ratifying that treaty, Russia's chosen force structure could undermine continued adherence with START I. This might not be consistent with U.S. efforts to pursue continued reductions in the threat posed by Russia's nuclear weapons.

Potential Limits and Force Structures under START III

As mentioned above, Presidents Clinton and Yeltsin agreed that they would negotiate a START III Treaty, reducing forces to between 2,000 and 2,500 warheads, after START II enters into force. President Yeltsin and others in Russia have long sought an agreement that would reduce forces to this level because it is consistent with the number of warheads Russia would retain if it retires its older weapons systems and does not construct significant numbers of new missiles or submarines. Hence, as Table 4 below shows, Russia could easily deploy a force within these proposed START III limits without developing a new MIRVed ICBM and without retaining all of its aging Typhoon submarines.

Table 4: Illustrative Russian Force Under Prospective START III Treaty

ICBMs	Launchers	Warheads
SS-19	105	105 (1 RV on each)
SS-25 SS-27	400	400 (1 RV on each)
SLBMs		
Delta IV	128 (8 subs)	512 (4 RVs on each)
Typhoons	40 (6 subs)	400 (10 RVs on each)
Bombers		
Bear H	55	880 (16 wpns on each)
Blackjack	6	96 (16 wpns on each)
Total	734	2,393

Implications for the United States

Although officials in the United States have apparently concluded that reductions to 2,000-2,500 nuclear warheads would not undermine U.S. security, they have not yet indicated how the United States would structure its forces under such an agreement. Table 5, below displays two alternative forces that would be consistent with a limit of 2,500 warheads; one retains 14 Trident submarines and reduces ICBMs and bombers, while the other retains 500 ICBMs and 71 B-52 bombers, but reduces the Trident fleet to 10 submarines.

As these tables demonstrate, START III could leave a significant discrepancy in U.S. and Russian SLBM warheads. Russia's force could include fewer than 1,000 SLBM warheads and the U.S. force could include more than 1,300 SLBM warheads if the United States retains 14 Trident submarines. Many in Russia would like the treaty to impose deeper reductions on U.S. SLBM warheads to eliminate this discrepancy. As a result, Russia could propose that START III also reduce the limit on SLBM warheads from the START II level of 1,750 to perhaps 1,000-1,250 warheads. This restriction could force the United States to select the second force on Table 5, with only 10 Trident submarines. Many in the U.S. defense establishment have resisted a reduction to 10 Trident submarines because this would concentrate the whole fleet at one base and could sharply reduce the number of warheads at sea at any one time. Others, however, including some in the U.S. Navy, believe that the United State should reduce to 10 Trident submarines because this would reduce operating costs and eliminate the need to spend billions of dollars to backfit older submarines with the new D-5 Trident II missiles. Congress and the Department of Defense are likely to take a closer look at these issues if the United States and Russia begin START III negotiations in the near future.

Table 5: Illustrative U.S. Forces under a Prospective START II Treaty

	With 14 Tridents		With 10 Tridents	
	Launchers	Warheads	Launchers	Warheads
Minuteman III	350	350 (1 RV on each)	500	500 (1 RV on each)
Trident	336 (14 subs)	1,344 (4 RVs on each)	240 (10 subs)	960 (4 RVs on each
B-52H	60	490 (8 wpns on each)	71	568 (8 wpns on each)
B-2	20	320 (16 wpns on each)	20	320 (16 wpns on each)
Total	766	2,494	831	2,348

CONCLUSION

The preceding discussion indicates that, although Russia continues to maintain a sizeable nuclear arsenal, the quantity and quality of its forces have declined since the demise of the Soviet Union. Arms control and economic pressures have led to the elimination of hundreds of deployed missiles and bombers that had carried thousands of nuclear warheads. Testing, training, and modernization all continue, but these efforts have slowed as well. As a result, although some continue to express concerns about the pace and direction of Russian nuclear force modernization, many analysts have focused on the potential implications of weaknesses in Russia's nuclear force structure and command and control assets. These problems could introduce new threats and risks of unintended launch if Russia continues to raise the profile of its nuclear weapons in its foreign and defense policy. On the other hand, these weaknesses, and Russia's apparent inability to invest considerable sums of money in its nuclear forces, could strengthen interest and improve the prospects for the further reductions in U.S. and Russian strategic offensive nuclear weapons through START II and a prospective START III Treaty.

CHAPTER 9

START II IN THE RUSSIAN DUMA: ISSUES AND PROSPECTS

AMY F. WOOLF

BACKGROUND

The United States and Russia signed the second Strategic Arms Reduction Treaty (START II) in January 1993.[1] START II limits each side to 3,500 warheads on strategic offensive delivery vehicles -- land-based intercontinental ballistic missiles (ICBMs), submarine-launched ballistic missiles (SLBMs) and heavy bombers. The treaty also mandates the elimination of all land-based multiple warhead ballistic missiles (MIRVed ICBMs) and limits each side to no more than 1,750 warheads on SLBMs. The United States and Russia can reduce their forces either by dismantling and destroying bombers and missile launchers, or, within limits, by removing warheads from deployed bombers, ICBMs and SLBMs, a process known as "downloading."[2]

The United States Senate gave its advice and consent to the ratification of START II in January 1996. The Russian Duma, the lower chamber of the Russian legislature, has held committee hearings and some initial debate on the treaty, but the Duma has not yet completed its review and no vote is scheduled at this time.[3]

Several officials in the Yeltsin government, including Defense Minister Rodionov and General Sergeyev, head of the Strategic Rocket Forces, have

---

[1] This treaty followed the 1991 Strategic Arms Control Treaty (START I), which limited each side (at the time, the United States and Soviet Union) to 6,000 accountable warheads on their strategic offensive forces. This treaty entered into force in late 1994, after Ukraine, Belarus, Kazakhstan and Russia each ratified it as successors to the Soviet Union.

[2] For more details see START II: Central Limits and Force Structure Implications, by Amy F. Woolf. CRS Report 93-35F, updated May 9, 1995.

[3] The Russian parliament consists of two entities, an upper chamber known as the Federation Council and the lower chamber, the Duma. Both chambers must approve treaty ratification. This report focuses on the Duma's role in START II ratification for a number of reasons. First, the Federation Council has shown little interest in international affairs, and may be inclined to follow the leadership of the Duma on this issue. Second, the Federation Council has shown less animosity towards the Yeltsin government than has the Duma, and, therefore, may be more amenable to approving treaties favored by the Executive Branch. And, third, Duma members have been far more vocal in their criticisms of START II than have members of the Federation Council. For more information the Russian parliament, see U.S. Library of Congress, Congressional Research Service. Russia's New Legislature: Context and Implications for U.S. Interests. CRS Report 96-878F, by Jim Nichol, October 31, 1996.

argued in support of START II ratification.[4] They contend that Russia cannot afford to maintain its forces at START I levels and, therefore, must reduce to START II or lower levels for economic reasons. They argue that, with its forces declining anyway, Russia can only maintain parity with the United States if START II compels the United States to reduce its forces as well.[5] At the same time, though, some observers in the United States believe the Yeltsin government has not expressed enough support for START II because even those Russians who favor ratification identify problems with the treaty. Many U.S. analysts believe this approach has hurt the chances for ratification in the Duma.

Many members of the Duma (and other analysts in Russia) have expressed strong doubts about START II. Some oppose the treaty because they generally oppose the national security policies of the Yeltsin government and START II is a symbol of such policies. Others have enumerated concerns that derive from the provisions in the treaty and other areas of U.S. and Russia's security policy. It is difficult to compile a comprehensive list of these criticisms, or even to state which is most important to members of the Duma, because each critic seems to have his own list and the lists often change. Nevertheless, this report highlights the issues raised most often during statements and speeches by members of the Duma and identifies some solutions proposed by Duma members. These issues include concerns about the force structure and economic implications of START II; concerns about the effects of U.S. missile defense deployments on Russia's nuclear deterrent; and concerns about the effect that NATO expansion might have on Russia's military security and political stature.

DUMA CONCERNS

CONCERNS WITH START II PROVISIONS

Force Structure Issues

Some members of the Duma have argued that the START II Treaty is not in Russia's national security interest because it will eliminate the core of Russia's nuclear forces -- the large MIRVed ICBMs. In contrast, they note that treaty does not ban MIRVed SLBMs, which constitute the bulk of the U.S.

---

[4] Charles Aldinger, U.S., Russian Ministers seek START-2 ratification, Reuters, October 16, 1996.

[5] Vladimir Lukin, Chairman of the Duma International Affairs Committee has also raised this point, stating "if we do not ratify it the United States will keep more than 8,000 warheads. Then we will become a second-rate nuclear power... If we ratify it, we will keep parity with the United States in nuclear force." Yuri Svirko, Russia may set conditions on nuclear arms treaty, Reuters, January 31, 1996.

strategic offensive force.[6] Others have noted that Russia will have to eliminate many more missiles than the United States to reduce to the 3,500 warhead limit. This is because the United States can take greater advantage of the "downloading" provisions in the treaty.

These provisions permit both parties to reduce their forces by removing warheads from deployed missiles, rather than by eliminating the missiles altogether. However, the treaty only allows the parties to remove a maximum of 4 warheads from each missile. Because the majority of Russia's MIRVed ICBMs carry 10 warheads, downloading by 4 warheads would not leave these missiles with a single warhead. As a result, Russia will have to eliminate the missiles entirely. Most of the U.S. MIRVed ICBMs, in contrast, carry only 3 warheads, so the United States can download these missiles to single-warhead status. In addition, because the treaty does not ban MIRVed SLBMs, the United States can download, rather than eliminate, its Trident missiles to reduce these forces to the treaty limit of 1,750 warheads on SLBMs. Because the United States can take greater advantage of the treaty's downloading provisions, critics in Russia argue that the United States will also have a greater "reload" capability if it chose to withdraw from the treaty and restore its forces to higher levels.

Economic Issues

Many Russian experts, both inside and outside the Duma, note that the economic burden created by Russia's strategic nuclear forces would exist with or without START II. Russia will have to bear the costs of eliminating dozens of nuclear-powered ballistic missile submarines and many of its older MIRVed ICBMs because of their advanced age and in response to limits in START I. Hence, some support START II because they believe that the economic costs would be far higher if Russia had to replace these aging systems to maintain its forces at START I levels.[7] At least with START II in place, Russia could be

---

[6] A report prepared for the CPRF (Communist Party of the Russian Federation) faction of the Duma stated that "The START II Treaty virtually preserves the existing structure of American strategic offensive weapons and calls for relatively little effort in the conversion of the land-based component of U.S. ICBMs." See CPRF Report on START II Ratification, FBIS-TAC-96-001-L, October 2, 1996, p. 19. In addition, an unidentified member of the Duma Defense Committee reportedly said some of the defense committee's members believe the treaty's provisions concerning the "destabilising role of inter-continental ballistic missiles with separable warheads" are discriminatory because the provisions cover ground-based missiles, which are the bulk of the Russian missile forces but do not similarly affect sea-launched missiles, which "spearhead" the U.S. force. Duma 'Expert' Predicts Difficult START-2 Job for Perry, FBIS-SOV-96-201, October, 16, 1996.

[7] Alternatively, in theory, Russia could allow its deployed forces to fall below the levels maintained by the United States, but no one in the Yeltsin government or the Duma has publicly advocated such a position. Many believe that Russia's nuclear forces are one of the sole remaining indicators of Russia's superpower status and it could be politically unacceptable Russian officials to advocate that Russia allow itself to become

sure that the United States would also reduce its forces and Russia could maintain parity with lower levels of expenditures.

Others, however, argue that START II will add to the economic pressures created by Russia's strategic nuclear forces. First, they note that the treaty would require Russia to eliminate its MIRVed ICBMs by the year 2003, several years before these missiles reach the end of their service lives.[8] In addition, critics note that the elimination of older MIRVed ICBMs will reduce Russian strategic nuclear forces to around 2,300 warheads; Russia would then have to produce several hundred single-warhead missiles if it wanted to reach the START II level of 3,500 warheads.[9] Thus, Russia would have to invest greater sums than it would need without START II to accelerate both the elimination of the older weapons and the production of replacement weapons.

Suggested Solutions and U.S. Responses

Members of the Duma, and other Russian critics of START II, have proposed three possible solutions to the problems they cite with START II. First, some believe that Russia should not ratify START II in its current form. They argue that parties could either modify the treaty so that Russia could keep some MIRVed ICBMs or replace it with a START III Treaty that would not only permit Russia to retain MIRVed ICBMs but also to impose greater restrictions, if not an outright ban, on MIRVed SLBMs. They argue that restrictions on MIRVed SLBMs could correct an imbalance created by START II and reduce the U.S. advantage in "reload" potential by forcing the United States to eliminate more MIRVed missiles and replace them with new single-warhead missiles.[10]

Supporters of this type of solution also argue that removing the ban on MIRVed ICBMs would allow Russia to maintain parity with the United States, even if the U.S. retained its forces at START I levels, without building hundreds of new single warhead missiles. Russia could keep its older missiles as long as it deemed necessary and then replace them with new MIRVed systems -- either a 3-warhead version of the Topol M (known as the SS-25 follow-on or SS-27 in

---

less of a nuclear superpower than the United States.

[8] During meetings in Washington in October 1996, Alexei Arbatov, a member of the Duma Defense Committee, referred to START II as the "most wasteful treaty in the history of arms control." He pointed out that Russia's MIRVed ICBMs would have to leave the force at least 5 years before the end of their service lives.

[9] The Chairman of the Duma Defense Committee, Lev Rokhlin, stated "we would have to create an extra 500-700 single unit missiles -- with one warhead -- to find ourselves at the level allowed by the treaty." He estimated that it would cost Russia $40-50 billion to manufacture these missiles, silos and their infrastructure. Rokhlin Says START-2 Will Cause Rearmament, FBIS-SOV-96-181, September 17, 1996.

[10] This point is raised in the CPRF Report on START II Ratification, FBIS-TAC-96-001-L, October 2, 1996, p. 40.

the United States) or an entirely new type of MIRVed ICBM -- when funding became available.[11]

Most experts doubt that the United States would accept changes in START II that permitted Russia to retain MIRVed ICBMs; the United States believes this provision is central to efforts to maintain stability at lower levels of forces. As a result, if Russia wants to retain MIRVed ICBMs, the Duma may have to reject START II in any form.

Second, many members of the Duma have recommended that the United States and Russia extend the reduction period in START II beyond the 2003 deadline currently written in the treaty. Some note that when it was signed in 1993, START II presumed a ten-year draw-down period with its deadline of 2003; an extension of 3-4 years would restore this original schedule and allow both sides to spread the costs of reductions over a longer period of time.[12] Some in Russia have also noted that an extension of 5-7 years would allow the time-frame for weapons eliminations to coincide with the planned life span of Russia's older MIRVed ICBMs. This change would not only spread the costs of elimination over a longer period of time, it would also provide Russia with more time to produce new single-warhead missiles. The lower annual production rate would reduce the annual budget needed to support the new production.[13]

Officials in the Clinton Administration have not offered any public response to suggestions that the United States and Russia extend the deadlines in START II. However, many analysts doubt that the United States would agree to an extension of 5-7 years. This would undermine one of the central provisions of the treaty by allowing Russia to keep its MIRVed ICBMs far longer than intended. On the other hand, some U.S. analysts believe an extension of 3-4 years is reasonable in light of the delays that have occurred in treaty ratification. And, since most Russian experts argue that such an extension is absolutely necessary to win Duma approval of START II, it is possible that U.S. officials will consider this proposal in ongoing discussions with their Russian counterparts.

---

[11] During meetings in Washington in October 1996, Duma Member Alexei Arbatov argued that the deployment of a 3-warhead version of the Topol-M would permit Russia to maintain higher numbers of warheads at a lower cost.

[12] During meetings in Washington in October 1996, Alexei Arbatov stated that the first step in winning ratification of START II would be to extend the implementation deadline by 3-5 years. He said this was a necessary, but probably not sufficient, step.

[13] The CPRF Report on START II notes that, to deploy 800-900 ICBMs by 2003, "Russia will have to secure the annual production of around 80-90 single-warhead Topol-M missiles. Because of its economic difficulties, Russia probably will not be able to attain this objective on schedule. Stretching out the deployment ... might be a possible solution." CPRF Report on START II Ratification, FBIS-TAC-96-001-L, October 2, 1996, p. 19.

Third, many in the Duma have suggested that the United States and Russia agree now that they will reduce their forces further, to perhaps 2,000-2,500 warheads, under a START III treaty. Some Russians have argued that a framework for START III would allow Duma members to know that Russia would not have to build several hundred new single-warhead missiles under START II that might only be eliminated later under a START III treaty.[14] The lower limits in a new treaty would also help Russia maintain numerical parity with the United States by requiring U.S. reductions to a level that Russia is likely to reach as it eliminates its aging MIRVed ICBMs and older submarines.[15] In addition, some in the Duma, and others in Russia, believe that a START III Treaty might correct some perceived weaknesses with provisions in START II.[16]

In the past, the Clinton Administration has stated that the United States would participate in START III negotiations only after START II entered into force. However, after Secretary of Defense Perry failed to convince Duma members to support START II when he met with them in October 1996, the United States began to explore options for a START III Treaty to address some of the Duma's concerns. Reports indicate that Administration officials have discussed START III with their Russian counterparts in recent meetings. For example, the agenda for the February 1997 meetings between Vice President Gore and Prime Minister Chernomyrdin contained discussions on START II and START III.[17] Although Gore and Chernomyrdin did not release any information about the substance of these discussions, they did announce that Presidents Clinton and Yeltsin would address the issue during their summit in March 1997. Some analysts believe that, at that time, the Presidents may announce a broad framework for further reductions. However, the United

---

[14] At the same time, a "framework" would not have the legal standing of a treaty and could be changed with further negotiations. As a result, some Russians, including Duma member Alexei Arbatov, have argued for a "legally binding framework" for START III. However, under U.S. law, an agreement would not be legally binding without congressional approval, and it is unlikely that the President would seek such approval for a framework that represents opening positions in international negotiations.

[15] Vladimir Lukin, Chairman of the International Affairs Committee has stated that deeper reductions in a START III treaty would enable Russia "not to construct new missiles and to secure parity at a lower level." See Foreign Committee Chairman on NATO, FBIS-SOV-96-196, October 7, 1996.

[16] Rokhlin highlighted this option when he noted the possibility of an alternative to START II ratification where "the treaty is ratified but on the condition that a START-3 treaty be worked out that would foresee deep cutbacks in the Russian and American arsenals." He also noted that a new agreement could take into account "aspects of START-2 we deem negative." See Rokhlin Says START-2 Will Cause Rearmament, FBIS-SOV-96-181, September 17, 1996.

[17] Transcript: Background Briefing on Gore-Chernomyrdin Talks. The White House, Press Briefing by Senior Administration Officials, February 6, 1997.

States might still insist that START II enter into force before formal negotiations begin on START III.[18]

CONCERNS WITH BALLISTIC MISSILE DEFENSES

Some Members of the Duma have linked their disapproval of START II to U.S. plans to develop and possibly deploy a national ballistic missile defense system, particularly if such a deployment exceeds the limits in the 1972 Anti-Ballistic Missile (ABM) Treaty.[19] Some argue that Russia should not enter into another arms control agreement with the United States if the United States is unwilling to abide by past commitments. Others contend that a nationwide missile defense system in the United States would undermine Russia's national security. Few believe that the United States will limit its missile defenses to a small number of interceptors directed against threats from rogue nations. They note that some Members of Congress have suggested far more extensive deployments and that, even if the United States begins with limited intentions, it might eventually deploy a more extensive defensive system.[20] But several Duma members argue that Russia will find it difficult to maintain an effective nuclear deterrent without multiple-warhead ICBMs if the United States deploys nationwide defenses because MIRVed missiles provide a cost-effective means to penetrate ballistic missile defenses.[21] As a result, many argue that Russia cannot accept the limits in START II unless the United States remains bound by the ABM Treaty.

Some in the Duma have also argued that U.S. plans for the deployment of advanced theater missile defenses (TMD) could undermine Russia's deterrent because defenses deployed close to Russian territory could intercept Russia's

---

[18] U.S. says START-2 must be sealed before new talks. Reuters, January 17, 1997.

[19] This treaty, and its 1974 Protocol, limit the United States and Soviet Union to one ABM site in each nation. The treaty also limits each nation to 100 ABM interceptor missiles at its single site and it limits the size and location of ABM radars.

[20] The CPRF Report on START II states that "the United States plans to begin deploying a territorial ABM system after the sides have implemented the terms of the START II Treaty by 2003. The territorial ABM will be based on existing tactical ABM complexes." CPRF Report on START II Ratification, FBIS-TAC-96-001-L, October 2, 1996, p. 31.

[21] The CPRF Report on START II states that "In the presence of countermeasures -- i.e, if the other side has an ABM system going beyond the framework of the ABM Treaty -- the renunciation of MIRVed ICBMs could have a negative effect on nuclear potential." CPRF Report on START II Ratification, FBIS-TAC-96-001-L, October 2, 1996, p. 20.

long-range ballistic missiles.[22] As a result, some have argued that the Duma should not approve START II until the United States and Russia reach agreement in their discussions on a demarcation line between ABM systems and TMD systems.[23] And many believe that this agreement should limit not only the capabilities of U.S. TMD systems, but also their numbers and locations.

The United States is unwilling to accept a formal linkage between Russian approval of START II and continuing U.S. compliance with the ABM Treaty. Officials in the United States have long argued that the two treaties are independent and each enhances the security of both parties. The Clinton Administration has also stated that the United States does not, at this time, plan to deploy any defenses that exceed the limits in the ABM Treaty. At the same time, though, many U.S. officials conclude that the two sides probably have to complete the ABM/TMD demarcation discussions before the Duma will approve START II. Negotiations resumed in February 1997, but it is not clear whether they will reach a conclusion any time soon.

CONCERNS WITH NATO ENLARGEMENT

Many members of the Duma, along with other officials in Russia, have linked their disapproval of START II to NATO's plans to offer membership to several nations in Eastern Europe. Some highlight a military link between NATO expansion and START II by noting that NATO expansion will bring NATO's conventional and possibly nuclear forces closer to Russia's borders. They contend that tactical nuclear weapons along Russia's borders would be able to strike "strategic" targets inside Russia.[24] These critics note that Russia cannot offset the increased threat from NATO forces with its own weakened

---

[22] Georgiy Drasheninnikov, a staff member for the Duma Defense Committee has stated that "a deployment of ground- and sea-based TMD would permit the United States to block the main bases of Russian SSBNs." See the Arms Control Reporter, January 1997, p. 603.B.289. Such a configuration could be a problem for Russia because many U.S. analysts believe that, in the event of a conflict, Russia would not send its submarines out into the open ocean, but would, instead, seek to launch its submarine-based missiles from port or nearby bastions.

[23] The ABM Treaty only limits defenses against strategic offensive missiles; it does not restrict those designed to intercept shorter-range missiles. However, the treaty does not define the difference between strategic and theater missile defenses (TMD). The Clinton Administration has engaged in negotiations with the Russians to develop such a definition so that the United States can develop TMD systems without raising questions about compliance with the ABM Treaty. Because Russia fears that some of these defenses could intercept longer-range missiles, it has proposed more restrictive provisions than the United States is willing to accept.

[24] Rokhlin has noted that the "inclusion of East European countries into NATO as members and the possible deployment of nuclear weapons in them would create a new threat to Russia: tactical nuclear forces thus turn strategic." See Ivan Rodin, Perry Fails To Persuade Duma Deputies, FBIS-SOV-96-203, October, 18, 1996.

conventional forces. Hence, Russia must maintain nuclear forces to guarantee its security in the face of an expanded NATO.[25] Some believe Russia should rely on non-strategic nuclear weapons, such as short range missiles and aircraft, to counter NATO's conventional superiority. This is analogous to NATO's reliance on nuclear weapons during the Cold War to counter the advantage of Soviet and Warsaw Pact conventional forces. Others, however, believe Russia should respond to NATO's enlargement by increasing its reliance on strategic nuclear forces. Where increased reliance on non-strategic nuclear weapons would represent a military response in the absence of sufficient conventional forces, an increased reliance on strategic nuclear weapons would represent more of a political response. Those who support this type of response contend that no nation would threaten Russia with conventional or nuclear weapons if Russia maintained a strong and credible nuclear deterrent. Strategic nuclear forces would not only serve as a key measure of this deterrent's strength, they would also remind nations that Russia is a nuclear superpower to be reckoned with.[26]

Although the United States and its NATO allies have held extensive discussions with Russia in an effort to ease concerns about NATO enlargement, officials in the United States do not see any link between NATO's plans and the START II Treaty. Instead, most agree that the Duma and others in Russia have linked the two in an effort to gain leverage and attract attention for Russia's views on NATO enlargement.

PROSPECTS FOR START II RATIFICATION

During 1996, many U.S. arms control analysts believed that the Duma would eventually approve the START II Treaty. Many expected a vote to occur after the June presidential elections in Russia and November elections in the United States. At the same time, many experts expected the Duma to attach conditions to the treaty linking its implementation to continued U.S. compliance with the ABM Treaty and, possibly, to plans for NATO expansion. Some also expected the Duma to offer amendments to the Treaty to extend its elimination deadlines and, possibly, to alter provisions relating to MIRVed ICBMs and warhead "downloading." Because most believed that the United States would not accept some of the conditions and amendments under consideration in the

---

[25] Vladimir Lukin, Chairman of the Duma Committee on International Affairs has stated that NATO's expansion would bring "a powerful military organization ... close to Russia's borders," and, under these circumstances, "Russia has no way out other than maintaining its nuclear deterrent force at a proper level." See Deputies Tell Perry of Concerns Over NATO Expansion, FBIS-SOV-96-203, October 17, 1996.

[26] The CPRF Report on START II notes that "Russia's possession of nuclear weapons under these circumstances [NATO's expansion] guarantees its ability to avert a nuclear attack or broad-scale aggression by conventional armed forces and arms against it or its allies." The report also states that "Russia cannot be assured of keeping the status of a great power under present conditions without keeping its nuclear status." See CPRF Report on START II Ratification, FBIS-TAC-96-001-L, October 1, 1996, p. 9.

Duma, many experts questioned whether the treaty would enter into force even if the Duma eventually approved the treaty's ratification.

After Secretary of Defense Perry received a strongly negative response when he addressed the Duma in October 1996, growing numbers of analysts in the United States began to doubt that the Duma would ever approve START II. Not only had the Duma's suspicions of U.S. and NATO intentions increased, but the list of START II issues of concern to Duma members seemed too long and the nature of their concerns seemed too complex to solve without changing the treaty or other areas of U.S. policy in ways that the United States would find unacceptable. Russia's continued hard line against NATO expansion in early 1997 seemed to confirm this view.

Nevertheless, reports indicate that the United States has sought to address some of Russia's concerns with START II by opening discussions on a potential START III agreement. On February 27, 1997, the White House announced that strategic nuclear arms control would be one of the key areas of discussion when Presidents Clinton and Yeltsin meet in Helsinki in March. Although the United States probably will not address all of the concerns highlighted in this report, it is possible that progress in some areas, when combined with economic problems that could force Russia to reduce its strategic offensive forces regardless of its treaty commitments, might eventually convince enough Duma members that Russia's interests would be better served by approving START II and moving on to further reductions after that treaty enters into force. On the other hand, weak support from the Yeltsin government, the ongoing political confrontation between the Duma and the Executive, and lingering concerns about the substance of the treaty could continue to stall START II ratification.

CHAPTER 10

NATO ENLARGEMENT: A CRITICAL VIEW FROM BELARUS

DENIS KRIVOSHEEV
Minsk, Belarus; Manchester, UK

INTRODUCTION

The end of the Cold War has been a serious trial for European security. The break-up of bipolarity in the international system and unravelling of hostilities have often been perceived as promising peace and stability to the whole world, and even more so to Europe. However, domestic instability in the post-Communist countries, the raise of nationalism, and disintegration of several states have almost immediately challenged this optimistic vision (Simai, 1997). It was commonly perceived that these developments had to be countered. However, one of the measures suggested in this relation, namely NATO enlargement, has only furthered the unease in the region. It involved a large number of states into the situation of contention, and, opposite to the desired, heated the nationalist trend in Russia. The prospects for NATO enlargement have also changed the geopolitical situation of several less influential countries in the region. In the case of Belarus, for example, the country has been pushed towards a stronger compliance with the Russian policy, let alone the increased tension within the society.

The question of NATO's place and role in the post-Cold War Europe is central to the operation of the security system in the whole subcontinent (Camilleri, 1993: p. 81). After the dissolution of the Eastern Bloc, Western Europe has become a gravitational centre for most of its former Eastern adversaries, who now pursue admission to the Euro-Atlantic structures. The preparation of a positive decision on the first new admissions to NATO will has been a central issue in the recent European security discourse and politics. It has raised a number of salient questions concerning the directions of changes of the European security system, NATO's place and role in it, the validity and real motives of Russian claims on non-enlargement of the Alliance, and the prospects for regional stability and security itself.

A first-hand exposure to the East European perception of European politics gives sober grounds for a critical approach to the issue. I will suggest an analysis of the host of problems related to NATO enlargement in the new, post-Cold War, strategic context in Europe, and assess the evolution of the North-Atlantic Alliance's place and role in it following the interplay of the interests of the major parties concerned. I will then critically evaluate their mainstream arguments and, finally, suggest an alternative understanding, implication for the future of the current changes in the European security system - as prompted by an alternative international perception from a post-Soviet perspective.

THE POST-COLD WAR STRATEGIC SETTING IN EUROPE

The new strategic setting in Europe is essentially different from that of the Cold War era. The global military, political, economic and ideological confrontation that lasted four decades and was centred here, has ended. In the late 1980s Soviet power underwent a rapid demise producing military, political and economic uncertainty in the area between its western borders and Western Europe. The Eastern military bloc (Warsaw Treaty Organisation - WTO) collapsed, and the political identity of this sub-region (now referred to as East-Central Europe - ECE) has been questioned[1]. Shortly after, the USSR broke up into several states that vary in size, strength, military and political orientation, in their commitment to liberal economic and political reforms, levels of domestic stability, and influence. Most of them have been engaged in integrationist projects (Commonwealth of Independent States - CIS), including in questions of security and defence (the Tashkent Agreement of 1992), but the real accomplishments of this have been very modest. In the situation of fragmentation in Eastern Europe, Russia emerged as the biggest of the Soviet successor states. It has acquired most of the former USSR's territory, economic and military potential, and acceded to most of its international commitments, most importantly in the military and security areas. Consequently, Russia has assumed the USSR's posture as a major power in the East of Europe.

Western Europe succeeded in preserving its identity as a collective multi-national economic, political and military power on the continent and as the United States' major partner, although its prospects for further integration are, probably, no less problematic now than before. Meanwhile, and despite claims about its hegemonic decline, the USA has preserved its status as a superpower, as well as its military, political and economic engagement in Europe. However, the nature of its presence on the continent after the end of the Cold War has been questioned (Gummett, 1997; Ruhle & Williams, 1997). The legacy of the Cold War also includes a system of security-related organisations which have had to adapt to the post-confrontational realities. Of these, NATO has become an

1 The notion of ECE applies to Poland, the Czech Republic, Slovakia and Hungary. Similarly, identity and priorities of other post-Communist countries, those of South-Eastern Europe, have been subject to change. Among other consequences of the end of the Cold War is the break-up of the former Yugoslavia and emergence of military conflicts on part of its territory.

independent actor in the European security politics with interests, influence and policies of its own (Cornish, 1996: p. 752).

By the mid-1990s, the strategic context in Europe evolved gradually into its present state, when the debate on NATO enlargement reached its peak. The ECE countries have reasserted their decisiveness in wishing to join the North Atlantic structures, especially after the accomplishments of their sub-regional integration project - the Visegrad process - proved to be very modest (Dunn, 1992: p. 27), while the prolonged uncertainty of the political and economic transition (Andor, 1996: p. 218) became apparent[2]. Most of the East European countries, including Russia, have failed to consolidate efficiently their political and economic life. In Western Europe, the regionalist projects have been extended into the area of foreign policy and security, highlighting debates concerning the EU's Common Foreign and Security Policy, European defence identity, and the idea and policies of Atlanticism. The strategic relationship with the US has been re-affirmed, and Washington has confirmed its military engagement in Europe. NATO has been suggested as the basis of the European Security and Defence Identity. (Gummett, 1997; Cornish, 1996)

Within this pattern of the new European context, the major interests, as related to NATO enlargement, may be roughly grouped around the principal actors in the process: the European NATO member states (of whom the position of the major powers - Britain, Germany, and France[3] - is the most pronounced, although different in several respects), the United States; the ECE countries who seek Alliance membership; and Russia, who opposes it[4]. Among these, NATO became a crucial actor in its own right, although its fate has been quite ambiguous. The Alliance's active position included some major adjustments to the new situation that required assumption of a new role. In 1991, the Strategic Concept was adopted which highlighted changes in the Alliance's military and political strategies. In the absence of potential adversary, its capacity is now re-oriented to be able to face new risks and challenges. Contacts and co-operation with non-member states have been fostered (Smith, 1997). In response to the absence of military threat and hostilities, NATO's structure and planning have been made more "transparent" which has been paralleled by nuclear and conventional force reduction (Ibid.). Much of it, however, has been synchronised with similar measures taken in the USSR/Russia, and become possible due to reciprocity. Unilateral presentation of the figures to argue for the contemporary NATO's "peaceful" posture, as suggested by Smith (1997), is inadequate for Russia-NATO debate.

After the dissolution of the WTO and end of the Cold War, finally signalled by the collapse of the USSR, the rationale for NATO's further existence, with its emphasis on

2 There is an alternative vision, according to which the ECE countries have by now become *de facto* "part of the West" (Latawski, 1997), which, however, appeals more to their sharing main values, but not to the state of their economic, political and social life.

3 France still remains formally outside the Alliance's military structure.

4 For the convenience of analysis, the diversity within Western Europe, and the interests of South-Eastern and former Soviet states (other than Russia), will be spotlighted, unless specifically mentioned when important.

military-strategic functions, was seriously questioned on very explicit grounds (Rotfeld, 1996: p. 282; Cornish, 1996: pp. 751-3; Camilleri, 1993: pp. 84-6). Its primary purpose, according to the Washington Treaty, was, and still is, collective defence (Article V). In practical terms, it was a military alliance created specifically against the USSR/Eastern Bloc, with the military doctrine being based on the concept of deterrence. There was ambiguity about the Alliance's future until the Dayton Agreement of 1995 and the successful performance, subject to the UN mandate, of the NATO-led Implementation Forces (IFOR) in Bosnia. The effect produced by this efficient intervention in the prolonged and turbulent arena of conflict in Europe was reinforced by the subsequent French *rapprochement* with NATO (Cornish, 1996: pp. 755-60). The Alliance's popularity and prestige have grown immensely, and its posture in contemporary Europe is no longer under stress.

National and Collective Security and Defence in Contemporary Europe: A New Role for NATO

The question of achieving and maintaining security (national collective and international) by military means needs some discussion at this stage. The direct utility of military force has nowadays been seriously questioned. The reasons for this were suggested by the revolutionary changes in the military technology, operation of the so-called security dilemma, declining effectiveness of warfare as a political instrument and its immense cost (Buzan, 1987). The incredible military, primarily nuclear, build-up undertaken by the major powers during the Cold War had the major purpose of prevention of the military means from being used (the doctrine of deterrence evolved into that of mutually assured destruction). Apparently, such a purpose could not be assigned to national/ collective military forces after the end of the Cold War, in the absence of a virtual powerful adversary. Moreover, the major threats involving the use of military forces in Europe comes from domestic conflicts, rather than international ones[5].

Nowadays, military forces in Europe are an important attribute of statehood and a political factor. Their use, however, more often serves purposes other than the traditional defence of national territory, with the most "popular" being peace-keeping, peace-enforcement and conflict resolution elsewhere. The advantage of military alliances - combined military strength - is not offered for similar purposes, with their multilateral composition being a "moral" advantage for their international use. Nevertheless, the political significance of national/ collective military forces may have even increased, and their use in national interests, other than national territory defence, is becoming still more evident. In Europe, national military forces add weight to political bargains. Hence, the number of options available to NATO campaigners has broadened.

---

[5] Of all the major contemporary conflicts in Europe, only that between Greece and Turkey qualifies as a definitely inter-state one. The conflicts in the former Yugoslavia and between Armenia and Azerbaijan first emerged between the subjects of federal states.

The momentum for NATO enlargement is driven by various developments and interests. Europe is a vibrant political and economic organism where multiple processes, some of which are contradictory, need to be accommodated. NATO enlargement has offered a mechanism, through which a host of various parties' interests could be channelled. When interests differ, some of them can still be achieved through the same process, although a degree of mutual adjustment may be necessary. NATO enlargement is such a case. However, being instrumental in the policies of Western Europe, ECE, the US and NATO, it proved to be uncomfortable for Russia and some of its neighbours.

The actual idea of NATO enlargement was brought about by the ECE countries after the fall of Communist regimes in Eastern Europe and Soviet withdrawal from the region. There is an intimate link between the considerations of national security, affiliation with stronger powers (in the case of smaller states), military expenditures (the alliance with the USSR gave the advantage of a certain degree of free riding here) and broader economic considerations[6] (Andor, 1996: p. 212). Within the East European security discourse, these issues were matched with, if not overrun, by an apparent desire to establish a closer association with Western Europe and eventually join its economic, political and security area, particularly through the membership of its two key institutions - the EU and NATO (Latter, 1996: pp. 1, 3). For the ECE countries, membership of the Euro-Atlantic structures is associated with potential advantages that would contribute to their progress on the defence-military political and economic levels (Andor, 1996: p. 218; Latter, 1995: p. 1). At the stage when no real external threat is observed, economic considerations tend to predominate in the formulation of national security and foreign policy (CFDP, 1996: p. 93; also Rotfeld, 1996: p. 290). They clearly stand behind the arguments that favour NATO membership (Cimoszwicz, 1996: p. 3; Kwasniewski, 1996; Millard, 1996: p. 218).

These ECE arguments are derived from several central notions: regional security (understood as stability and mutual guarantees - extended from the West to ECE), national security (reassurance against potential threats), superseding the Cold War-time divisions in Europe, ECE's independent role in European politics (as opposed to its dependency on the policies of major powers ever since gaining independence), and interrelations between membership of NATO and EU (Rotfeld, 1996: pp. 289-91; Cimoszewicz, 1996: p. 3; Havel, 1996; Kwasniewski, 1996).

Western Europe's motivation in expanding NATO is quite pragmatic, and is broader than the desire to reassure itself against unforeseen threats. The process can be instrumental in dealing with several issue-areas. These include: reassuring NATO's availability for European defence mechanisms (ESDI) and fostering mutual adjustment; reassuring US military engagement in Europe, American technical and financial support (Gummett, 1997: pp. 221-5); "anchoring" Germany to a cohesive West (Camilleri, 1993: p. 84); in response to the ECE countries' pressure, giving them first admission to the

---

6 This may be expected as an effect of establishing closer links with economic powers in the region. Also, some believe that military expenditures may prove to be smaller in the long run (Financial Times, 26.03.1997, p. 3).

Euro-Atlantic structures (EU enlargement is economically undesirable at this stage (Hopkinson, 1995: pp. 21-2; Millard, 1996: p. 218; Andor, 1996: p. 218); reinforcing Western political, economic and ideological (Western values) leverage in ECE and advancing it further east, etc.

Western European objectives are compatible with ECE's expectations as long as ECE does not see itself as (having a potential for) a distinct region. This enables Western Europe and ECE to share most of the arguments.

Considering public opinion and Congressional hard line on huge overseas expenditures (Kull & Rosner, 1997), there is a degree of uncertainty about American full support for NATO enlargement. The United States' rationale in favour of that process includes several themes: reinforcement of American status of superpower in Europe and elsewhere; advancement of its military, political, economic and ideological leverage; safeguarding NATO as an instrument of its overseas policies together with strategic support of its European partners; encouragement of European role in and contribution to the Alliance and NATO's "out of area" operations; and arms market promotion (Clinton, 1997; Solomon, 1997; Ruhle & Williams, 1997).

NATO enlargement is also instrumental in diversifying American assistance to Eastern Europe; fostering liberal economic reforms there; employing NATO for the tasks of non-proliferation, combat of terrorism and drug trafficking. American argumentation for NATO enlargement is important not only for Russia, its major opponent, but also strong domestic opposition articulated around a populist "America first" agenda (Bienen, 1993)[7]. Therefore, American national interests are more explicitly pronounced than those of West European countries (Clinton, 1997; NATO, 1995).

It is only natural that Central-East European and Western arguments in favour of enlarged Alliance, which I will analyse below, well supplement the reasoning of NATO officials[8]. NATO welcomes new members, and looks forward to a new budget and enlarged scale of operations. As for the discourse itself, the Alliance primarily has to find more arguments to refute Russian concerns and persuade the Americans. Despite the difference of purposes of the major non-Russian parties, there is a solid base for cohesion of their policies. ECE is making its way into the North-Atlantic structures willingly abiding by the rules set. Western Europe is restructuring its integration models. The US is advancing its strategic aims. NATO, once its existence is no longer questioned, has to face these requirements and correlate its role with that of other European institutions (OSCE, EU, WEU). As a multi-lateral structure, it has to

---

7 The major concern for Americans is the financial burden caused by the process, and also situation in Russia. There are also voices of criticism in Western Europe and ECE. They point to the undesirable implication of the process for the region (strained relations with Russia, inability to accept all the applicants, etc.), Russian and their own domestic politics (insufficient public support, financial burden), NATO's efficiency (Rotfeld, 1996: p. 287; Cunningham, 1997; Millard, 1996: p. 218).

8 There are also voices in Western Europe, ECE and the US that argue against NATO enlargement. Most of them follow the Russian argumentation, taking seriously its anxiety (Rotfeld, 1996: p. 287; Millard, 1996: p. 218).

accommodate a variety of opinions, but also to make the result self-sustaining. Therefore, its official position, summarised in *Study on NATO Enlargement* (NATO, 1995) represents a "political compromise within the Alliance" (Rotfeld, 1996: p. 285).

The central idea of NATO's argument is that the Alliance's enlargement will improve the security architecture in Europe by providing long-term stability further east (NATO, 1995: chs 2,3). Membership of NATO, as well as the process of enlargement itself, will counteract the tendency towards disintegration along ethnic and territorial lines, and foster co-operation and problem settlement between the countries in ECE and elsewhere through their adaptation to its entry requirements. The amplified stability, according to the logic suggested in the above document, will improve security for all countries in Europe, including Russia and other non-members. Thus reassured stability is presented as "inclusive and comprehensive security structure" (NATO, 1995: ch.2) for the members and non-member states. The new security structure will embrace the new strategic setting in Europe, and will be directed against no one (Latter, 1996:5-8).

Most of these points abstract and generalise regional security operation processes. Concrete procedures and policies may well work for or against this logic. NATO's formal obligations on which Russia insists (not to deploy nuclear weapons and foreign armed forces in ECE) are aimed at decreasing the ambiguity, while the Alliance's reluctance to do so out of caution is discouraging.

Most other arguments in favour of NATO enlargement also leave Russia uncomfortable. Logically, the discourse on membership in a military alliance requires emphasis on the question of national defence, as well as the existence of a relevant threat, actual or potential. When the immediate security of a country is not at stake (which is recognised by the ECE governments [Cimoszewicz, 1996:4; Rotfeld, 1996:189-91]), the discourse becomes inconsistent. Its "classical" product is the security dilemma (Herz, 1950). In the ECE context, it also brings uncomfortable connotations for Russia. Articulation of potential threats is very cautiously worded: "risks", "new challenges" (Ruhle & Williams, 1996: p. 110; Clinton, 1997: p. 6). However, when "historical experience" (Cimoszewicz, 1996: p. 4) is voiced by an East European as an excuse for membership in a Western structure, it points further east. Calling Russia "a power with great gravitational potential and with security partners of its own" (Havel, 1996) gives the same hint[9].

Undivided Europe, mentioned in different way by *every* proponent of NATO membership, is an attractive symbol, but unless it refers to a pan-European structure like OSCE, its meaning is double-edged. ECE's "Western" past is an even more symbolical notion, which besides negates independence of all the ECE countries except Poland. The argument that ECE has *de facto* become the "new West" - politically, economically, etc. - after the Cold War (Latawski, 1997) is an overstatement which disregards the voices of East Europeans themselves (Andor, 1996). The correlation between membership of NATO and of EU (Cimoszewicz, 1996: p. 3, referring to all ECE countries; also in

9 Direct mentioning of Russian threat to the ECE counties is also commonly expressed (see for example Radu, 1997: p. 39), but certainly not by those speaking in an official capacity.

Kwasniewski, 1996; Rotfeld, 1996: p. 290) which, in my opinion, is essential motivation for the ECE governments, is not emphasised by their Western counterparts.

The vision of future NATO membership of those ECE governments who are the strongest candidates, presents it as open and excluding no one *a priori* (Cimoszewicz, 1996: p. 5; Kwasniewski, 1996; Havel, 1996). However, this does not comply with the logic of their arguments that put NATO, not OSCE, at the centre of a new European security architecture. As noted Cimoszewicz, the then Polish Foreign Minister, arguing for Poland's rapid accession to NATO, "One of the concepts of a pan-European security system is based on a radical reform of the Organization of Security and Cooperation in Europe. Yet, even if a radical transformation of this institution, with its membership of more than 50 states, were possible at all, there would be uncertainty as to whether it would be an effective vehicle for an international security and whether all the important powers would participate in it" (1996: p. 6). The tone of such notions suggests that Russia is not welcome in the "effective" security structures in Europe.

NATO enlargement is a major change in the European military and political context, and Russia's strong reaction to it is not surprising. The matter has been discussed for several years, and its results are as yet discouraging: "the West did not (and could not) find arguments which would convince the Russian society" (CFDP, 1996: p. 94). It is important to see the two sides of the undesirability of the Alliance's enlargement from Russian and other East European (for example Belarusian, Ukrainian) perspectives: this process undermines the delicate political balance (not yet stability) within the countries where it is generally negatively perceived, and it changes substantially the geopolitical context in Eastern Europe which, in turn, poses tremendous constraints upon the newly independent states and their politics. It could be a matter of long debates which of these two aspects, domestic or the international one, is more significant. Probably, they are both inseparable.

The prospects of NATO enlargement worsen the political situation within Russia and other countries that see this process as *a priory* discriminatory in relation to them (Pierre & Trenin, 1997). It is conductive for the political forces like the Communists and nationalists in Russia, or the pro-Russian leadership in Belarus, who oppose economic and political liberalisation and the growing Western influence in Eastern Europe. The "liberals" in Russia have been marginalised, and their appeal for a policy of co-operation with then West has been completely invalidated. In Belarus, the proponents of a union with Russia have gained an invaluable argument both domestically and in relations with Russia. Even Russian Government, by far an adversary of any merger with Belarus, had to accept and act upon their appeal for closer political and military links. This makes the neighbouring countries extremely uneasy given their similar with Belarus status in relation to Moscow in the past. Ukraine has consistently attempted to take a constructive attitude in relation to all the parties concerned with NATO enlargement. However, the recent developments in Russian-Belarusian relations challenge its delicate neutral position (Pavliuk, 1997). On the other hand, the prospects of NATO enlargement have dismayed the weak political opposition in Belarus who advocate this country's independent of Russia foreign policy and openness towards the West.

Some analysts suggest that Russia's negative perception of NATO enlargement is grounded in the false attitudes of its own establishment. It may be suggested, for example, that NATO enlargement has emerged as the overriding factor in Russian foreign policy due to a false notion that there is a national consensus against it (Prakhalina, 1997); or that Russian strategists think in terms of the old geopolitics (Latawski, 1997). However, it is not plausible to blame Russia for its insolent attitude. As I have already tried to show, the arguments in favour of NATO enlargement often have anti-Russian connotations, if not direct mentioning of Russian threat. Clashing with Russia's objections, they mutually reinforce each other. Moreover, investigation of both sides' strategic interests reinforces this point about the inescapable Russian-enlarged NATO contention.

Although Russian counter-arguments to the Alliance's expansion have been underpinned by the changing domestic situation, and its official position has not always been consistently formulated[10] (Rotfeld, 1996: p. 288), the general line has been persistently negative. Russian reasoning points to the fact that the East-West confrontation has ended, and while the Eastern military potential has been disbanded, the Western Cold War military alliance has been preserved, and is now expanding towards Russian borders. Lacking clear rationale as a military preparation, it is associated not so much with a military threat to Russia, but with the policy of isolation (Interfax, 1997) which was systematically practised by the West against the USSR. For the economically, politically and socially distressed Russia, the implications of isolation are appalling (Pierre & Trenin, 1997: pp. 6-8). This feeling is reinforced by the understanding of the meaning of the ECE countries' endeavours. They try "to leave the East behind" - to join the Western area of security and prosperity which would preclude mighty and turbulent Russia. It is also clear that the West would prefer to be able to control, if not the Russian domestic situation, at least Moscow's international moves. The rhetoric of "enhanced stability" in the whole of Europe precisely describes this situation. Granting NATO a special place in the European security system, developing its capabilities to fulfil so-called non-Article V functions (peace-keeping, peace-enforcing and crisis management - in technical-military terms, these require offensive capacities) and keeping its membership controlled by the internal procedures, produces the phenomenon of a new power structure in Europe. Regional stability, grounded in a new order and power relations, does not equal security. It is quite obvious that while contributing to the security of its members, NATO enlargement cuts the edge of security on its own borders, denying it to its as yet not suitable applicants, let alone the few countries in the post-Communist Europe who look for alternative security arrangements.

---

10 In 1993 Yeltsin gave signs of no objection to the Alliance's enlargement in ECE (Financial Times, 19.10.1993: p. 32) Later, the emphasis of Russian objections would vary subject to the differences between the position of Russia's Communists and military experts, and that of Russian "liberals", and their relative influence upon the official Moscow.

This vision comes from an extreme, but its logical body is clear, and it complies with the traditions of European geopolitical reasoning, both in the East and West. It should, obviously, underpin the arguments of the strategic analysts in Moscow and other European capitals. However clear at the stage of analysis, this vision cannot be presented at an official level, as this would mean to call the Cold War back into existence. Therefore, Russian arguments follow the language of the opponents (in which the allegiance to power politics is the strongest expression of (mutual) criticism). The expression of Russian opposition to NATO enlargement points to new division lines in Europe, unequal treatment, asymmetrical concessions made by the USSR/ Russia to the West and prospects of further disparity. Drawing the implications of NATO's plans for political stability in Russia is the most apt for the West, as it articulates the values that the latter puts at the forefront (CFDP, 1996: p. 94; see also Rotfeld, 1996: pp. 288-9).

Practical politics, however, not only "correct" the language, but also call for pragmatism. Russia is compelled to suffer the geopolitical defeat of the Soviet Union. Russia has no right to veto NATO decisions, and has to rely on its size and relative power, possession of armed forces and nuclear arsenal, manipulation of neighbour states like Belarus, or strengthening of ties with members of loose anti-Western coalitions. It may be argued then that since Moscow had no real means to stop NATO enlargement, its opposition to the process has been a tactical mistake and now it is facing a defeat. However few the concessions the West has given to Russia, the Fundamental Act, the recently achieved agreement between Russia and NATO, is a document that could have not existed at all.

A paradox, and also a reality of contemporary European security politics, is that Russia would hardly find itself in a better position - internationally, but not domestically - should NATO remain within its present borders. Russia is locked within the consequences of the Soviet Union's defeat, but also within the geopolitical constraints of its extensive territorial and military resources that lack an adequate efficient economic basis. The inescapable historical responsibility of the Russian state to manage these resources is ever more constrained by the Western pressure. This growing pressure is the reality of a new power structure in Europe that could have taken other than NATO enlargement form, but would be no less painful for Russia once ECE and other parts of the former Soviet sphere of influence have been seduced by the perspective of a new (or "rediscovered") identity with the West. The difference, however, is the immediate effect of the process on the domestic Russian politics and politics of its neighbours.

CONCLUSION

NATO is a key structure in the post-Cold War European security system. Its new place and role have been defined as a result of a multilateral process in a new strategic context in Europe, when the interests of its key members have formed a coalition to meet the requirements of the new security situation in Europe. The salient factors include the demise of the Soviet dominance in the Eastern Europe, military conflicts in Balkans, pressure from Eastern Europe for membership of the Euro-Atlantic structures, and extension of the West European integrationalist project into the area of defence.

To meet the requirements of the new situation and take a key place in the non-confrontational European security context, NATO has changed its doctrine (facing the absence of potential adversary, it now implies a response to risks and challenges to the regional security) and structure of relationships with the EU, and has adopted new functions (Smith, 1997). This has created a powerful rationale for its expansion into the area formerly controlled by the USSR.

The prospects of NATO's eastward enlargement have provoked Russia, the biggest Soviet successor state and heir to the most of the Soviet armed forces and its entire nuclear arsenal, into an active opposition. However, Russia's objections to the Alliance's enlargement have failed to stop the process. Having inherited the USSR's geopolitical posture, Russia is also compelled to accept the consequences of its defeat. European security discourse and politics around NATO enlargement have revealed a fundamental shift in the post-Cold War regional security order. Russian establishment's perception of the process and a sharp decline of Moscow's leverage in European politics are likely to suggest it a conclusion about a new power-structural realities in the region. In the course of negotiation with NATO, Russia was compelled to accept the prospect of its enlargement, although it has attempted to limit it through the *Founding Act on Mutual Relations, Co-operation and Security*. In light of the fundamental nature of the contemporary strategic changes in Europe and of Russia's as yet strong military posture, further tensions are likely to evolve. Therefore, NATO's first eastern enlargement, suggested as a measure for enhancing stability and security in the whole of Europe, is likely lead to further unease between its old and new members on the one hand, and Russia and its supporter states (Belarus, Kazakhstan) on the other. It can provoke a further Russia's shift away from the West.

An understanding of the inevitability of a fundamental shift in the regional security order and underlying it power structure, caused by disintegration of the Eastern Bloc and Soviet Union's geopolitical defeat and its consequent collapse, cannot preclude criticism of the process of NATO enlargement. Its fundamental impact upon domestic politics in Russia and a number of other East European countries, and its implications for the security environment in the region is an effect with far-reaching consequences. The impact of political forces that have been invoked by the prospects of the North Atlantic Alliance's eastern enlargement in Russian politics cannot be dismissed on the grounds that Russian political establishment has a false perception of the new European realities, and that its perception is guided by an outdated geopolitical thinking. The proponents of NATO enlargement have to recognise that this process has undesirable consequences, whether foreseen or not, for a number of countries of the region and, potentially, for the region's stability. A critical East European vision of the process and its implications suggests a sad conclusion about the persistent undesirable impact of contemporary

European developments in the area of security upon the political situation in the countries in the East of Europe.

References

Andor, L. (1996) "Economic Transformation and Political Stability in East-Central Europe", *Security Dialogue*, Vol. 27, No.2, pp. 207-225

Beinen, H. (1993), "America: the firsters, the decliners, and the searchers for a new American foreign policy", in Leaver, R. & Richardson, J. (eds.) *Charting the Post-Cold War Order* (Boulder CO: Westview Press)

Buzan, B. (1987) *An Introduction to Strategic Studies: Military technology and international relations* (London: Macmillan)

Camilleri, J. (1993) "Alliances and the Emerging Post-Cold War Security System", in Leaver, R. & Richardson, J. (eds.) *Charting the Post-Cold War Order* (Boulder CO: Westview Press)

CFDP (Committee on Foreign and Defence Policy) (1996) "Russia and NATO: Theses of the Council on Foreign and Defence Policy", *Comparative Strategy*, Vol. 15, No. 1, pp. 91-102

Cimoszewicz, W. (1996) “Building Poland's security: Membership of NATO a key objective”, *NATO Review*, No. 3, May, pp. 3-7

Clinton, B. (1997) *Report to the Congress on NATO Enlargement* (http://www.state.gov/www/regions/eur/9702 nato-report.htlm, 26 February)

Cornish, P. (1996) “European Security: the end of architecture and the new NATO”, *International Affairs*, Vol. 73, No. 4, October, pp. 751-70

Cunningham, G. (1997) "EU and NATO Enlargement: How public opinion is shaping up in some candidate countries", *NATO Review*, No. 3, May-June 1997, pp. 16-8

Dunn, J. (1992) *East-Central Europe: The Challenge of Freedom*, Wilton Park Paper 50, (London: HMSO)

Gummett, P. (1997) "Foreign, Defence and Security Policy", in Heywood, P. et al. (eds) *Developments in West European Politics* (London: Macmillan)

Havel, V. (1996) "NATO-The Safeguard of Stability and Peace In the Euro-Atlantic Region" (http://www.csdr.org/)

Herz, J. (1950) "Idealist Internationalism and the Security Dilemma", *World Politics*, Vol. 2, pp. 157-80 Hopkinson, N. (1994) *The Eastern Enlargement of the European Union*, Wilton Park Paper 91, (London: HMSO)

Interfax (1997) "Yeltsin stresses "intolerable" nature of NATO expansion", Interfax news agency, Moscow, Summary of World Broadcasts, 17 May

Kull, S. & Rosner, J. (1997) "The American Public, Public, Congress and NATO Enlargement", *NATO Review*, No. 1, January, pp. 9-14

Kwasniewski, A. (1996) "Poland and NATO" (http://www.csdr.org/)

Latawski, P. (1997) "Expanding Security Institutions in East/Central Europe and the Baltics", paper presented at *Conflict and Conflict Prevention after the Cold War* (Northern Universities/RUSI Seminar, 7 May)

Latter, R. (1996) *Britain and Germany in the New Europe,* Wilton Park Paper 113, (London: HMSO)

Latter, R. (1995) *Strengthening Stability and Security in Central Europe*, Wilton Park Paper 101 (London: HMSO)

Millard, F. (1996) "The failure of nationalism in post-Communist Poland 1989-95: An historical perspective", in Jenkins, Brian & Spyros A. Sofos (eds.) *Nation and Identity in Contemporary Europe* (London: Routledge)

NATO (1995) *Study on NATO Enlargement* (http://www.nato.int/docu/basictxt/enl-9501.htm, September)

Parkhalina, T. (1997) "Of Myths and Illusions: Russian Perceptions of NATO Enlargement", *NATO Review*, No. 3, May-June 1997, pp. 11-5

Pavliuk, O. (1997) "Ukrainian-Polish Relations: A pillar of regional stability?", in Wohfield, M. (ed.) *The Effect of Enlargements on Bilateral Relations in Central and Eastern Europe* (Paris: ISS, WEU) Pierre, A. & Trenin, D. (1997) "Developing NATO-Russian Relations", *Survival*, Vol. 39, No. 1, pp. 5-18

Radu, M. (1997) "Why Eastern and Central Europe Look West", *Orbis*, Vol. 41, No. 1, Winter, pp. 39-58

Rotfeld, A. (1996) "Europe Towards New Security Arrangements", in *SIPRI Yearbook 1996* (SIPRI, Oxford University Press)

Ruhle, M. & Williams, N. (1997) “Why NATO will Survive”, *Comparative Strategy*, Vol. 16, No. 1, pp. 109-16

Simai, M. (1997) "Multilateral Co-operation and Systemic Hangs : implications of the breakup of the Soviet bloc", in Robert W. Cox, *The New Realism*, (United Nations University Press, Tokyo)

Smith, R. (1997) "A Changing NATO", *NATO Review*, No. 3, May-June, pp. 8-11

Solomon, G. (1997) "Prizes and Pitfalls of NATO Enlargement", *Orbis*, Vol. 41, No.2, Spring, pp. 209-21

CHAPTER 11

RETHINKING SECURITY: QUESTIONING THE INDIVISIBILITY THESIS

DENIS KRIVOSHEEV
Minsk, Belarus; Manchester, UK

INTRODUCTION

Security is a persistent problem in individual human life, domestic politics and international relations. For the current international relations agenda, it is international security which is of primary concern. However, any contemporary security discourse is bound to consider security on all the above three[1] levels. At the height of the Cold War, and ever since, various attempts to re-conceptualise security have been made. For decades, an immense international tension has been focused on Europe, and considerable resources fed attempts to counter it. In the aftermath of the Cold War, the globe split into several regions, some of which gained in security while other had to face its continuing decrease. Eastern Europe, unlike the former Yugoslavia, does not fall into an extreme case of being below the line of security. Yet, the situation in a number of the post-Soviet states is often perceived, not least by their own citizens, as that of just above the bottom line. This perception of lack of insecurity is fed by various factors, of which the military ones come probably the last. Even NATO expansion, so far negatively viewed by many East Europeans, and its implications for regional security, has more social and political, rather than military, connotations. Instead, considerations of maintaining the former standards of living, social stability and quality of life, come to the fore. In Belarus, for example, the effects of the nuclear catastrophe on Chernobyl atomic power station in the neighbouring Ukraine, cause grievous preoccupations of the survival of the whole nation (Marples, 1997: chapters 3, 4). The ecological problems, however, are coupled with numerous others. Similar problems, preoccupation with the quality of life, and similar desire of secure existence, are characteristic of people formal parts of the contemporary world.

---

1 More than three levels of analysis may be suggested (other may include communities, social groups, state bureaucracy, etc.).

The predominant concepts of security, and their particular policy implementations, have always been subject to constant criticism, both in the West and East, in the North and South - to use the major expression of dualism of the post-Cold War times[2]. One major criticism has always been addressed against the limits of realist thinking about security and the language of division associated it, and its expression in the foreign policies of the major powers during the Cold War and after (Tickner, 1995: pp.181,189). The other aspect of contemporary alternative security thinking is its accentuated humanism. The introduction of humanist appeals into the discipline has been both challenging and productive for its agenda. It requires greater attention to be paid to the economic, societal and environmental issues that were marginal to the traditional analysis of security in political and military-strategic terms. It also demands that we think of international security as indivisible, that is, no genuine international security is possible unless there is security at all levels, and for every element, within the international system. However, there are certain difficulties in applying the notion of indivisibility to international security, which I suggest to examine and elucidate.

A brief reference to the history of the post-W.W.II security discourse will show the major steps in the development of alternative security thinking. This will disclose how international security came to be understood as indivisible and what is implied by this notion. I will then consider the concept of security - its possible definition, referent objects and the theoretical grounds upon which its indivisibility may be conceptualised. I will then consider the question of international and national security policy and estimate to what extent the notion of indivisible security may be relevant in international politics, notably when applied to the whole of the international system and not just a group of countries of the West (the North). Given the determinant role of national policies and the inherent asymmetries in the contemporary international politics, I will argue that indivisible security is unlikely to be realised within the framework of the contemporary system of international relations.

OPENING UP THE SECURITY AGENDA

The history of post-World War Two international security discourse, however uneven, has been marked by a number of important developments. During the Cold War, security discourse was dominated by the realist thinking that emphasises the role of states as self-interested agents in international relations. This state-centric model, conceptualised as national security, was predominant both theoretically and politically. However, the very interest in security studies was genuinely driven by an attempt to overcome the traditional

[2] The East-West division characterises the realities of the bipolarity during the Cold War. Validity of the use of the concept of North-South division has been questioned by the process of economic and political diversification among the countries of the "South". However, it is still practical for the purpose of the argument presented in this work when referring to the economic, political and military gap that separates the rich and the poor countries. Also, it is frequently used by many contemporary writers in the field.

in International Relations focus on the concepts of power and peace and the limitations of this approach (Buzan, 1991: p. 3). One of the first important insights into the nature of international security was made by Herz (1950), who suggested the idea of the 'security dilemma'. According to it, the security preparations of one state inevitably increase the insecurity of the others, which leads to spiralling military build-up. This idea points to the important elements in human behaviour and interdependence in security relations. This concept was adopted and successfully developed by various authors in the 1970s and 1980s (R. Jervis, H. Bull, A. Wolfers, K. Booth, R. Ashley, S. Hoffmann, L. Beaton, others), whose contribution to the discipline have offered a systematic critique of the state-centric approach, the traditional realist preoccupations with the issue of states' military capabilities and zero-sum vision of the distribution of power in the international system. By the mid- and especially the late 1980, these ideas and approaches gained general awareness, if not acceptance, and could be equally encountered in the works of East European writers in the field (Podlesnyi, 1989; Grela, 1989; Kiss, 1989; Behar, 1989). They can be traced in the concept of the "new political thinking" suggested by the Soviet leader in the same decade (Gorbachev, 1987). Strategic Studies, an academic field that had accommodated much of the then security studies in the West, pointed to the nature of military technology, state bureaucratic decision-making, and dominant military doctrines as important mechanisms through which security the dilemma operated (Buzan, 1987). There was also an appeal in the academic community to recognise that individual humans should be the ultimate referent point of any international relations agenda (Bull, 1977: p. 22).

The political and ideological realities of the Cold War perpetuated the feeling of collective and personal insecurity. To break the vicious circle of the security dilemma, new models of international security politics were investigated. The approach with probably the strongest international impact was that of the independent Palme Commission which suggested the idea of *common security*. It proposed to move beyond ideological antagonisms, and pursue genuine international security through joint actions based on common interests (Mack, 1993: p. 8). Later, there were also important attempts, although of limited success, to decrease military hostilities in Europe through the policies of non-offensive or non-provocative defence (Butfoy, 1995). In parallel, economic, societal, environmental considerations were becoming an essential part of the international security agenda[3]. In order to incorporate them into a broader multi-dimensional approach, the concept of *comprehensive security* was introduced (Mack, 1993: p. 5).

With the end of the Cold War, this extended international security agenda has been widely acknowledged (also by some neo-realist thinkers, for example Buzan (1991)), and gained major international political attention (Boutros-Ghali, 1993). The early 1990s was a time of shared optimism about the prospects for international peace and security based on a broad multilateral consensus on the questions of conflict resolution and crisis management (Simai, 1997: p. 96). However, after the great East-West division was overthrown, the world turned out to be no less insecure and turbulent than before. The bipolarity did not

---

3 In fact, this understanding was not entirely new, as the UN Charter clearly proves (Bretherton, 1996: p. 132).

evolve into a new system of international stability. It disintegrated abruptly, together with the Soviet Union, lifting constraints from many potential conflict situations and giving way to actual conflicts. As a result, the arrangements for global stability and security that had developed since the Second World War collapsed (Ponton, 1996: p. 74).

The major sources of insecurity at this stage may be found in the polarisation of North-South division (economic, political and military), rise of nationalism, arms proliferation, terrorism, global ecological degradation and scarcity of natural resources. Recent works on international security examine these issues as part of a broad international agenda. Coming up with the ideas characteristic of comprehensive security, many authors raise further questions - concerning the meaning of the end of Cold War (Ponton, 1996); the role of the state as a major provider of security in the international system (Buzan, 1991); hierarchy of individual and collective values and questions of emancipation (Booth, 1991); growing number of threats, their ordering and possible national and international responses (Tickner, 1995); North-South relations (Ravenhill, 1993); regional/ global power structures, economic-security nexus, effects of globalisation, social forces that shape contemporary international security relations (Falk, 1995; 1996; Strange 1994) internationalisation of ideological conflict (Huntington, 1993; Rodan, 1996); relevance of conditions of existence to the international security agenda, the role of international organisations (Brethherton, 1996). All these different authors share an understanding that the traditional attitudes and policies are inappropriate for the persisting and new challenges to the international security, and they are motivated by the desire to find a new comprehensive and appropriate approach. Development of an adequate new vision is crucial for the countries of the post-Soviet area where, as I have shown above, perception of insecurity has penetrated different spheres of life in the face of these countries' international political marginalisation, their unprecedented economic decline and ecological degradation.

The idea of common security, shared by all alternative approaches, contains an important notion of indivisibility of international security. Such an understanding of international security, combined with its multi-dimensional comprehensive vision, has become an important part of the contemporary security discourse (Bretherton, 1996: p. 130). This notion points to the supra-national nature of international security - as irreducible to 'securities' of separate states - and emphasises the effects of security dilemma and cross-national operation of the major non-military threats in the modern world. Secondly, the notion of indivisible security adds to the meaning of international security, which is 'most clearly revealed through three objectives: peace, development and democracy. They are interlocking and mutually reinforcing' (Boutros-Ghali, 1993a: p. 3 in Bretherton, 1996: p. 130). If understood in this way, internationally accepted and supported by the UN documents, the concept of security should be a clear 'guide to action' for the international community. However, there is still much ambiguity about such an approach. First, the indivisibility of security as relevant to international relations may be questioned in theory. Second, despite the general concern with international security issues by all states, including the major Western powers whose leverage in international politics has increased after the break-up of bipolarity, there is little evidence of policies consistent with this notion being implemented.

SECURITY AS NEGATIVE INFINITY

There is a substantial body of literature that focuses on security. However, giving a comprehensive definition to security remains problematic. Even well-recognised European authors writing on the problems of security, like Buzan or Booth, and many others, refer to someone else's definitions and/ or suggest their own in a descriptive rather than precisely worded way. In fact, despite many shared insights into the nature of security, it is still an 'essentially contested concept' (Buzan, 1991: p. 13). Security is not just difficult to define, it is supposed to have various definitions, not least because its definition is essentially a question of (state) policy, whereas policies may vary significantly. Another problem with the definition of security is its negative approach. Of the significant number of definitions that may be found in the literature (for example, in Buzan, 1991: pp.16-7, and Tickner, 1995), all define it in a negative way[4] - as an 'absence of', or a state of being 'protected from' various threats. A 'positive' definition seems to be fundamentally absent. Indeed, security suggests a look outside from within an area controlled by the subject. Like the Universe, it suggests that the area outside will always be greater - fundamentally infinite - whereas that 'inside' is always limited.

This simple analogy of the subject-universe relationship represents a useful model that depicts a possible vision of security and security policy. It suggests that absolute security can never be achieved. Minimal physical security (survival) can be temporarily guaranteed, but there is still greater 'space' outside whence different risks come. This sense is captured by the multi-dimensional security agenda. Relative security, by contrast, is possible and desirable, and it plays a fundamental role in international relations. The influential neo-realist theory of international politics (Waltz, 1979) around which many debates in the academic field of International Relations have evolved, puts the idea of security at the centre of state's behaviour motivation. According to Waltz, in the actual (anarchic) international system only relative security can be achieved, and only by acquiring greater relative capabilities vis-à-vis other states. This point has been contested in various ways (see Keohane, 1986). The idea of common security, one of the alternative approaches, suggests that security can only be achieved 'with other states rather than against them' (Mack, 1993: p. 8). Such an approach should help to solve the security dilemma. However, even if we fully accept that neo-realism does not sustain this argument, we cannot easily reject the logic suggested by it.

Various definitions of security establish relationship between three principal elements: the subject, the area in which its existence is realised, and actual/ hypothetical threats posed to it. For example, an often quoted definition suggested by Lippmann (in Buzan, 1991: p. 16; Bretherton 1996: p. 127 and elsewhere) states: "a nation is secure to the extent to which

---

[4] With the exception of the definition suggested by Waever who explores politico-linguistic aspects of security.

it is not in danger of having to sacrifice *core values* if it wishes to avoid war, and is able, if challenged, to maintain them by victory in such a war". Here, the subject is a nation (but, as we know, it can also be the individual, community, state, international community of states), which is threatened by the possibility of having to sacrifice its 'core value'. The notion of *core values* in a general and precise way grasps the essential element of any definition of security - the referent objects of security. These may be freedom, individual life, health, territory, well-being, ideology, etc. - depending on the vision of security. This notion is equally useful whether the understanding of security is narrow, and focuses primarily on military threats, or broad and multi-dimensional, and whether it is applied to the individual, collective/ national or international levels. The problem evolves when we realise how differently the *core values* may be conceived in particular cases, whether taken from the same or different levels, and when we draw the implications of this observation to the notion of security's indivisibility.

INTERNATIONAL SECURITY BY MEANS OF NATIONAL POLICY?

Threats vary in nature and scope. Although some subjects are relatively more secure than others, they are all necessarily insecure to various extent. The set of *core values* may be broad and in a certain way, unlimited. As Buzan (1991: p. 19) puts it, the "bottom line (of security) is about survival, but it also reasonably includes a substantial range of concerns about the conditions of existence". The modern world is complicated not only because of the nature of the problems it embraces in an era of technological progress, social dynamism and environmental degradation, but also because of the diversity of co-existing standards of human life. Hence, while the security preoccupations of many people in the poor South are about the 'bottom line', those in the richer North are about the maintenance of certain levels of income, decrease of environmental risks, and accommodation of social discontent under much more favourable conditions than in the South. The threats are unevenly distributed (Strange, 1994: p. 48), both across individuals and nations. It is only when the survival of humanity as a whole is immediately threatened, do the *core values* for everyone coincide. So far, only the peril of nuclear holocaust has been such a threat, and that was when the concept of common security came into being. All other global threats, including the ecological ones, do not immediately and equally affect the *core values* of all people (UNDP, 1994: ch.2). The *core values* of different subjects do not coincide.

In the previous section I introduced the notion of security's indivisibility along with the understanding of *international* security, in Boutros-Ghali's formulation, which importantly exceeds the narrow focus on military hazards. There have been attempts to postulate security as indivisible on other than international levels as well. Buzan (1991: pp. 103-6) asserts that no state is truly secure unless it is secure internally, i.e. its various subjects do not pose threat to each other[5]. Booth (1991: p. 139) applies this logic further 'down': "True (stable) security can only be achieved by people and groups if they do not deprive others of

5 Buzan presents this vision in his discourse on "strong" and "weak" states.

it". The United Nation's stress on humanism rounds up these approaches: "Humane security is *people-centred*" (UNDP, 1994: p. 23, italics in the original). However, whether security is truly indivisible, particularly when filtered through international politics, is dubious.

Two distinct policy approaches to the problem of international security are possible. The one that stresses its indivisibility is based on the belief that "today there is no longer any such thing as someone else's problem" (Boutros-Ghali, 1993: p. 96). It is grounded in the observation that "[w]hen security of people is endangered anywhere in the world, all nations are likely to get involved" because the consequences of any such danger "travel the globe" (UNDP, 1994: p. 22). These become apparent, for example, through the issues of migration: émigrés escape the hazards of war, famine, unemployment in their own countries and often bring economic, social and political discontent, if not the same problems, to the countries where they find refuge (Castles & Miller, 1993: ch.6). In practice, however, the corresponding approach finds the consent of, or is undertaken individually, by national governments mainly in the areas where the threats affect strongly and more or less equally every country (so far, in relation to a limited scope of military and ecological issues). The other approach, in fact the most common one, takes national ends as the priority of any national policy, from which security is not an exclusion. The fundamental problem with international security is that it is highly demanding in national contributions, whereas the final effects and benefits are dispersed through the whole system. Policy-making is based on cost-effect calculations. When the cost of a problem's solution is high whereas its immediate effect can be tolerated at a lesser expense, the decision comes easily.

There is a certain 'deep culture' through which security is achieved and/ or maintained. Strange calls it security structure and defines it as the "framework of power created by the provision of security by some human beings for others. The protectors - those who provide the security - acquire a certain kind of power which lets them determine, and perhaps limit, the range of choices, or options available to others" (Strange, 1994: p. 45). Strange's definition refers to political economy, but this framework is equally applicable to security relations in any social environment, of which international politics is not an exception. Where patterns of power operate, some units are necessarily privileged versus others. In a society of humans, this contradiction can be resolved or finessed by the institution of democracy. In the international system, however, similar mechanisms are missing. The normative international commitment to 'democratic governance' and attempts to make political conditionality a cornerstone of the global agenda (Brethertone, 1996) are very often just another expression of the power of the strong who can 'conditionally' use them in certain, but not all cases. Under the conditions of anarchy (absence of authority), when the major agents are sovereign states[6] with an immense difference in capabilities, democratic procedures are hardly possible. The United Nations, the most representative universal organisation with the most democratic constitution, is based on the principle of

6 Various views are possible on this matter, however. Some theories emphasise the role of non-state actors; others suggest that the role of the state is vanishing, being overtaken, for example, by certain social forces that operate on the global scale (for example, see Falk, 1996).

sovereign equality of all its member states. This principle, combined with the non-democratic procedures within the Security Council, its most efficient body, leads to scant efficacy of the democratically taken decisions, and the privileging of the strong in taking the authoritative ones (Bretherton, 1996: pp. 132-4)[7]. Combined with the uneven pattern of distribution of the threats common for all countries (of those related to individual safety, food supply, employment, healthy environment, etc.) across the globe, this situation points to a structural inequality in the international distribution and maintenance of security. This is empirically evident and well documented (UNDP, 1994: ch.2).

The structural barriers that hamper realisation of equal universal (although still relative) security for all nations will exist at least as long as some parts of the international system are privileged vis-à-vis the others. This privilege means not only a lesser degree of vulnerability to those most common threats, but also the practice of setting the rules for the whole system while protecting their own, broader set of values separately. Huntington has expressively showed that such a combination of universal dominance, self-interested international policies and privileging one's own values is historically characteristic of the Western powers (1996: ch.3, pp. 183-6). He warned about the threats to the Western 'civilization' because of the emergence of non-Western "movers and shapers of history", and summoned policy-makers, in his own words, to "maintain Western predominance, protect Western interests and promote Western *political and economic values*" (Huntington, 1993: pp. 23, 40, italics added).

However extreme, Huntington's opinion is instructive in that it points to the real situation when the protection of Western values is juxtaposed with the provision of elementary rights to the underdeveloped countries and their people. This is most pronounced in the economic sphere where the cost-effective model has found its almost absolute expression. Observation of the structural inequalities of the global economic life has brought several authors to the notion of 'global apartheid' (Falk, 1995: pp. 49-55; Tickner, 1995: pp. 179-81; Parkins, 1996: p. 49).

The nature of economic insecurity can be variously perceived, and so its relevance to our analysis could be questioned. Buzan puts economic threats among the five major issue-areas that threaten national and international security. However, he assumes that economic insecurity cannot be equally relevant for security analysis except for when a poor economic performance weakens the state's military capabilities (Buzan, 1991: p. 127). He stresses that the market economy (or capitalist economy, in his own words) which is predominant in the world today, "is founded on a considerable degree of permanent insecurity for all the units within it" (Buzan 1991: p. 235). Therefore, most of economic insecurities are "normal day-to-day consequences of life in a competitive international environment" (Buzan, 1991: p. 115). However, economic issues cannot be excluded from our security discourse, at least because the poor economic performance of many countries of what was previously called the Third World, and now increasingly of countries in Eastern Europe, becomes a matter of international tension. Economic insecurities do not affect equally all states and leave much

7 Whether the principal agents are states, social groups, multi-national corporations, or individuals, the argument is equally relevant taken their structural inequality.

less leverage to the less secure ones. Operation of free market on both national *and international* scale is often understood by the governments and some academics in the North as their *core values* (FCO, 1996; Fukuyama, 1992: p. xiv; Huntington, 1993; 1996: pp. 57-9), while it raises the question of survival for the poorest people in the South (Gill, 1996: p. 215). Even if we adopt the logic according to which free market operation will ultimately serve the development of the poor parts of the world (which is still questionable in theory (Halliday, 1993: pp. 22-4) and empirically dubious (Cheru, 1997: pp. 221-2)), for the period of transition the insecurity of the disadvantaged will maximise, not lessen.

The international economic system is just one of the areas where interests of different actors compete rather than match or compliment each other, and where the "deep culture" of power relations operates. Taken as an example, it helps to disclose the complicated situation in which security is distributed and maintained unevenly through the international system.

The implications of this point in one direction: as long as there are advantaged and disadvantaged parts in the system, the concept of indivisible security can hardly come from theory into the "real" world of international politics. The advantaged parts of the system (countries or their groupings) will always be tempted to set a wider range of *core values* and defend it by all their effective means against the "external" pressure - in fact, a narrower scope of *core values* of others. This situation creates tension, and often evolves into conflicts, which contradicts the conditions of a stable universal comprehensive security - an indivisible security, as we would all to see it, from the different parts of the world.

CONCLUSION

There is a very big temptation to speak of international security as indivisible. However, realisation of security as indivisible fails in practice, once it is understood in the broad terms, with all its dimensions - its economic, societal and ecological, as well as political and military - being equally important. Theoretically, security is always related to a subject. When the subjects are multiple and when their security requirements and expectations differ, they may not all accept the same conditions to be qualified as security. This situation is real in international politics, and can be well illustrated by international economic relations. The situation when some parts of the international system are privileged and have more capabilities versus the others, precludes full adoption of policies coherent with the notion of indivisible security. This situation, in which security and stability of the whole system is affected, is likely to persist as long as inequality of different states is a matter of fact.

REFERENCES

Behar, N. (1989) "The Debate on European Security in Bulgaria", in Waever, O., et al. (eds) *European Polyphony: Perspectives beyond East-West Confrontation* (London: Macmillan)

Booth, K. (1991) "Security and Emancipation", *Review of International Studies*, Vol.17, No. 3, pp.313-26

Boutros-Ghali, B. (1993) "Empowering the United Nations", *Foreign Affairs*, Vol. 72, pp. 89-102

Boutros-Ghali, B. (1995) *An Agenda for Peace* (2nd ed.) (New York: UN)

Bull, H. (1977) *The Anarchical Society: A study of order in world politics* (London, Macmillan)

Bretherton, C. (1996) "Security after the Cold War: Towards a global Paradigm?", in Bretherton & Ponton (eds) *Global Politics: An introduction* (Cambridge: Blackwell)

Butfoy, A. (1995) *Critical Reflections on Non-Offensive Defence*, Working Paper 14 (Centre for International Studies, Monash University).

Buzan, B. (1987) *An Introduction to Strategic Studies: Military technology and international relations* (London: Macmillan)

Buzan, B (1991) *People, States and Fear* (2nd ed.) (New York: Harvester Wheatsheaf)

Castles, S & Miller, M. (1993) *The Age of Migration: International population movements in the modern world* (London: Macmillan)

Cheru, F. (1997) "Global Apartheid and the Challenge to civil society: Africa in the transformation of the world order", in Cox, R. (ed.) *The New Realism*, (United Nations University Press, Tokyo)

Falk, R. (1997) "State of Siege: will globalization win out?", *International Affairs* 73(1), January, pp. 123-36

Falk, R. (1995) *On Human Governance: Towards a new global politics* (Cambridge: Polity Press)

FCO (Foreign and Commonwealth Office) (1996) *Global Free Trade and Foreign Policy* (http://www.open.gov.uk/index.htm)

Fukuyama, F. (1992) *The End of History and the Last Man* (London: Hamish Mamilton)

Gill, S. (1996) "Globalization, Democratization and the Politics of Indifference", in Mittelman, J. (ed.) *Globalization: Critical reflections* (London: Boulder)

Grela, S. (1989) "The Debate on European Security in Poland", in Waever, O., et al. (eds) *European Polyphony: Perspectives beyond East-West Confrontation* (London: Macmillan)

Halliday, F. (1993) "The Cold War and Its Conclusion: Consequences for International Relations Theory", in Leaver, R. & Richardson, J. (eds.) *Charting the Post-Cold War Order* (Oxford: Westview Press)

Herz, J. (1950) "Idealist internationalism and the security dilemma", *World Politics*, No.2, pp. 157-80

Huntington, S. (1996) *The Clash of Civilizations and the Remaking of World Order* (New York: Simon & Schuster)

Huntington, S. (1993) "The Clash of Civilizations", *Foreign Affairs*, Vol. 72, No. 3, Summer, pp. 22-50

Keohane, R. (ed.) (1986) *Neorealism and Its Critics* (New York: Columbia University Press)

Kiss, L. (1989) "European Security: Hungarian interpretations, perceptions and foreign policy", in Waever, O., et al. (eds.) *European Polyphony: Perspectives beyond East-West Confrontation* (London: Macmillan)

Latham, R. (1996) "Getting Out From Under: Rethinking security beyond liberalism and the levels-of-analysis problem", *Millennium*, Vol. 25, No. 1, pp. 77-108

Mack, A. (1993) *Concepts of Security in the Post-Cold War*, Working Paper 8, (Department of International Relations, A.N.U.)

Marples, D. (1997) *Belarus: From Soviet rule to nuclear catastrophe* (London: Macmillan)

Parkins, C. (1996) "North-South Relations and Globalization", in Bretherton & Ponton (eds) *Global Politics: An introduction* (Cambridge: Blackwell)

Podlesnyi, P. (1989) "Non-Military Aspects of Security: The view of a Soviet scholar" , in Waever, O., et al. (eds.) *European Polyphony: Perspectives beyond East-West Confrontation* (London: Macmillan)

Ponton, G. (1996) "The End of the Soviet Era: Implications for Global Politics), in Bretherton & Ponton (eds.) *Global Politics: An introduction* (Cambridge: Blackwell)

Ravenhill, J. (1993) "The New Disorder in the Periphery", in Leaver, R. & Richardson, J. (eds) *Chartering the Post-Cold War Order* (Boulder CO: Westview Press).

Rodan, G. (1996) "The Internationalization of Ideological Conflict: Asia's new significance", *The Pacific Review*, Vol. 9, No. 3, pp. 328-51

Simai, M. (1997) "Multilateral Co-operation and Systemic hangs implications of the break-up of the Soviet bloc", in Robert W. Cox (ed.) *The New Realism* (United Nations University Press, Tokyo)

Strange, S. (1994) *States and Markets* (2nd edition) (London: Pinter Publishers)

Tickner, A. (1995) "Re-visioning Security", in Ken Booth and Steve Smith (eds.) *International Relations Theory Today* (Cornwall: Polity Press)

UNDP (United Nations Development Program) (1994) *Human Development Report 1994* (New York, Oxford: Oxford University Press)

Waltz, K. (1979) *Theory of International Politics* (Reading, Mass.: Addison-Wesley)

INDEX

T

U

V

W

Y